Kissing
The Hag

The Dark Goddess and the Unacceptable Nature of Woman

First published by O Books, 2009
O Books is an imprint of John Hunt Publishing Ltd., The Bothy, Deershot Lodge, Park Lane, Ropley,
Hants, SO24 0BE, UK
office1@o-books.net
www.o-books.net

Distribution in:	South Africa
	Alternative Books
UK and Europe	altbook@peterhyde.co.za
Orca Book Services	Tel: 021 555 4027 Fax: 021 447 1430
orders@orcabookservices.co.uk	
Tel: 01202 665432 Fax: 01202 666219	Text copyright Emma Restall Orr 2008
Int. code (44)	
	Design: Stuart Davies
USA and Canada	
NBN	ISBN: 978 1 84694 157 3
custserv@nbnbooks.com	
Tel: 1 800 462 6420 Fax: 1 800 338 4550	All rights reserved. Except for brief quotations
	in critical articles or reviews, no part of this
Australia and New Zealand	book may be reproduced in any manner without
Brumby Books	prior written permission from the publishers.
sales@brumbybooks.com.au	
Tel: 61 3 9761 5535 Fax: 61 3 9761 7095	The rights of Emma Restall Orr as author have
	been asserted in accordance with the
Far East (offices in Singapore, Thailand,	Copyright, Designs and Patents Act 1988.
Hong Kong, Taiwan)	
Pansing Distribution Pte Ltd	
kemal@pansing.com	A CIP catalogue record for this book is available
Tel: 65 6319 9939 Fax: 65 6462 5761	from the British Library.

Printed and Bound by Digital Book Print Ltd
www.digitalbookprint.com

Kissing The Hag

The Dark Goddess and the Unacceptable Nature of Woman

Emma Restall Orr

BOOKS

Winchester, UK
Washington, USA

CONTENTS

DEDICATION

I offer this book, in thanks, to my grandmothers -
the vicious pixie, Nina, for her pain and her poetry,
the glamorous wanderer, Alma, for her beauty and untamed
heart.
With my words, I offer the peace of acceptance. We live within
each other.

ACKNOWLEDGEMENTS

This book is drenched in the inspiration of my home in the heart of England, the beauty of its landscape and the cycles of its seasons. I raise a cup to the spirits of the quiet valley and dark forest.

For their inspiration and beauty, I give thanks to all the women who talked to me about their lives, who offered me their stories, their laughter and their tears, and in particular the Black Frog, Freya's Cat and, of course, in the final edit, the irrepressible BMCs. I acknowledge too every man who has found the hero within.

STORIES

Amidst the exploration of ideas, as is often the case with my writing, I have placed brief anecdotes, memories and sketches of moments. Each of these stories is true. Though each is written in the first person, they are not all my own. In speaking to women over the period of my research, in living my life's journey alongside others, I have collected many tales; some of these I here share. In order to protect the sources, at times two stories have been woven together. Names have all been changed.

Those who know me well will know which are my stories; those who know me a little will no doubt guess and be both right and wrong; those who don't know me should not worry either way. Further, I would dissuade any speculation as to whose stories they are. Details may change, but through millennia of human lives they have all been lived a thousand times and more.

FIRST WORDS

Hag is not a nice word.

Yet there comes a time in every woman's life when *nice* is tedious, when nice is insipid, seeping into the soul like souring milk, warping the mind. Indeed, nice can, at times, be all that is offensive.

Hag: it's a fascinating word. As I speak it aloud, the sound is as smooth as an out breath. Aspirated, its vowel is extended and then clipped as if with a warning kick of death. It is a primal word, formed with barely any effort required. It whispers of cold wind, of thick fog and the stench of stagnant water. It is a word robed in spiders' webs, dusty and worn, unsure where to place itself on the shiny veneers of today. Lingering at the edges of life, it waits to run a broken nail down some blackboard of the soul.

No, hag is not a nice word. Like princess or pole-dancer, the word quietly slips us a picture, and though for each of us the image may differ slightly, it invariably embodies all that is declared to be simply and irrefutably *not nice* in woman.

This book is about her.

It is about us all.

The Tale

I sit here in the soft light of another new day.

My eyes ache to be closed, lids sliding as I watch, and breathe, conscious of tired muscles lifting and falling about my bones. My skin is rough, like linen too often washed in haste, dried in the salty breath of another seamless wind. It stretches, too loosely, over the scaffold of my face.

A few strands of hair dance before my eyes, picked up by the breeze, and silently I wonder at their lack of substance. Thin, like the last long grasses of autumn, scoured by the wind, burnt by the first frost, they touch so lightly, grazing against the weight of my bloated body. I am full, swollen with all that has been my life, holding within me its rich emptiness, and as I chuckle my belly shivers, lying upon itself in the folds of its idle carelessness.

I sit here, and watch, as life hurtles by.

Inside this body my words echo, thoughts half formed and drifting in the vast stillness of a lifetime's breathing. Words unspoken, tumbling past the chill of damp stone, an ancient well, ever seeking out the dark of water far below. It roots me, this stillness, feeding my ambivalence. So does the ache in my ankles, swollen, unmovable, like pillars in the mud wrapped up in dry ivy, dusty like the memories that hold me from crumbling. Where once there was life, sweet earth and grass soft and fresh, dew wet beneath bare toes, there is now just a glimmering of some distant dream.

And it seems to me as if now, were I simply to exhale, knowingly exhale, releasing the stories of my soul, the winds would take me for an old seed husk, up and far far away into the darkening skies. There is nothing more to do.

Let me tell you a tale

Let me spin you a yarn and use, if I may, long strands pulled from the language of our ancestral blood, threads rough and skin-scratchy, dyed red with old hemp and purpled with woad, threads that have held together the pathways of our souls generation after generation, since the days when the great ocean steadily rose to cast adrift these islands from the great unceasing forests beyond.

Listen. Sit back and listen, to the call of the crows, the breeze in the old leaves, the words of our grandmothers.

~ ~

It was a time like so many times that have come and gone within these lands, a time when men found themselves living with peace.

Yet by 'peace' I don't mean a peace that comes to the soul and fills the heart with the divine breath of tranquillity; this was, like most, the peace that comes when, by some quirk of fate, there is a lull amidst ages of cruel fighting. Such times are always rich with victory for some, while death and pain are the taste of others' lives.

They are strange, such times. Men long used to battle, hearths used to scarcity, at first celebrate with feasting and wild colourful games, releasing the energy held still in reserve for the anger of the fight. Then there follows the quiet, when the tide recedes and exhaustion seeps across the land, with the longing and bitterness that accompany grief and violent change. Slowly, as the seasons turn, men start again to see the footprints of daily living. A few are able to sigh deeply enough to set aside the pain, but many stumble on the furrows of the newly sown fields, wandering into the forest, searching for distractions that will keep their minds from memories. There is left a deep craving, one that is felt ought not be mentioned, the craving for purpose, the longing again for the rush of the kill.

It doesn't help that the land, too, takes longer to forget. Blood soaked into the mud may disappear, the scorched earth is soon covered with chickweed and groundsel, the mess of the hooves of war is soon enough ploughed over, but drifting in the breeze linger the stories of the dead. Their cries are trapped like horses' hair tangled in the thorns and twigs of the old forest. No, the land does not easily forget.

So it is that at such times men come together, squabbling like young village dogs, and this time was no different.

The feasting hall still smelled of cool dust and damp mortar, for the stone masons weren't long gone, and the hangings draped across it were bright with the colour of their dyes, letters in gold thread celebrating victories so newly won. That night, as each one since winter had come creeping in, the voices of the men grew steadily louder, shouts echoing, reaching into the dark heights of the ceilings, laughter clattering with the slamming of fists upon the tables as one claim evoked another, as challenge provoked challenge, as ridicule was countered with insult and threat.

I don't recall what it was that, the next morning, hastened them all so from their warm beds, but it was some wager I do not doubt, on the killing of a stag or a great tusked boar, a stake of honour set high enough to ensure the court was emptied of the shimmering energy of their frustration before sun's rise. A couple of the young maidens, the wild ones who could, went too, hair tied back and riding hard like squires, the knights calling to each other in the wind as they galloped over the meadows towards the forests below and beyond. Only a few watched them go; the wife of Cedrin, her gown tight across her pregnant belly, and a few young boys kicking stones on the track outside the castle gates, one the son of Tanna, the king's blacksmith.

The paths, white with hoar frost, were soon mud beneath the sleeping trees as the chase careered through in a blur of dawn's icy breath, and before long the gathering was scattered, hounds chasing a dozen scents in each direction, yapping and yowling, horses chafing at the reins to follow the tension of their riders' lust. It seemed the deer that day were all about them, yet too elusive to be seen, and the young hunters leapt at every hint of a

5

lead. Distracted by the sound of a branch dryly breaking, it wasn't long before the young king found himself alone, the clamour of the others moving quickly away.

For a moment he stood dazed; there was a strange quiet in the air, a familiar scent he couldn't place yet which clung to him, intriguing him. Beneath a canopy of ancient yews, the winter light dim, he tried to catch his breath. His horse's hooves had sunk deep into the mud of a stagnant pond that now sucked and squelched at each foot the creature lifted. Staring into the black water, every nerve awoken, he remembered the smell: that of death. His vision clouded, his heart pounded, as the images of battlefields again flooded through his mind, fuelled by the kick of it, the adrenaline of instinctive fear. The great fires were burning, smoke searing his eyes again, fields of ripe barley, swelling golden in the breeze, laid waste in the cause of barbaric war, and that smell, now a stench of blood and piss, thick in every breath. Holding his head, trying to shake the vision, from amidst the trees he heard the *shlice* of metal slowly unsheathed. Catatonic, half blind, he searched the grey light for the sword.

The horse that came towards him was blacker than night. So huge was it that the king's own stallion was quite dwarfed before it. Some say the rider was wore gleaming black armour from his mask and helmet to the spikes upon his boots; some say he wore a long cape of blackest cloth, lined with the colours of the midnight sky; and some say he wore no armour, but a cloak of cormorant feathers and his eyes were of molten gold so that none may ever bear his gaze. But we shall not know, for on that day no one saw him but the king.

His sword glistened darkly as if wet with blood. He spoke in a whisper which could not be misheard. "Arthur Pendragon. Come fight me. For your crown."

The young king later told his queen that as he reached for his sacred sword, that cast by the Pheryllt back in the mists of time, he heard the screams of every man who had died in fighting, every starving child's cry, every wail of grief, yet the sounds were not in his mind but in the very wind around him. And when he realised that he had left Excalibur behind, bringing with him only his raw dagger, arrows and bow, he knew for a moment that he would die, that he would die for all who had died upon the fields of war. And listening to his words, with fingertips wet with her tears she touched his face so gently, flowing through him with wisdom like the waves of the seas that washed and shaped the shores of his kingdom.

The black knight, his horse moving with ease through the deep muddy water, put back his head and laughed and laughed, a laugh that rumbled through the land like rocks falling, crashing down a mountain side, splitting his mind, "You are mine," he roared, his great sword lifted to the skies. Then lithely he brought it down to point directly at the king's cold bare throat.

As the tip touched the skin, he whispered slowly, "Your land is mine"

For a moment the young king wondered how he had every thought it to be otherwise.

Closing his eyes, he tasted the blood in his mouth, the taste of his living. He longed only for the touch of his lover's cheek upon his own. He longed for the sweet shrill moment of release, ice breaking, blood flowing, perfect death.

But it did not come. Aware of his own breath, moving not a muscle, Arthur looked up into the trees and the knight, shaking his head, slowly spoke again, this time with a sigh of a thousand years. "Too easy." And he laughed again, hard and sharp, "Too easy, too ... easy". The sword's tip dropped from the throat to the heart of the young king whose fingers had tightened bloodless about his reins. "I will ask a question of you."

The young man wanted to scream, *What?! What is your question?!* but if any sound could have come from his throat it would quickly have been silenced: a great raven landed on a branch behind the great knight.

"I will give you three days. After which time you must return, and to this very place. If you answer well, I will leave you your kingdom, and your life. If you do not, you lose both to me. And I ... " again he laughed, wild as distant thunder, "I will be High King, of all this land." The raven watched the young king, his sleek head tilted, listening.

When quiet draped again the yews, he raised a hand before him, cupped as if holding a liquid treasure, a glint in his eye. "The question?"

"Tell me," demanded Arthur, in all the voice he could muster, "and let this be done."

The knight's whisper pierced the mist like a rusty scythe. "What is it that women ... most desire?"

There was a pause, a silence softened only by the horses' breathing in the cold damp air. Then pulling on his reins, he turned as the steed reared and, splashing down into the dark mud, within moments both were gone.

Anger rose in the young king, quickly and coarsely. Nobody had patronised him, had threatened and treated him as such a child since the days before he was proven king. Nobody but the Druid, and for a moment he wondered if this were some new trick of the wily old man, another way of forcing him to learn the dirty lessons of life's web, and rage grew inside him as, forgetting the hunt, he pulled at his horse and rode as fast as the beast could take him, veering through the trees, out into the meadows and up towards the castle walls.

Guinevere was on the floor rugs before the fire, winding wool, laughing with the women that sat around her. She looked up when he strode in, so happy to welcome him, a curl of hair like sunlight upon her cheek, but her open smile faded before the anger in his eyes. She spoke quickly and softly to her companions who, in a swirl of skirts upon stone, were hastily gone. Alone, she watched him, keeping her distance as he prowled the floors.

Slamming his fist against the wood, he threw the door open to the parapet and walked out into the winter cold.

A blanket wrapped about her shoulders, she quietly followed, the wind blowing her hair every which way. A flurry of doves took to the air, circling and landing on the thatch of far off barn roofs, and she waited as he searched the landscape, scanning the forest that lay below them like a sea of pale grey, islands of evergreen, his eyes focused somewhere within his own soul. When his gaze settled tenderly upon the fields down the valley, his sigh encouraged her to look into his face.

He whispered, "This land is torn apart".

She smiled, murmuring sadly, "It's the hunger now killing, my Lord".

In the clarity and love of her pale blue eyes he felt her pushing him, and he turned away, filled again with irritation. Why did she feel so much older when the difference in their years was believed nothing at all? Why had he surrendered, without a fight, by the forest pool? The memory of his submission hung about him like a shit-soiled rag.

When later she held him, the winter's air was in his hair, and she breathed in the sharpness of its cold clarity, feeling the muscles of his body still taut. He had ridden out with Kai, desperate to quell his restlessness, and their friendship had soothed and strengthened his soul but a little. Taking his hand, she led him into the warmth of their chamber. There, in the dark dyed rugs of their bed, she kissed his face and spoke softly of her day, the sickness in the village, an accident at Willow Cross, the laughter of the children playing with baby kids in the pens. Not listening, he relaxed beneath the stroke of her fingers and the play of her voice, until he found that he was telling her of the dawn's early hunt, and the black-robed knight.

Before she was able to hold it in, the laughter was bubbling through her and his angry indignation only made it worse until tears were running down her cheeks, shining on the cream softness skin of her face already flushed by the fire. "Wench, will you stop that!" he shouted, struggling to find his feet, but she pulled him back down, gasping her apologies as she tried to suppress her giggles. He stared at her, shaking his head amazed, wanting to tell her of the fear, really tell her of the fear, but she rubbed her eyes and touched his lips with her soft fingertips, touching him so gently, tangling his mind.

"Tell me his question again, my Lord?"

"If you tell me why you laugh."

"Because your bravery is beautiful."

He turned away.

"And because, my Lord, what a woman most desires is *you*, a noble husband, a king, brave and true."

In the feasting hall that night, amidst the celebration of the stag caught with young Sir Aleric's arrow, the talk was only of the Black Knight's challenge. There was no mention of the danger they might be in, but only the glory that could and would be won. Their good king had again offered purpose to his warriors and the mead horns and flagons were emptied with laughter and with agitation. The court's women were asked, maids, wives, kitchen girls, grandmothers of every rank and in any turn, and many stood up in the great hall, declaring their words true, but each gave a different answer. Love was all a woman desired, loyalty, truth, an unwavering devotion. Wealth, another swore, enough for gowns of silken thread, lace and silver buttons, or jewels of gold. But surely it was beauty, and the revellers laughed, a bust that was lush and a bottom of velvet. No, surely just love. Yet what good was love without bonds of trust, so without doubt it was vows made on stone that a woman craved. Salvation, one said, a woman of the new gods who wore no jewels about her neck, and a moment of silence followed her words before a knight declared that it must be a spanking, for discipline was what a woman desired. Laughter broke across the tables once more that long night, as a young maid teased him, "I'll be disciplining you," she cried, "with the back of my spoon!" and so the bids continued on.

Three days Arthur had to solve this strange riddle and each knight, each soul, wished to be the one to bring him the key. Feigning tiredness, he listened with an uncharacteristic detachment. He wondered at the faith these people had in his ability; not one seemed to consider that he might not succeed. He wondered at their inability to imagine he could die.

At one point, old Finnian, a little worse for the ale, drove his knife into the bench and said, "I do believe these women have a hatched some plot against us, for here we are discussing all that they would most desire and we, sires, listening like pups at a skinning. It's a conspiracy. I declare there is no one reply!"

A new antagonism spread around the tables, peppered with wit, and behind its veil Arthur rose and quietly slipped away. His Lady, within a moment, was by his side.

In their chamber he laid his head upon her belly and closed his eyes.

Taking blankets and provisions, the court emptied the next morning as every free hand went questing the answer so needed by the king. The women of every village were stopped and questioned, and with young children whining, tugging at their skirts, arms filled with muddy turnips, jugs of water, suckling babies, they each smiled or shrugged, looking into the skies, offering a vision of their own deepest longing. One woman, by the old mines, paused from her log cutting to survey the young knight. "What we've ever wanted, sire, and no doubt will ever want - a man who don't want to fight," she said and slammed her axe into the wood.

Sir Praid went up into the Blue Hills to find the wild man who could see the paths of life ahead. Another even journeyed to the abbess of Haughton Ford. It was said that Bards had been sent to the Cells of Song to dream-vision, and one was preparing to offer the verses of Mon at the Old Stone.

Arthur sent word to the Druid. The response came quickly: "You must reckon the price and pay it with honour". Slamming his fist down upon the table, his patience broke as he threw his cup, yelling, "Why won't he tell me clearly?" His voice was so loud the young runner jumped with fear and surprise. "Tomorrow, I will go. I myself will find it."

He was not seen in the feasting hall that night, and though there was laughter as stories were told, it was hard not to look up and see his empty chair.

When, early the next morning, the young king made his way alone from the courtyard, a good many watched, a gravity sinking.

He had been riding all day, without knowing why he chose this track or that. And even though he had passed many farmsteads and villages, though he had slowed the pace of his horse, all he had really seen was the hunger in the land. One old man looked up from the fence he was mending, saying, "Good day, son". And not knowing the rider, he added, "Is it as bad where you come from?"

Arthur shook his head, baffled by his own uncertainty, his gaze upon the ragged sheep and skinny silent children in the yard. "But, sir, the Saxon wars have not come this far, surely?"

"The foreign butchers? No, son, this famine is from lack of rain all summer long. The land has turned sour, and that is the truth of it." The man looked up into his face, sad and tired, "Were you in the fighting, son?"

Making his way down through the valleys, his coats wrapped high about his shoulders, he found he could not shift the desolation within him. The Druid's words lingered in his mind, like mist hanging low above a swamp meadow.

"What have I done?" he whispered into the scarves about his face, the warmth of his breath white in the evening air. "I saved my people." *Isn't that what I did?* He threw his words out into the silence, to the Druid, to his father's Druid and all those before him. And silence returned to him.

A snort broke the air.

The hilt of his sword clasped tightly in his hand, the young king quickly turned, the hunter instantly awake to the sound of wild boar. His eyes scanned the forest, waiting for the scent of it. But he saw no boar. Just ahead, at the joining of three muddy roads, there was an ancient oak, vast and winter grey with a girth the stretch of three good men, and in a crook of its gnarled roots he spied a heap of filthy rags. There were blankets and grain bags, and a dirty shock of crimson cloth and from beneath them came again that mucous-thick snort. While a part of him was revolted by what appeared to be the destitution of some forest vagrant, he wasn't completely sure that it was human at all. Curiosity provoked him from his horse and, sword unsheathed, he tiptoed towards that strange pile of shreds and tatters, wondering at the smell.

When she looked up, he flinched.

She smiled; at least, it could have been a smile, for her cracked lips parted and she showed her teeth, three black crooked teeth, as sharp as they were broken. She shuffled in her heap of rags and horror overwhelmed him as the stench intensified. She lifted her arm towards him, her skin white and raw with cold, flesh hanging from bones that were hideously bent. Slowly she uncurled a twisted finger, the nail extending further, and she beckoned.

Come, she seemed to say, *come here.*

And though every cell in his body seemed to fight against it, Arthur took another step closer. She beckoned again. He swallowed and stepped again, aware of the smell sickening him to his belly. Her eyes were black as beads between red, swollen lids, wet and streaming. Her nose was hooked as a goshawk's beak, her great nostrils flared and oozing a green mucous that was collecting, congealing, on the ridge of her top lip.

He stammered, "G-good day," and her mouth opened again. She nodded her head as her face broke into that horrifying smile, and her body began to shake as a croaking, choking noise emerged from somewhere within her, a coughing and barking that soon, to his alarm, rose into a snorting, cackling, squealing roar.

She was laughing.

He stepped back, and she stopped abruptly.

In one deft movement, she shrugged the blankets off completely, revealing the dark crimson of the robes she wore. And with her head on one side, like an old bird listening, her black eyes boring into his soul, she spoke, slowly, clearly, directly. Her voice was little more than a hoarse dry whisper, like a wind that files rocks to the grain.

"What's troubling you, sire?"

Before he knew why, he had begun, and as he was speaking he found he could not stop, perhaps because if he had he would have dishonoured her. More likely it was because her eyes denied him the choice to disobey. So the king stood, beneath that great oak in the grey forest of his land, in the pool of her stench, a thousand years from his castle and the warmth of his lover's embrace, and he told the dreadful hag of the Black Knight's challenge and the quest that had since the meeting so consumed him, and his words tumbled over themselves as pebbles in the surf.

She watched him, and when his head hung, his eyes closed, confused and tired, she smiled again and whispered, "That's too easy". She waited until the young man looked up into her face. Pushing away a wisp of hair, like colourless straw, she sucked her teeth, snorted, swallowed. And smiled again.

"Do you ... know the answer, my Lady?"

She breathed deeply and sighed, the stagnant smell of her breath seeping into his lungs. "If I tell you, you must vow to grant me one wish."

"What would you wish?"

Lifting a crooked finger, the knuckles swollen and gnarled, she said, "Any wish I like".

He nodded, suddenly eager to hear her words and get away, back to the world he could hold and understand, "Anything at all. You have my word, my sacred word".

Though he slept in his beloved Guinevere's arms, it was fitfully, his dreams jarring him awake again and again, dreams of a mouth dark and cavernous, the broken black teeth, about to devour him. Reaching for his wife, he whimpered and sighed, and her soft fluid warmth held him close in the darkness. She never asked what had happened, or why he looked so bleak. He wondered if, through some mystery of women he did not understand, she knew already.

When he rose before dawn, she helped him to dress.

At the gates, Kai was already astride his horse. "I'm beside you, my Lord," he said, his chin rigid with the determination of his loyalty. But Arthur raised a hand, looking at nobody as he rode on through the gates, calling behind him, "No, sir, I must do this alone. Do not dishonour me by speaking again".

Guinevere watched. Some young child reached up and she took the cold little hand in her own, listening to the wind as her husband rode away.

There was little done at court while he was gone. People seemed somehow stuck in long moments, gazing at nothing, dreaming visions that disappeared, numb and wondering. Young knights gathered by the gates, and they bickered and fidgeted, scuffing their boots on the ground beside their horses, debating when to disobey and follow their king down to the forest below.

She was sorting loaves for the village widows when the young lad skidded on the stones, yelling as he tumbled through the doors into the kitchens, "The King's horse has been seen!"

"But is he upon it?"

The scout shrugged, "I dunno, Mam," and he turned on his heels and skidded back down the passage. She dropped the bread and hurried after him, making it into the courtyard as the gates were drawn open. Arthur was indeed upon his stallion, but his face was so pale he could ride through the band of knights, to the stable boy waiting to take the horse from him, with not a word said by anyone. Dismounting, he took her hand and they walked inside.

"My Lord?" she whispered.

In the great hall before the hearth he slumped into a chair and, rubbing his forehead, he stared into the flames devouring the wood before him. He seemed not to have noticed that he had been followed by so many of the court. Shaking his head, he turned to Guinevere. She motioned to a slave girl, "Bring ale, child, go, now," and, crouching before him, she whispered again, "What is done, my Lord?"

"It appears, my love," he sighed, "it appears my answer was that which he desired. Or did not desire, for his rage brewed some extraordinary darkness of a storm that seemed to come from the land itself, from beneath the old trees, with spirit winds that screamed ... " His words drifted as if he were remembering something he could not understand.

There was a murmur from the crowd behind them and Guinevere squeezed his hand, "So it is done, the challenge met?"

Frowning, he looked at her, her eyes of pale sea blue, and he half smiled, "Yes". Yet everything about him seemed to question her as if he were suddenly in awe of all that she was.

"Then what is your pain, my Lord?"

"I have met one, and found myself another."

16

There was silence in the hall. Then footsteps rung upon the stone as Aleric walked forward, his hand about the hilt of his sword.

"Allow me, my King, to take this weight from your soul."

"No," Arthur shook his head. "Not you, sir."

Letting go his queen's hand, he got to his feet, painfully carrying his anguish, and turned to face those gathered in the hall behind him. "I have made a promise I do not know how to fulfil." And he told them of his ride over the hills and down into the valleys beyond, he told them of the vile hag, of her stench and the hideous nature of her appearance, and he told them that, in return to the answer sought by the Black Knight of the pool, he had agreed to grant her any wish she desired.

There was a stillness as every soul waited, barely breathing.

"She asked for a knight, of this court, to wed."

The gasp was chilling. He closed his eyes and sat again in his chair before the fire. Guinevere took his hand as he shook his head. "I cannot ask any man here to give his life in such a way. It's inhuman. I cannot stand by my word. It must be broken."

For every soul in that room the revulsion was like a tide receding, drawing them silently back from the threat, horrified, unnerved, away from the young king who sat with his head held in his battle-scarred hands. Only one fought the tide.

Sir Gawain, soft faced with youth, stepped forward onto the empty floor.

Of course, a dozen men, as many women, begged him not to do the deed, exploring in their own minds how repugnant such an act might be, telling him with such graphic detail what would happen from the moment they were wed, how his life would be ruined, his body and his reputation soiled, explaining to him how he would have to leave the court (for the court would not tolerate such a stinking beast). There were others who, so overwhelmed by the idea, did all they could to avoid him about the castle, as if the young knight were already sullied with her gruesome stench. Some wondered if the young knight were so naive he did not understand what was meant by marriage and a few made such a suggestion directly to him. But Gawain listened to no one. In his heart he held the pride of being the one, the only one, who had upheld his king's honour. To anything else he was blind. He sensed that he would have to be.

Preparations were made for the simplest of ceremonies as Arthur, taking a simple wain, rode out with the young knight to the far valleys beyond the hills, there to find the bride. Nothing was spoken for many miles, not a word between them, both men tense with cold and pride. As they neared the crossroads of the ancient oak, the king turned to the younger man. With his eyes he offered him one last chance to escape this fate. Gawain nodded, lips pursed, and they hurried on.

The ceremony was a succession of steps needed to be taken. It lacked any hint of fluidity for it lacked joy, the guests hiding their horror and melancholy with varying degrees of success. The vile appearance of the hag could not be concealed despite the fine robes lent by the queen and, before the crowd, at her side, the young knight walked as if in a trance.

The feast that followed was quieter than any meal at court since the worst tragedies of the wars. The Bards played their lutes, the harps and drums, but even the jigs sounded desolate, mournful as twilight, though the songs, upon the orders of the queen, were those of honour, not of love. Plates were left uneaten. One man of the court even wondered whether the meat had turned, and called questioning a servant maid, but his wife hushed him quickly, whispering, "It's sour in your mouth, my Lord. Eat and be glad of it".

Though he waited as long as he could, the time did come when the young knight could put off the deed no longer. Guests were falling asleep across the tables, the king and queen had long since excused themselves and left the feasting for their chamber. Rising, Gawain turned to the hag, barely looking upon her face at all. He offered his hand, murmuring, "My Lady". As her chair was drawn back, she stood, bent as she was, and together, step by step, they left the hall arm in arm. As they walked down the dark passageways, a swell of voices rose behind them.

Terror had long since flooded the young man's mind and, blank, he ushered her into their marriage chamber. The great iron bed was hung with lace and veils and shadows hovered in the firelight, draughts playing as ever with the candles' flames. She moved awkwardly, as if in pain, making her way to sit upon the bed.

He stood before her, his legs stiff and shaking, knowing he must say something but unable to find words. There was a sparkle in her swollen, watering eyes, and for a moment he wondered if she were crying. Perhaps, in that moment, he saw her for the first time. The folds of her face seemed scarred with deep lines of age, her black beady eyes half hidden between puffy pink lids, her mouth misshapen by the wreck of her teeth, her skin deformed with warts and boils, the beak of her nose, yet in that moment Gawain saw her as a human being and his revulsion was broken by a wave of compassion. He realised that he had no idea how old she was. He knew only, suddenly, in the flickering light, that she must have lived through days he could not conceive.

She spoke and he blinked, for he realised he'd been staring.

"You are a knight indeed," she croaked. "A true knight of this land." There seemed softness in her gaze, as if she really did understand what he had been through that day. He stared still. Then drawn forward, trembling through honour, through awe, revulsion and sadness, bending towards her, he kissed her gently upon the rough skin of her cheek. She smiled, cracked lips breaking apart across her dreadful teeth. For a moment their eyes met. Until, shocked, turning away, Gawain stumbled into a chair,

"I - I will sit here a while. It has been a long day".

Pouring a drink from a jug of ale, he held his head in his hands and sipped. A part of him half listened, for her movement, her presence behind him, but he heard nothing. She made no sound at all. Not a breath.

When he turned, curious, what he saw shocked him senseless. Upon the marriage bed was sitting, quietly waiting, smiling softly, eyes shining, the most beautiful maiden he had ever dreamed he would behold. Her hair was spun silk of a thousand autumn colours; like moonlight in polished bronze, the fire seemed to dance within it. Her skin was clear and smooth as the blossom of the may, and the robes lent by the queen no longer hung about the shrunken shoulders but stretched over the fullness of her velvet breast. Gawain swallowed, wondering suddenly if the ale had been overly strong. His mouth fell open.

She laughed and the music of it drifted down through his soul.

"Who are you?" he murmured, fraught with disbelief.

"I am your wife," she said softly.

"What? How?" he pushed his hair from his forehead, stunned.

She just smiled. And, for an instant, the young knight glimpsed something of the mystery of woman. While another man might have leapt to his feet to hold such beauty in his own hands, Gawain was too much struck with awe. He stared at her, feeling his face change until a smile stretched from one ear to the other. She laughed at his wonder with a warm affection. "Come."

Staggering to his feet, he came to her, scared that touching her would break the guise, but she reached for his hand and put it to her cheek.

"Feel me," she whispered.

The emotion poured through him, overwhelming his senses, and she laughed as he sunk into the warmth of her, burying his face in her hair, hiding the tears that wet his face, muffling his gasps of relief and disbelief, amazed at the body his hands were holding.

"My Lord," she whispered, "yet you need make a choice."

Breathing in her sweet scent, he lifted his head from her bosom, "What choice?"

"I cannot be like this all the time, Gawain. You must decide if you would have me fair by the day or through the night. If I am beautiful by day, the court will be proud of you, the other knights envy you. But by night I would revert to the wild hag you have seen."

The young man flinched, looking up into her face, "Oh please, no. Surely you would not".

She pushed him a little away.

"If you would have me like this by night, in the privacy of our bed chamber, where we can enjoy the pleasures of each other's touch, then by day I would be still in the form of the old hag. The court would pity you, perhaps shun you for my ugliness that so revolts them." She touched his brow, combed her fingers through his hair and whispered, "What would you have me be?"

He stared at her, horrified, confusion skidding through his mind. Stumbling to his feet, he paced the room, speaking half words, pushing his hair from his face. He lifted the cup of ale and put it down untouched, staring at her again.

"I cannot," he protested.

"You must."

He picked up the fire rod and dug roughly at the burning logs, shaking his head. "By the gods, how can I make such a bloody decision? I would lose either way." And flinging it down upon the hearth stones, he came back to the bed where, sitting beside her, he touched the softness of her skin, running his finger along the line of her jaw, and he sighed from the depths of his soul. "You must decide."

Looking into his eyes, she smiled, filling his soul again with sound of her laughter.

"Then you shall have me fair, day and night, my Lord. For you have given me what a woman most desires."

"What have I given you?"
"My own way."

When the sun's early light crept into the bed chamber, Gawain lifted an arm lazily from the curved belly of his beloved wife, slowing the trail of his fingers across her skin. Opening his eyes, he smiled, amazed still by the sensation that flooded through him with every touch, and as he gazed at her sleeping face the excitement in him rose, intensifying with the remembering of what she had been. He hardly dared think of it, yet at the same time his mind sung as if with the tension of some acute exertion, as if he'd just outrun a furious storm and, panting, knew all too well that, somewhere out beyond the horizon, the skies were being torn apart with the wildness of their very nature. He pulled the rugs up higher about them and smoothed the hair from her eyes, overwhelmed.

As she awoke, her own smile melted the young knight all over again and, when he closed his eyes beneath the wash of pleasure, her laughter was as soft as rain. Moving her hands across his thighs, she let her fingers play upon his skin, her kisses searing his mind again until the excitement had filled his soul like an ancient ocean, the surge of the waves throwing him into a freedom that took him soaring through clear high skies. He hardly knew whether he should laugh or cry. All he knew was that his love was as pure as worship.

"My Lady," he whispered, "I am utterly yours."

She breathed in as if breathing in all that he breathed out, sighing a thousand sighs, closing her eyes, giving up her body to the hunger of his hands.

They slept and loved and slept again, and when finally a slave girl crept in to set the fire, they hid beneath the rugs and giggled like children, knowing all too well how beyond their chamber the castle would be wondering what had happened in that dreadful wedding bed all night long.

With the fire ablaze, she drew away, rising to find water in the chamber's dressing room, and alone beneath the rugs, he stretched as if pushing himself into the form of a man grown now suddenly a little older. He rubbed the soft down of his youthful beard and rolled from the bed, drawing the drapes from the window slits. And as he breathed deeply the morning air, misty and fresh, he was quite sure he caught a hint of the first scents of spring.

The court, though at first alarmed, were too relieved to insist too closely upon knowing the nature of her change and many assumed it was a hex that had been placed upon her, a hex dissolved by the purity of the young knight's compassionate heart. Though it took a while for some to overcome their fear of such a powerful and mysterious magic, most still would have admitted that the couple's love was the beauty of the castle all that summer long.

Gawain himself did not know what spell had been cast upon her, what could have caused such a ghastly countenance, nor did he ask. Sometimes something made him pause and he would watch her as she whirled, singing in the fields that grew rich with their barley gold, dancing in the meadows chasing swallowtails and laughing, laughing, or playing upon the shore lifting her skirts before the waves, and he would wonder.

Perhaps he feared it was the form she wore now that was the guise.

Perhaps he knew.

CHAPTER ONE

The Wild and Dark

The whispers of the tale

To lay a foundation, I began with a story. An old tale, the lives of its heroes were woven long ago into the fabric of our heritage. They are lives, fears and faces that exist within each one of us, tangled in the lines of our blood and evolution. It's a story that can be found in very many forms, in old myth and legend, in folklore and music, in the history of our people, in the laws of religion and the laws of men, in the 'burning of the witches', the slander of modern bitching, the statistics of divorce, the crises of self image, in the babble of psychology. It's her story, a hag story and one of many; and just as they all do, it teaches us of both love and terror, and not necessarily in obvious ways.

As a book about the hag, the journey across these pages is, too, an exploration of desire and fear, love and betrayal. Yet my interest is here not in the analysis of that tale. I don't seek to unravel it in order to find its validity or relevance logically. More than anything else, the tale is told to hang silently as an illustrated backcloth, to linger in our memories as we journey on, allowing our perspective a little of its rich colours, its emotion. That is the nature of the old stories, each telling holding within it some of the ancient threads that remind us how we are connected, through centuries within ever-changing worlds, as individual human beings and as communities, to the magical landscapes of our far off ancestry, where history is drenched in misty scents and dreams. With slight variations, every story told has been lived before, and told before, again and again.

In many ways the tale is also the holding force of this book. As if it were its magical encompassing circle, it holds the matter that brings me to this desk to write at all, to listen for inspiration in the crackling of the hearth fire. For what drives me to chase words here, stumbling, laughing, frustrated, amazed, is that quest for understanding played out in the old tale. It's an enigma that has raged through my own life, not only flinging down challenges and barricades, but creating moments of intense wonder and sheer exhilaration. It is the place where *woman* and *nature* meet.

For a long time in our Western culture, intellect, understanding and reason were thought unnatural in women; it was with grace, silence and obedience that we were expected to hide our natural savagery. Our grandmothers fought to be heard, and in many forums of society we continue their work, but these pages aren't concerned with our ability to reach or match some standard set down by men: women's wit and ability can outdo or be outdone by men's in equal measure. Instead, what I am exploring are those parts of us that we as women continue to hide - and what happens when we don't. For though we can be brilliant in so many ways, womankind is not often sunlight upon soft ripples, spring dew upon petals, the smiling and gentle ease of mothering comfort; grace, silence and obedience are not qualities that the average woman can sustain for any length of time. *Sugar and spice and all things nice* isn't the whole recipe: we too have snips of string and apple cores, bugs and slugs, tails, snouts, conkers, splinters and mud in the mix. Gloriously, it is not our failings but our very nature that is constituted of black clouds, cacophony, sudden storms and wild, treacherous mire. Here, in the muddy, bloody, raw essence of woman, we glimpse the face of the hag, the pith and fibre of woman that is just not *nice*.

Round-bottomed, soft-bellied, irrational, magical, too caring, too carefree, proudly demanding, unfettered by dependence, sexually unashamed, hairy, hungry, unpredictable, silently present, intangibly distant, ceaselessly gossipy, alarmingly uninhibited, seething with potential, incomprehensible,

25

altogether unfathomable, dangerous and deliciously powerful, she is the hag. She bleeds. She laughs so hard her belly shakes, she snorts and farts. She is the dark side of woman, the inside, the raw side beneath the surface skin we are taught so well to cleanse and tone and remedy with paint. She is the woman whose self-expression is not quite under control. Mysterious, intuitive, emotional, curvaceous, lustful, needy, selfish, natural and free, she is the *me* we long to - but know we shouldn't - reveal.

Feeling suppressed, we can rant and complain, blaming those of our peers we perceive to be competing for the lucrative success of acceptability, teetering on the thin ice of their own insecurities. We can blame the younger generation, the older generation, both clearly judging us against their own biased measures of experience and expectation. We can blame men for wanting some artificial perfection of sexual plaything, efficiency and subordi-nation. Any number of elements of modern society are perpet-ually and effectively asserting an agreed vision of what is acceptable. Yet rather than decrying our society, I would rather remove the notion of blame, and focus upon ourselves. Perceiving the wild, muddy, determined and selfish within us, we tend towards feelings of shame, worthlessness, the self-negation of fear, not because others necessarily declare the hag unacceptable (though they may), but because fundamentally *we* do. And in turn we judge others as quickly and as poorly.

If we hold to this belief that swathes of our nature as women are so unacceptable, inevitably we live in a state of perpetual tension. We consistently disable ourselves, too afraid to express our barefaced creativity, crippled by our inability to live as fully as we would wish. We suffocate all that we would hope to be, sabotaging our honesty, our relationships and our potential. With no medium for our creativity, no chance of satisfaction, we live unfulfilled, frustrated, bored and alone, seeking out the cocktail bars and chocolate bars of repetitive and addictive quick-fix absolution.

The hag, the wild soul of woman, lingering in the verges of our mind, shudders at such hollow and ineffective escapism. Any lapse of self-awareness, the briefest loss of self-control, a slip of the tongue or foot, a disconcerting confrontation, is an opportunity for her to slide her wrinkled butt out of the shadows and into our limelight, soaking us in an ice-warm flood of humiliation. It is the nightmare that is the exposure of our own raw and uncivilised nature, revealed in its naked state of emotional release or clumsy physicality, her stench filling our mind with the chilling fear of rejection. And such a fear makes us crazy, emotional, irrational. The frustration can erupt as hysteria, perhaps even exploding into psychotic behaviour, as destructive and uncontrollable as any creature scared and wild. More often it leaves us closed, numb and bewildered, feeling utterly alone, and lost as to the point of living at all.

So is this book an exploration of the hag, her cravings and our fears: the love and the terror. It's about learning to live more wholly, weaving the longing for darkness with the usefulness of light - not in some need to find balance, but in order to express the exquisite fabric of honesty. It is about learning how to access and express the richness of our potential, pouring out our soul creativity with laughter and with pride. It is about learning how to touch and be touched by another, surrendering ourselves into the wild flood of lust, love and celebration. It's about learning how to live without escapism, without inhibition, yet with full responsibility, getting what every woman most desires: her own way.

The book is written from the perspective of woman. In doing so, my hope is that, as a female reader, you can find yourself sitting within my words, looking out at the world through those moments of frustration, outrage and despair, of aching empathy, tears and laughter, that we share with other women. There will doubtless be times when my words veer away from your experience, but their validity still hums in that these are the stories of the women around us. While I have not written to allow the same intimate empathy within the male reader, I welcome him too, inviting him to read on, to watch and listen, that he may come to know the women in his life a little better, and particularly those whose wild, awkward and difficult nature both intrigues and enrages him. Further, there is an undercurrent beneath what I suggest to be women's nature that is in reality fully a part of human nature, indeed nature as a whole.

My perspective doesn't come from a standpoint of personal development. The New Age movement that promotes its plethora of nice, clean guides to life seems to me tipped towards a secularised, godless search for a loving truth and blessings of light. I write instead as an animist in the British Pagan tradition, a polytheist who acknowledges numerous gods and is utterly devoted to a dozen or more. A priest of the land that is my home, the islands of Britain, I have trained as a Druid perceiving nature as both sacred and merciless. I am often in the presence of death, I know pain and I am no optimist. My quest is not enlightenment. There is no sentimentality in my vision, but instead a profound and potent current of wonder and fealty to the gods, the land, the ancestors - to nature, human and nonhuman - and as such a deep desire to explore the creativity of living *well*.

My religious tradition is explored fully in many other texts, written by myself and others, elucidating its essential practice and the ongoing quest to learn to live with honour, with and within nature. As a reader, it is not necessary to share my theology, for where I speak of it here my focus is the hag and the primal deities that inspire her: the many faces and forms of the dark goddess of nature. An elemental and primitive force, she is all that is beyond our control, pushing us, pulling us, shocking us witless, threatening to raze our world, tearing us down with the power of her need to be expressed. Within humanity, she is revered as countless ancestral gods of myth and folklore, from the Morrigan to Black Annis; I shall not limit her reach here by naming her. If to you she is an archetype crafted by human nature, it would not alter the foundation of my thesis.

Nonetheless, she is honoured from the outset here, for her dark nature whispers, like a cold and quiet wind in the last leaves of autumn, through the tale that begins this book, and each page from there on.

The wild and nature

He puts his arm around me and immediately I want to kill him. There is a chivalry in his action, but within it an assumption that I need or want his guidance. I smile at him and almost imperceptibly shake myself free, moving from the sensible route between the puddles, fallen leaves and twigs into the deep pile of leaves that lines the path. He steps forward as if to stop me, to support me, but I dismiss his concern with a movement of my hand, and throw him a complex question about government policy and legislation.

It's an obvious ruse, but he understands it and, though disquieted, he tries to answer, watching me nervously as I shuffle through two feet of autumn leaves, dirtying my elegant shoes, the hem of my skirt becoming wet and muddy; I lift it a little to avoid excess drag. What he's telling me is information I need to know, but I hear very little, my soul transported to the age of four, in red welly boots and anorak, remembering throwing great armfuls up into the air, the gold and russet and dark brown, the brittle dry and tiny yellow ones floating down, the wet leaves falling faster, over my head and all around. I'm soaked in the experience. I can taste the thrill of the moment like a shimmer in the breeze, the hint of autumn's chill, the soft chatter of my parents moving slowly behind, the *shlush* of the pram wheels through the leaves and puddles.

Stopping to look up at the enormity of the trees, their

branches arching over the path, I feel so wonderfully small. My brother is hollering for me to 'Come on, slow coach!', the others running ahead, throwing leaves, playing like puppies, and standing there in my red boots such an extraordinary peacefulness fills me. A leaf is falling, dancing above me, heading slowly down towards me.

I realise he's stopped. I've stopped.

"I'm sorry," I smile. "It's just so beautiful."

It occurs to me that if I were with Pagan friends we would be playing, kicking up leaves, running to catch this one, that one, chasing each other like squirrels, laughing until the tears were running down our faces; we'd be taking some time to sit and watch the fall. I sigh, then watch his face begin to frown with a nervous smile. He lifts his briefcase in defence as, with a great armful of leaves, I shuffle through the pile towards him.

The wild is exciting. But it's best held in a cage, surely, for the wild is unpredictable, and that means trouble. After all, though nature is all that births us, holds us, feeds us, it is also all that actively destroys us. Since our ancestors claimed their first scrap of land, nurturing fire for warmth and a dry place to sleep, a meadow where seed sown was worth protecting, people have done what they can to tame the forces of nature. It's an inherent part of our evolution, to accrue control in order to reduce a threat.

Where nature is not held back by technology, the majority, urbanised, civilised, view it with suspicion, nervous of the uncontrollable, the unknown and the unknowable. There is a fear of the wild. Turning determinedly away from the inevitability of storms, floods and quakes, we bow to the call of big business and the media, of pharmaceutical · and chemical companies who encourage us to cleanse away every last invisible smudge of bacteria, odour and decay. Immune-deficient, asthmatic, chronically fatigued, allergic to life, we poison ourselves with the toxins we ingest as pills, sprays, wipes, fumes, detergents and toiletries.

Yet all the time the wild intrigues us. Despite our fear - because of our fear - we play with fire. In awe, we watch movies of nature's killers, from tigers to twisters. We peer into dark corners, play in the snow, face death mountain climbing or dive in deep water. Knowing we can return home to the safety and reassurance of a warm bath, we go for a long walk in the chill air, we holiday in the 'third world'; life is routinely comfortable for the majority in Western culture; most of the time it is possible to pretend we have nature under control, for on the whole it is kept safely outside the front door or on the television. And the wild, in a cage, can be good entertainment. The same is true of human nature.

We watch emotional or physical violence, on the big screen or small, empathising, feeling the rush of fear and the flood of relief, allowing the movie to affirm for us the safety of our own reality. Where it doesn't, infrequently that same empathy can act as provocation, encouraging our natural violence where otherwise it relieves it; but for most, even those who relish the bloodiest action on screen, the reality of bodily fluids is distasteful and alarming. Human odours, dead skin, shit, spit, sweat, piss and blood: once again, those disinfectants are ready to hand, our fear exaggerating far beyond any actual need.

The intangible in our nature is equally alarming, uncontained emotional release deemed as bad as the physical dribble. Grief, love, jealousy, rage, the desperation to have a child, the hunger for power or revenge: human nature can be as incomprehensible or uncontrollable as any mudslide, virus or typhoon. Taught to hide it, deny it, clean it up, suppress it, our collective social mentality supports the use of alcohol, prescribed and even illegal drugs, the continuous chatter of television, anything that will distract and stupefy, encouraging us not to worry, to shrug, not to bother, not to care. All too often, our fear of nature promotes passivity, the blind denial of the problem only adding to our disconnection from nature, which in turn only allows the situation to grow worse.

Many girls grow up without a functional understanding of their own nature. Too often self-exploration is brought to a halt with gates being firmly closed as we are told to *behave*. Our adventuring is frustrated, curiosity negated, convention denying us the necessary mess of self-expression and creativity. With adults obsessed by safety, children - especially girls - are now seldom allowed to explore alone, no longer sent from the house after breakfast, told to 'stay out of the way', and 'keep yourself occupied', roaming with adventure and freedom, learning from every fright and bruise and revelation. Just as a culture loses its understanding and so its connection with its environment, so girls disallowed from exploring their own nature grow to be women disconnected from the basic cycles of their being, the tides of their hormones, appetites, talents, cravings and emotions.

In some ways it might feel as if we are comfortably removed from nature, hands clean and hair brushed, safe from the chaos, but the separation is an illusion crafted of fear and ignorance, and such a divide only generates confusion. With no clear idea of the depth of our power, we live with a gnawing fear about what might happen if we *were* to let go. Surely the grief is so very deep we'd cry forever; surely the anger is so immense, if we opened the dam we'd demolish the entire bloody world around us. If we were to do what we wanted, to express our frustration, to swirl or sing or slide into our lust, to love with all the intensity we feel inside, our lives would surely break up into a thousand sharp and slippery shards. Too many women don't even begin to express their true creativity because the energy and ideas they know they'd reach into are just too frightening. The fear of what they might unleash is crippling: the unpredictable storms of nature, the wildness inside.

And, in just the same way that we disconnect from the environment, as we lose our sense of the deep inner power of our own nature, our life force humming, we lose our respect for it too. We begin to abuse it. The wildness that is nature within us is chained and tamed, both with the drugs of our culture - sugar, alcohol, antidepressants - and with the entirely acceptable conditioning of our very own self-negation.

The wild goddess, the hag with her wicked grin and muddy fingers, is not only shunned as indecorous and dangerous, but dismissed with the benumbed wave of a hand. And as she leaves, she takes with her our potential, our creativity and our fulfilment.

Fear of the dark

With all my strength I pull. For a moment it seems an impossible task, then suddenly it shifts. The back of the armchair touches the wall above me, and the blanket is secured. I sit back and look around. A cushion needs adjusting, the blanket straightened. Apart from a sly twinkling narrow slip of light along an edge, the whole den is dark.

Wriggling into the heap of cushions, satisfied, I sigh, and nestle down to dream. The wildwood is all around me, crickets and bird calls, a toad by a pool absolutely still, butterflies in the breeze, bright green moss on a branch low and soft enough for me to lie on. Stretching out big black paws, claws flexed then retracted, I listen to the sound of the jungle and drift into half a snooze.

It isn't long before I stretch again, leaping indolently from my tree to meander off into the thick of the forest, prowling, listening, watching a troop of howler monkeys passing above me, getting distracted by vultures chattering. I chase a dragonfly near a stream, splashing in cool water. I snooze, listening to distant music ...

And a long while later, out of the darkness of the trees, voices emerge.

"I'm not exactly sure where she is. She disappeared after breakfast." For a moment, the words make no sense, then I hold my breath so as not to move a muscle, listening, waiting, hoping they'll go on out into the garden. "I expect she's up in the tree house, in some world of her own." I can hear the smile in my mother's voice. The man half laughs and murmurs something in the way that grown ups do as I snarl silently, *go-away-go-away-go-away* ...

Sliding again I see them walking through the jungle, a huge and powerful tiger close by, mean and hungry. The sky is clear blue, sun no doubt baking the bare earth as I lie in the cool dark shade of my vast avocado tree.

"Here she is!" The sky is torn off my world. Above me suddenly, looming over me, big naked faces, a white ceiling and walls that are closing in. There's nowhere to run. Light, like some sticky liquid, covers everything around me, blanching it to bones. The world is stiff and rigid. Wide eyed I glare, shocked. My mother's expression quickly changes and she winces, closing her eyes, "Oh, sweetheart". Carefully spreading the blanket back over the chairs, she whispers, "I'll put some milk and cookies under the sofa ... "

The other voice is louder. "Should she be in the dark like that, straining her eyes?"

I hear my mother shrug, and smile, "She likes it."

It is not surprising that we have an innate fear of the dark. In the dark, we lose the reference points of familiarity that offer us a measure of certainty in an ever-changing world.

Furthermore, what exists in this uncharted state is not only the unknown, but also all that we have rejected or denied as real. The most frightening energies we sense in our blindness are the demonic little entities who we know would defeat us if we allowed confrontation. These are the emotions we've feared, the jealousies and envies, the physical or emotional desires we've deemed perverted or dangerous, all entangled with vague memories from childhood, films and stories. While some are based on experience, some are now twisted by trauma or suppression, elements of our soul in need of release or healing, there is so much in that shadowy darkness that is held by unnecessary fear, parts of ourselves that still smell of wild, raw (hag) nature.

The fear itself is self-perpetuating. If we were able to catch it as it seeped through the soul, consciously identifying its nature and containing it for as long as were necessary, we could use the power as a guiding yet directed propellant for our own benefit. Instead of reacting out of control, we could act with intention. Usually, however, fear is a destructive and destabilising energy.

Simply identifying and admitting it can be hard enough. The emotional energy has been evoked because our data bank of experience tells us this is dangerous: be afraid, close down, get away. Some of those beliefs are obvious and important for our survival, but others were crafted out of our first encounters with the dangerous unknown. Rooted in childhood, for the most part these are beliefs based on circumstances that no longer apply (if they ever did). Our rational adult minds may tell us there is nobody else in the room, but still the child inside us might panic when the light is out and something inexplicably falls from the chair. The dark wild leaps out at us, breaking up our fragile veneer of certainty, knowing and familiarity.

Beliefs about relationship and value are even harder to grasp. Many core issues we hold around our self esteem are too painful to face, those that declare internally that we are not good enough, not loveable, not worth bothering with at all. Yet even while we refuse to face them, these undercurrents are disabling.

Terrified, all too often we fight our way out of that boundless dark of potential with assumptions we declare to be facts, with aggressive pedantry, blind faith and dogma. Stumbling, we grope for tangible stability, or we curl up and withdraw, once more craving the simple security that feels like being held. This is as true physically as it is with an emotional obscurity. For with nothing to hold onto that is safe or real or certain, we lose a sense of what defines us as individual human beings. As an under-current to everyday life, this is the pull that makes us so insecure: determining what is real, we live according to beliefs built on realities that no longer exist, beliefs carried now on rafts tied up with the artificial twine of asserted fact. In stronger currents, in white water, it leaves us shaken, defensive and afraid. When it persists, surging into floods, we begin to lose our faith in that declared reality, losing our ability to self locate, eventually drifting over the edges of sanity. We get lost in the dark.

This is not a fear we are born with, but one that develops in the first years of life, exploding at that point when a young child's grasping for knowledge first catches hold of a sense of himself as a separate being. Our response is to turn on a light, to create a pool of knowing with the glow of the night lamp, a comfort zone of familiarity. Not only do we do this for our children but we do it for ourselves, throughout our lives, recreating moments of relief, often out of all proportion to any actual need. The social culture of politics, revealed religion and science makes official such desires for certainty through debating and asserting agreed perceptions. Tabloid journalism and soap operas do the same for those not wanting or able to think, affirming a shared reality that can be used as a crutch of certainty. Overeating, promiscuity, drugs that mollify and distract, compulsions and work addictions, are all comfort zones, padding for the soul who is afraid of the dark.

Fear of the dark is socially *normal*, reckoned to be sensible, so is seldom addressed. Indeed, in the vast majority of religions across the world, darkness embodies all that is to be shunned. The perennial mono-myth that is the battle between the forces of light and dark is taken up by monotheisms who extend and intensify the natural fear as they encourage us to reach for their 'one true light'. Those seeking power and status as warriors in the fight, like knights in the old Crusades, leap up on their charges to champion the light. Desperate to overcome nature's gusts of chaos, its wild darkness, they hand out bite-size biscuits of knowledge for us to accept and gratefully believe in, soundbites to hold onto with confidence. Some of these make sense in terms of natural law, but many are without any foundation whatsoever, crafted out of wishful thinking and political device.

The nature of the dark

Yet, darkness is not evil; it is simply the not knowing. Throughout the history of our people, as far back as stories allow we see evidence that some have explored the power of the dark. In the long barrows and passage graves of Britain and Ireland, five to eight thousand years old, we find clues as to how peoples reached out to understand the forces of darkness and death that loomed over them. It is unlikely that the crawl through the narrow mud tunnels into the chambers of these ancient tomb shrines was something done by anybody; more probable is the idea that a chosen few would make these journeys on behalf of the tribe, a man or woman who was able to overcome the fear and return alive, and sane, with visions and confidence that would benefit the others. We could imagine these to be the earliest priests, people who were sufficiently different from the norm to be able to undertake such tasks; for it isn't just courage that is needed. Courage often comes with limited sensitivity. It takes a mindset that is willing to perceive and accept the unknown, the unknowable, that which is almost unthinkable, and find a language to explain to those who can't.

Yet surely to go purposefully into the dark, to explore its depth and celebrate its power, to dance in wild unknown landscapes, is to risk encountering 'evil' or even to side with it? Science, ever exploring beyond its own boundaries, delving into the unknown, has found acceptability in most reaches of society by asserting facts that can be apparently proven. Those who explore uncharted lands simply for the love of it, without need for validation of their journey or proof of their experience, remain suspect to the warriors of the light - both religious and humanist. To teach about the dark, its beauty, its nature, is anathema.

Yet, this is the work of the Pagan. Indeed, every mystery school and occult movement that has existed through these millennia, emerging and dissolving, is rooted in these ancient journeys, over time layering upon them the clarities and complexities of maps, signposts and pathways. The dusty alchemical tomes, the grimoires of the mage, the ladders leading from earthly hell to enlightenment, the prophecies of human annihilation, of ascension and final judgement, are all just well-thumbed Baedekers of the wild lands of the dark. The shaman's visions, the lunatic's burbling, memories retrieved from high fever and trance dance, the drug-soaked ramblings of the poet, are equally travellers' tales.

To the animist, it is the goddess of the dark, she that embodies nature's darkness with its inherent and essential purpose, that we journey to encounter on such spiritual questing, driven by a desire to understand her power and her intent. If we understand that the gods exist regardless of human acknowledgement, she is one of the most ancient gods, far older than any that create or offer light. And by her touch we are woken to the darkness inside our own soul, allowing us better to perceive - and at the same time reflecting - that which is all around us. Without sufficient reverence, we are lost. The universe is very dark.

As my son's old space book tells me, if our sun were a washing machine, Earth would be a pea some 60 metres away from it. In actual distance, that is about 150 000 km. It's another 5 750 000 km from here out to Pluto. The nearest star in our galaxy, Proxima Centauri, is 40 billion kilometres from our sun (on the scale of our solar washing machine, that's a microwave on the other side of this planet). Galaxies themselves spin in vast areas of what is, for the most part, absolute nothingness. Furthermore, astronomers now speak of 'dark matter', invisible material that we cannot see or understand, of which there is estimated to be thirty times more than anything creating or reflecting light. A hundred million light years (multiply by 9.5 trillion to find the distance in kilometres) of dark space exists between some galaxies. Light, as flickering specks dancing in the cosmic breeze, fire sprites in an endless night, is a minute part of what we can perceive to be the forces of nature.

Lay science informs us (too simplistically) that our planet circles this sun-star, its tremendous gravitational pull holding us in a spin with its fire at the centre. It is said that life would not exist with out it. Unquestionably, we rely on its heat and light; it is not surprising that so many religious and philosophical systems hold it as a pivotal focus. Yet life does not emerge from the light. The source of all creativity, of all creation, of imagination and potential, is by its very nature a place of darkness. That dark womb of creation is the core of woman; together with its currents and tidal flows of hormones, of blood, fertility, emotion, it is what makes a woman, drawing her into the tides and cycles all around her. It is her very nature. It is the centre of her creativity.

But we're afraid of the dark.

When the fear came upon my son, I used techniques I use with students of Druidry, and very quickly his fear dissolved. During the day, with eyes tightly closed, he learned how to sense the world around him. Feeling the carpet underfoot, rugs and floors, he discovered a confidence in his subtle perception, remembering how to listen to his feet. With hands awake and outstretched, he explored obstacles and edges until he could sense something's presence without needing to see or touch it. When night fell and his trust was sufficient, we made the same journeys, feeling, listening with fingers and toes, finding calm.

It can take adults longer than a few nights' practice, but the process is the same: reawakening skills innate in our human nature, we face our fear of the dark, at first on familiar ground, then moving into the unfamiliar. We use our imagination, our ability to remember and recreate a world out of what we've seen, as a positive tool. And as our own nature interplays with nature around us, so does our confidence build, allowing us to stride into the unknown.

The teachings of animism again place the emphasis upon the importance of relationships that provide a bond of connection: not just human to human relationships, but every way in which we interact with and within nature. Where we experience ourselves fully as an integral part of an environment, not a separate entity existing within it, it is the essence of those relationships that holds and guides us. This sense of connection comes from how we relate to the earth, the moon, food, wind, waters and sun, as well as those more transient creatures of nature - plants and trees, human beings and other animals. Fundamentally, it is the strength of those relationships that provides us with a source of valid and effective confidence. In a changing world, there can be constancy of intention that we can trust in a sound relationship, and that certainty within change is a powerful resource.

Creating a relationship with the goddess of darkness herself, she that obscures the world around us, is equally important. The animist knows she is merciless, her essence unmoved by human petitions, but reverence inspires a wakefulness that allows us better to comprehend her nature, ensuring our courage is sensitive and respectful.

However, the craft of creating relationships requires edges. In the light, we can see the edges of the other being and, stepping forward with a sense of our own identity, we can make contact. That other being may be a single leaf, a tree or an entire woodland; we may engage as an individual or as a community; however we come together, the edges are clear, and as such we are able to touch and be touched. In the darkness, however, those edges disappear.

The self and the dark

In a religious tradition focused upon the importance of relationship, maintaining our edges is accepted as crucial. Needless to say, I am not referring to personal boundaries that keep us defended to the point of being closed: such would be entirely counterproductive to any interaction. The edges I speak of naturally protect us, helping us remain healthy and strong, our soul energy cohesively intact. Without edges we are vulnerable to intrusion, to wounding, or being overly influenced; we can lose our sense of identity.

Of course, the edge we show the world is not always an undiluted expression of who we feel we truly are. We paint our edges with textures and colours as a glamour that protects our tender truth, presenting various personas for different relationships, adjusting how we are for every situation. Though this can be wholly manipulative or deceptive, doing so is not always dishonest or dysfunctional; at times it can be an expression of respect, altering the way we are in order to communicate more effectively.

Every creature of nature has many layers. Those I am concerned with here are the edges that delineate the area of the soul within and immediately around us into which we allow nobody but those we absolutely trust. Here lies our raw self, naked and vulnerable beneath the protection of guise and pretension. Our flaws and imperfections are all too evident and, though the hag shrugs, very often this inner self is rejected and abandoned. Staying busy, always in company, painted as we'd like to be seen, we find ways to keep her hidden. It is, of course, possible to do so for very many years, but in time her lack of nourishment becomes obvious; we start to look spiritually pale and thin, our essence fading, leaving the mere husk of a persona.

Allowing someone to get close enough to see through those painted edges is what we call intimacy. And if we are hurt by someone within that vulnerable intimate space, the wounds are the worst of our lives. For most women, the number we let into that place of trust we can count on our fingers, and often those of just one hand. Mothers share their intimate space (in healthy circumstances) from conception until the child start to find its own edges, usually between the age of two and three, skidding on tantrums of alternating frustration and fear. Where a father is accepted into the mother's intimate space, the child feels that closeness too. Yet, being human and struggling with their own issues, our parents make mistakes, emotionally backfiring, and most of us grow up with that intimate space already scarred.

Finding our independence, growing into women, we crave that intimate connection so deeply, longing to be held in perfect love and perfect trust, warm and secure, naked and flawed. In our hag truth, in the darkness of our inner self, we dream of the knight who would accept us for all we are: that perfect kiss ... Yet as adults, confusing love with that need, intimacy all too often doesn't extend beyond the first flush of a relationship when, blinded by emotion, for a while we forget our fear. When the blaze of fireworks fades, we step back, too afraid that an old cut may be repeated, and the relationship falls apart.

Where scars are still seeping, the edges of the intimate space become barbed wire or opaque barriers, screaming with protective aggressive signs saying: 'KEEP OFF', *don't touch, stay away*, as we defend our ugly broken self from further pain and rejection. In others, the intimate space becomes so damaged by abuse (drugs or violence) that the edges are vague, tattered or shattered, leaving no personal protective boundaries at all. Such people remain open to violation. In a world where trust is broken, intimacy becomes terrifying.

If the intimate space is so flinched that it is held completely within, the physical body can be abused while the individual feels still somehow untouched. *You can hit me, but you can't hurt me anymore.* Where the edges are permanently tight, the physical body reflects that tension as pain or disease. Scars on our edges develop rigidity in muscles and joints, down to the cellular level, creating areas vulnerable to damage.

In a healthy person, the edges of our intimate space are thoroughly flexible, flinching to evade intrusion, relaxing when the moment passes, allowing the body to relax in turn. Indeed, whatever the damage, with sufficient hard work it is possible to heal those edges, regenerating our soul's natural cohesion.

To describe the circle of our intimate space, I use the word *nemeton*. Coming from one of the oldest language roots of Britain, the word can be translated as a place in time and space that is both sacred and safe: a sanctuary. This was the temple grove of the ancient Druids, and those practising the tradition today still use the word; yet each one of us also carries that temple within our own soul. As we find healing and strength, experiencing our own integration within nature, as if rooted deep into the rich earth and freely breathing the skies, this personal sanctuary shines with the energy of our life force, vitality flowing unhindered, free.

Where our personal nemeton is whole, offering us such vibrant confidence, it is easier to make relationships with others, whether edges simply touch edges or we are open to share our sanctuary in a state of intimacy. The experience of connection, soul to soul, fills us. This is the greatest source of teaching and inspiration.

Of course, protecting ourselves usually appears the sane priority.

I move the curtains slightly, to breathe. They are heavy, dusty, obviously never stretched across the windows. Nobody's looking my way, everyone noisy and busy, running, laughing, pushing each other, trying to get to a chair. Another girl's out; she wanders off with a sigh and sits down at the side of the room, watching with big eyes, wishing she could still play. Her mouth moves as if she's still in the midst of it all, as the music starts up, the chaos of the game. I gaze at her, forgetting to hide myself again.

A heavy hand touches my shoulder. "What are you doing in there? Come on out and play with the other children, go on." I'm pushed out into the noisy room. I drift in my bubble, touched now and then by the hot breeze of the game, making my way to a patch of quiet in an alcove by the stairs. And there I stand, and watch, dreaming of stardust and the wide-wide dark of empty space.

He stands beside me for a while without saying anything, then speaks without looking at me.

"You shouldn't worry about what they say." His voice is soft, almost husky. He's a bit taller than me, a bit older. Maybe about eight. I shrug. I can feel him beside me. He's calm and quiet. "Why do you limp anyway?" I shrug again, not willing to gather up the words to tell him. "They think you're odd, that's all." And he looks at me.

His eyes are green.

"Have you ever sat in a space bubble?" I whisper.

He frowns, shakes his head, and smiles.

In our modern society there is a pervasive current, running through psychotherapy, philosophy and New Age spirituality, that encourages each of us to *find ourselves*. Yet many mystical traditions, including Western animistic Paganism, teach that at the very core of our being there is no self to find. At our centre, there is simply the empty darkness of nothing. In part, this is why Paganisms are reviled by those who value only light. It is also why deeply esoteric journeys can indeed take us to brink of madness: searching for who we truly are, we discover we are nothing. Yet here too is our dark goddess, she that is the formless unknown of complete release and pure potential. Deep within us, she is a well of serenity. Perceived through fear, however, she is the ugly horror of our eventual and inevitable annihilation, and another reason why we craft ways in which to deny her presence. For the woman who has not hidden the hag within herself, that darkness at the centre of the soul is a magical sanctuary. In Druidry, we speak of it as a nemeton deep within the soul, a place of exquisite peace and natural healing. Indeed, it is often referred to as a great dark cauldron; it is only when a woman is able to sit, balanced and grounded, upon the three feet of that inner cauldron, that she is able to find the strength of her soul's creativity, an ancient and bottomless pot containing that infinite universal darkness, this is the great cauldron of myth and legend, and mumbling beside it is her inner hag who, like Cerridwen, the old witch goddess of the sickle moon, stirs her brew of transformative inspiration.

Branwen, another goddess of the Welsh tales, has a cauldron that possesses the power of rebirth, dead warriors thrown into its abyss coming back to life to fight another day. The connection is the same in mythic tales all around the world: from the mystical depths of the cauldron, the wonder of new life emerges. Radiating the exquisite brilliance of life-potential, shimmering with miracles waiting to happen, this cauldron is the womb, both magical and physical. As nemeton, it is both the sanctuary and the source of a woman's true creativity. The more we are able to identify ourselves as centred within it, the richer our experience of life becomes.

Since the beginning of time, the mystery of birth has fascinated mankind. As a wild screaming bloody flood of women's magical power, men have been obsessed with their need to understand and control it. As bewitching as it is horrifying, over time and through men's teachings, this womb temple - the dark nemeton cauldron - has been progressively civilised, refined by a mentality that still quested its mysterious power yet feared its wild depths. Like women who behaved themselves, submitting to male authority, fragile and clean, the battered ancestral cauldron of the hearth fire underwent a transmutation, re-emerging within the tales as the shining chalice. As myths were Christianised, the mud of Paganism removed, this cup, the Holy Grail, became the focus of the most sacred quests, the seeking of the source of life linked back to Christ's death and regeneration. It was said that the grail held the very essence of divine creativity, and young men sacrificed their lives to discover its truth.

Women stayed at home. For the tales of the grail are tales of men's dreams. Unless she has assiduously gagged and chained her hag-self in some dungeon of denial, a woman doesn't go out seeking this divine creative power by daylight. To do so would be fruitless, for the mysteries and the answers lie within our own bodies, our own soul-intention, our very nature. Though it may be hidden from our consciousness, intuitively we know, because like every woman we hold the stories of our mothers, our grand-mothers and their mothers and, like herbs in the sacred brew, the awareness spits and bubbles in the darkness of our womb-cauldron, as intuition, as emotion, as desire. The wisdom of knowing and not knowing flows in our blood. Silently and eternally, the dark womb reflects the universe around us.

Questing the source of life for its own sake has always been a male concern. Sadly in the history of human politics and science, many have tried, seeking that universal truth that will confer the power of control upon the one who claims it. Believing themselves knights of the quest or even to have found the grail itself, they have stood by some crowning stone upon a high hill and claimed it, causing a wasteland of devastation as a result, some remaining barren places of conflict for millennia. No doubt others will do the same again. Apart from a few who feel the need to compete, the women watch with sadness, wondering at the futility as another one trips, falling, reaching for the cup, blinded by love, lust, deluded need: greed. With his knights around him, too often where he falls he is now surrounded by war, his grail-vision distorted by the delusions of wealth and power.

On the other hand, for a woman who knows the cauldron as a

nemeton or sanctuary, this is a place where she dissolves into the exquisite and infinite serenity of the dark, and in doing so explores the deepest magic of her heritage.

Sliding in is not easy. In so many ways it is utterly counter to our natural instinct for survival, or indeed what our society has taught us about sanity, value and clarity. Indeed as we make our journey, we face the demons who hover in the back alleys of our minds. It is not easy to stand and confront them, for they yell directly at our tenderest weakness, highlighting the vulnerability of our defended mortality. Yet the journey is thwarted, too, because these fear-demons are blocking our own potential, and so serving a useful purpose; for with a barrier that hides from us what we could be, we are not continually reminded of what we are not. Nor need we face the challenge of actively working towards it. Exploring our creativity, stumbling and failing along the way, is a much harder option than rambling along old familiar tracks, however unsatisfying.

The hag dances upon these roads without a care. When the centre is shaking, the world turbulent with change, when fear is provoked, instead of losing control the hag uses her nemeton, holding the emotional energy within that ancient dark cauldron. Hurricanes swirl and crash within its depths, the energy seething. Far from suppressing expression, the energy is contained, the process of action paused, until a perfect course of action is laid out and its full force can surge forward, flooding through into creativity.

Again, we must make sure that there is a clear understanding of the dark, one that does not hold the erroneous connotations that it has been given by theories and theologies that focus on light. The pitch-black scent of nothingness does provoke a natural fear. As utter darkness, with no reference points, the depths of the cauldron are a place of madness. Some slide in and never find their way out. Drug abuse, destroying the pathways of the brain, can send an individual into this world with no handholds.

Seekers and priests of that realm, the Druid, shaman, medicine man, mage, spend years learning how to go down deep and return with its dark treasure. The hag does it naturally.

In times past, those priests who walked in these worlds did not choose the path. It was only because of severe illness, an accident or birth disability, that they were taken and trained in the craft of the community's religion. Some kick of fate had tricked and hurled them into this dark groundless world on the edge of death. In our society today, it is manic depression and mental breakdowns, car crashes and war, or the disease epidemics of our era such as cancer and AIDS, that can drag people to explore what it is to be a priest of these ancient religions. A few seek it out through a burning curiosity they don't quite understand. Many make their quest through the (gentler) secular alternatives of psychotherapy and new age models of personal development. With some deep soul trauma, however, you have a head start, albeit unpleasant. Without it, those who wish to make the journey encounter the fears, one by one, from step one.

At first we move carefully, clambering on a steep downward path, into a twilight of lengthening shadows. The subconscious beliefs that linger in denial populate this land in the guise of monsters that must be faced, slain or befriended. Identifying the emotions and the beliefs that provoke them, making the changes that heal, we stumble at first, flinching, cowering, yelling, until we find ourselves strong enough to shrivel gorgons with a single glance.

From there, finding confidence, we move our hands off the cauldron's rim and onto the roots that hang down reaching into the depths, the roots that bring to the surface the subtle yet essential nourishment so needed by the soul. These roots, if we follow them, allow us to make the journey, sliding, lurching from foothold to slippery foothold, crawling in the darkness of not knowing, meandering back through time. So do we explore our ancestral stories, the patterns of our genetic inheritance, finding our own heritage, the wisdom gleaned by our blood kin and tribal communities. And if we are awake and willing to see, willing to be helped, we may come across grandmothers, wizened with piercing eyes, women who have walked the path before. Slowly we find a way, our way, out of the isolation and alienation that comes hand in hand with self negation, to a sense of belonging. We find ourselves sitting, tired and exhilarated, our minds emptied by the fullness of life's experience, and beside us chuckles the hag of our own wild nature.

Then one day, through carelessness, or recklessness, we fall. Or if we are lucky, that guide who is leading us lets go of our hand and we are suddenly alone, plummeting, breathless with immediate panic, *Alice*, grasping at anything that flickers with familiar light ... until gradually we find a way to fly. And gliding, on soul wings, like a manta ray in the deep ocean, we learn how to drink in the shimmering energy through which we drift and dive, sensing without considering, being without thinking, coming back out into the world of living balance, utterly renewed.

We learn how to love this place of absolute potential.

Use your elbows, he'd said. The basket he's carrying is disappearing into the throng ahead of me and a gust of determination takes me, fuelled by the panic of getting left behind. Stamping my feet with every stride, gritting my teeth, I dig my elbows into the legs of the grown ups towering around me. But for the occasionally indignant curse, "Cuidado, chica!", 'Coño!', few people seem to notice, so now I put all my strength into every shove and dig. It's like swimming upstream, with elbow-fins, through dangerous reeds and schools of slithery fish.

Breaking through the surge, the river current of people, I grasp at the bank, coming up for air. Dad is standing by a heap of cardboard boxes that are covered with messy birdcages, each one with its flustering nervous little birds. When I reach his side, he murmurs, "OK, love?" peering, short-sightedly, into a dirty wire cage. The man selling starts talking, with a slow, "Pues ... " before his Spanish floods out too fast for me to hear, his muddy accent strange and thick. My dad smiles and nods gently, but I think he's pretending. Every Sunday we come here to wander through the stalls, and the traders all know my dad, this eccentric Englishman who buys two or three dozen rather ordinary little birds at a time.

On the street corner a little way off kids dealing in football cards, skinny dark boys, mostly barefoot and dusty, swearing, "Joder!" and pushing at each other, "Ai, pero no jo!", "Si vale!". Watching them, I sit down on the curb, wondering if he'll get birds we can set free again, and I breathe in deeply, remembering what it feels like when a warm bundle of feathers breaks out of my opening fingers, flying off into the skies. I look up.

"Come on, little urchin," his hand is reaching down to me.

A little later and we're in the middle of nowhere, a blurry haze of heat all around us. I lift my face to the baking sun and he clips the rim of my hat, laughing, "Come on".

We're some way from the car which he left on the roadside. The grass reaches my arm pits, spiky dry and crunchy, crickets and bees buzzing, the smell of thyme. I pounce on grasshoppers, catching one, feeling it tickling inside my hand, watching it jump back into the grass.

Dad has a little bird box in his hand. I run up beside him. "Can I hold one?"

He smiles, not answering, just looking into the skies. I gaze up at the clear blue.

"What are they? Do they come from here?"

He nods, and for a tiny moment I feel sadness in his face, then he opens the box. There's a second of hesitation. Then fluttering wings on cardboard and suddenly they are gone, disappearing, camouflaged, into the wind. The rush of freedom hits me and I want to cry and laugh and ask lots of questions, but instead I sit down in the long dry grass and look up into the blue.

On the way back to the car, I whirl round and round.

As children, we exist in small pools of consciousness, beyond which the world is an unknown and magical place, filled with extraordinary and impossible things. Miracles happen all around us constantly, the unintelligible leaping out of the unknown, rabbits jumping out of a hat. We dream and play in a realm that is ever shimmering with total potential. Our limitations we shrug off, accepting them simply as a part of our childish size and lack of understanding.

Even where a child is abused, the human capacity to adapt is revealed in his ability to dream still of another world. It takes a great deal to break a child. We know intuitively just how much, for when we see it we know there is nothing more brutal and devastating in the human world.

The wild is an integral part of who we are as children. Without pausing to consider what or where or how, we gather herbs and flowers, old apples and rose hips, shiny pebbles and dead spiders, poems, tears and raindrops, putting each treasured thing into the cauldron of our souls. We stir our bucket of mud as if it were, every one, a bucket of chocolate cake to be mixed for the baking. Little witches, hag children, we dance our wildness, not afraid of not knowing.

But there comes a time when the kiss of acceptance is delayed until the mud is washed from our knees, the chocolate from our faces. Putting down our wooden spoon with a new uncertainty, setting aside our magical wand, we learn another system of values based on familiarity, on avoiding threat and rejection. We are told it is all in the nature of growing up. But it isn't so.

Walking forward and facing the shadows, stumbling on fears

like litter in the alleyways of our minds, we can find the confidence again. We can let go of the clutter of our creative stagnation, abandoning the chaos of misplaced and outdated assumptions that have been our protection. Then beyond the half light and shadows, we can slip into the dark and find ourselves in a world where horizons stretch forever. Once more we can acknowledge a reality that is unlimited, finding our true self, a wild spirit, free and eager to explore the extent of our potential, free to dance like fireflies, free to be the drum, free to love absolutely with every cell of our being, or lie in the grass watching stars and bats and dreams wander by.

We can live inspired, stirring the darkness of the cauldron within our souls, the source, the womb temple of our true creativity, brilliant, untamed.

CHAPTER TWO

The Blood

As women, our very nature is somehow alarming. If it weren't, we wouldn't spend so much time trying to hide it. We wash it and shave it, scent it and hate it, covering up the ever changing curves of our body, its growing, swelling, tightening, softening and sagging. The way we express ourselves is constrained, the dance of our movement limited by the visible and invisible corsets we wear, the expression of our passion disallowed by our shame. Every aspect of our creativity is diminished and dulled by what we consent to be unacceptable in our nature.

And what could be more alarming that the fact that we bleed?

Top of the Pops is on TV. Seven o'clock on a Thursday night and the room is filled, every sofa and chair, every inch of floor, covered in the sprawling bodies of girls gazing at the screen. Bryan Ferry's sleepy charm is like a dark flood seeping through them. I'm tense, half desperate to watch the man that so fascinates me, yet acutely aware of how uncomfortable it is to be in this crowd, wanting so to be out, alone, spinning, dancing, screaming silently, dreaming. I cling to the carpet, staring at the TV, captivated and disconcerted.

The song finishes, interrupted by some grinning idiot DJ, and as chattering rises around me, girls giggling and shouting, icily commenting, I creep behind the sofas to leave the room. The next song is Abba, confirming the validity of my escape.

I stand to leave and a voice behind me blurts out, "Oh shit, look at her jeans!"

A thousand eyes turn towards me as my hand slides on the brass door handle. I'm used to quips about my clothes; with my parents 5000 miles across the ocean in the heat of the tropics, I struggle daily from the school uniform into winter clothes that long ago ceased to fit my body or fashion. But the lull that lingers, a few seconds shattering into hours of dread, is broken not as I'd anticipated, with a snide cut at my embroidered pockets. The voice is disgusted. It says, "Looks like someone's got the *curse*!"

Locked in a bathroom, my fingers white beneath the rush of icy water, I scrub at the crotch of my old hippy jeans, bewildered as to how to get the blood from the seams. And where will I dry them? There is no privacy here, no space for it to be, no trust to allow it. Still scrubbing, the tears drip from my face onto the cold white enamel. I cross my legs tightly, desperate to stop the flow.

Too proud and scared to show the tears, I tap at the door, "Matron?" There's a squeak of a weary chair and the old woman comes out, her eyes still on the TV show chattering behind her. "What d'you want?" she says, distracted.

"I've started," I whisper.

"You've what?" she says, irritated, looking down at me now.

"I've started." I wince, biting my lip to hold back the tears.

"Oh all right," she says, "come on." And she sighs, leading me into the sickroom where she takes a note book from a drawer and taps it with a bony finger. "Put your name down there." With shaky hands I write my name in a column on the page, the letters blurring with my tears, and look up at her, waiting, flinching apologetically as she rummages in a cupboard. Handing me a heap of white plastic packages she dismisses me and shuffles back into her room and the television, "Now don't make a fuss. Go off and sort yourself out quietly".

The dormitory's empty, except for Jane, a silent girl with her head carefully hidden in a book, too square even to want to watch *Top of the Pops*. I stare at her, shoving the crinkling packages beneath my blanket, and I try to breathe calmly. My heart is racing. She carries on reading.

From the wall beside my bed, David Bowie looks straight past me.

Getting bloody dirty

As children we aren't so very different from the boys. We can kick and climb trees, run as fast and get as muddy, but just around the time when they begin to get bigger than us we get slammed by the 'curse' of our grandmothers' grandmothers. For a week in every four we are slow and heavy, our heads are thick with irritation and distant dreams; we need to work harder to stay as strong as our brothers.

With hormones flooding through our veins, waves crashing down and breaking up our moods, some of the boys start to back away, beginning to wonder who we are. Suddenly we seem strange, somehow mysterious; suddenly they seem young, and short, and life seems too complex. Without knowing how, we've ended up on quite another track, and there are rules to learn, completely new tangled rules. One of the first is one of the most important and most confusing of them all: never let it show. Indeed every woman I spoke to, whilst collecting stories for this book, said part of what they resented most about being a woman was the pressure they felt to hide their bleeding.

All too aware of that prime rule, bloated and aching, with low energy and a chocolate craving that really doesn't help at all, our body image can rapidly crumble beneath us. Sensing others' aversion, like a yell that has lingered on the wind for millennia, we feel an instinctive need to withdraw from the daily contact play of mixed society, and if circumstances don't allow it that same need shifts into the stress of pretending nothing is happening at all. As bleeding women we are a perfect example of all that is unacceptable; though others may not see it, overnight we become fat, hairy and ugly, and unbearably so. Smelling raw and musty, slumped in a heap of tired indifference, we are the hag as outcast, the defeated victim of the horrors of our own physicality.

Of course, some women are affected less than others. When a person isn't kicked by it, whether through the random nature of luck or gender, it is tempting to perceive those who are struggling as undisciplined and irrational: surely they can/could/should fight it! Our culture demands we do. Our modern world offers all we might need to conceal effectively every last dreadful symptom, from tampons to chemical deodorisers, medication to shame. We are prodded to get on with life, just like the menfolk, not to lose man-hours or show the weakness of our pain or unreliability.

Some of these modern gimmicks do make life a little easier. The exhaustion is as authentic as the water retention that bloats us. Our body scents do change, the cycle adjusting the oil in our pores, changing how we sweat. The change in hormones alters the rate at which we grow body hair. The blood is there, red and sticky, clotting and staining, expressing our nature. Yet the hag is not the disempowering force; it is our fight to keep her hidden that so wears us down.

It isn't simply disgust with the sticky dark fluid. Polite and squeamish society has taught us to be revolted by piss, sweat and faeces, and even the sexual emissions we're then asked to enjoy. The mess and muddle of physicality as a whole is a reminder of our animal nature and the course of our evolution, albeit one that a wide swathe of human consciousness would prefer to forget. But we are animals. Our hunting, gathering, scavenging ancestors lived for hundreds of thousands of years in the raw exchanges of existence, evolving from creatures whose lives were even less detached from it; this past ten millennia of emerging civilisation has not much changed our basic nature.

Indeed, until not so very long ago, the blood of a kill, the blood of confrontation, the blood of fertility, the cycles of nature, were integral parts of human society, the daily life of tribal community. In reality, but for small pockets of butchers and farmers, soldiers, doctors, midwives, morticians and miners, it is only in the past hundred years or so that our Western culture has removed itself from the wet mud and blood of living. For most, the very thought of immersing their hands in blood is abhorrent.

To the male 49 per cent of our population, blood equates with being wounded. Not long ago, when my husband accidentally stabbed himself in the leg with a craft knife, blood was everywhere, soaking into his jeans and spilling over the stone slabs of our kitchen floor. He was calm, as is his way, yet I watched with a curiosity as he dealt with this flood of his life force, suppressing the muddle of his panic and awe; this was the first time he'd had his own blood over his hands in over twenty years. I do it for a week in every four.

Indeed, the fear of touching blood is so deep in our culture that women who don't flinch from it are considered peculiar. Their attitude is distasteful and somehow dirty. We may bitch at the multinationals who supply 'sanitary' products at such high prices, adding complaints about the chemicals used in tampons and disposable pads. Many women know about menstrual products' pollution, blaming the government or water treatment companies for the tampons that drift at sea, washing up on our beaches. Yet the idea of using a natural rubber or silicon insertable cup (a Keeper or Moon Cup), or washable cotton pads, is not something that many would even consider. To do so would mean getting blood on their fingers.

It is only by women becoming aware of their own attitudes and fears, and being willing to break them, that changes will be made. So what stops us?

Five days with a bloody goddess

Over generations, women's dread of their bleeding week has

passed from mother to daughter. Feminism may have made a difference in the paths open to women, but it hasn't changed human nature: we are instructed to think of others and work for their needs. To do otherwise would make us selfish, socially incompetent, inadequate mothers, unacceptable wives, rotten lovers. It would compromise our ability to get the job we wanted. The fear of rejection, of being dismissed, ignored or alone, is compellingly acute. It's a human issue, a fear we share with men. The selfish man is a bastard, unable to hide his competitive aggression. The selfish woman has failed to hide her dark dirty nature: the hag has sneaked out to holler obscenities in the wind.

Compounding the fear that it will show, through our own mismanagement or clumsy emotion, there hangs heavily the suspicion that the hag's insanity is as contagious as the dirt on her fingers, which, of course, it is; for freedom, like laughter, is thoroughly catching. People like me are a bad influence.

Madness is horrifying.

When we bleed, our focus shifts. We internalise. We dream more deeply, more darkly, as our minds probe the edges of our consciousness, searching for new valleys and caverns to explore, for new ground to till and sow. The drive to conform, to walk in line and behave, just isn't quite so strong. We walk in unknown places, actively seeking out the powers of change, letting go our tight grip on the reference points of familiarity that assure us of our stability and our sanity. Our raw nature breathes.

To the Pagan animist who perceives deity as power of nature, here is another intensely potent goddess. As a natural force she appears to be in the blood, but she is not contained by it: independent of whom she moves through, she is more than simply the energy of life. Wild with her own potential for life, intrigued by death, she draws us within, as if to explore the life force not as observers but from a place where we are wholly immersed, deep within it. Here she drenches us with an immediacy of experience, heightening our awareness of every sensation, laughing as the intensity floods our soul. She is a goddess of the inside, and nature's craving to break open: she is a goddess of revelation. Through the hag, she is the darkness that demands unfettered expression.

It may be just five days, it may be a fortnight from the first twinges of premenstrual tension to the last dribble of our monthly blood shed, but our time with this goddess is never entirely comfortable. Closing our soul to her, enduring her presence with bitter resistance and self-deprecating rage, only provokes her. She is definitely a deity who likes attention.

Indeed, as any goddess of nature, she is always with us. Even when we are not bleeding, she hums in our veins, in the depths of our souls, calling to us from the darkness inside.

His eyes don't leave mine. He lifts up his glass and sips the red wine, leaving moisture for a brief moment upon his lips. Then he tilts his head, a glimmer of uncertainty washing through his mind, as half smiling, questioning, he wonders what I'm thinking. But though I look into his eyes, my inner gaze follows his hand as it comes to rest upon the table. Pushing through the density of silence, I find his fingers, the flesh of his palm, the film of creamy skin that covers the blue veins of his wrist, my fingertips finding the red pulse between the bones. And I listen with my fingers to the perfect rhythm of his life force. He watches the intensity of my focus, curious, waiting, my heart beating, bounding as if endlessly running over the wide green meadows of windswept time. In the pounding of the music that vibrates the air around us, we are living in slow motion. His eyes never leaving mine, my mouth slightly open, I am wondering how long I can balance on this precarious wall of anticipation.

Voices jar through my mind, my name is called and I pull away, look up, try and smile at the friend who is talking to me, loudly, laughing in a busy world of colour moving, people talking, glasses clinking, but his energy draws me back, and with a wash of relief we are again lost in the twilight silence, drifting in its sensation. He lifts his other hand, his fingers on my cheek, along my jaw, my neck, and suddenly we come together, mouth to mouth, as if the provocation were enough for the snake to strike. His pulse still in my hand, I can feel his serpent rise, fluid, satin, lithe, and so infinitely supple, weaving a dance around my own. And lost in our kiss, I'm half aware of the energy, half aware that I'm lost in it, wrapped up in the tangle of serpent smooth muscle, this power of life inside us, moving with a separate consciousness, almost a malevolence. I feel its power writhing, independent of him and me, of personality, mind and soul: life, just life.

I close my eyes and slide further. He responds to my every move, so intuitively that I know he's with me, and when he lifts his head, his throat bare, I can feel the hum of his living shining, and when his hand moves my chin, his tongue on my throat, I long to give him all I am, to dissolve from my body in a perfect moment of dying. It is as if to experience such intimacy, soul to soul, needs my willingness, for a moment, to offer my life itself. Absolute vulnerability. My trust is in the power of spirit and nothing less. Perfect sacrifice. We are entangled in a dance older than humanity. Animal to animal.

And then the music seeps back into our world, who knows why, drawing us back up to surface, to breathe again the light and noise, and we smile at each other, gently quietly pulling away just a fraction, enough to feel the snakes within turning, recoiling, returning to the darkness of the cave deep inside.

My body is seething with heat.

I blink, trying to focus.

The hag's black dog

Because when we are menstruating we naturally turn within, our awareness withdraws and it is harder to give freely and easily to others. Thinking again of the cauldron that holds our intimate space, the nemeton that is our sanctuary, we instinctively retreat during our premenstrual and bleeding days, finding shelter within its bounds. The edges of our safe haven tend to be sharper, more sensitive to touch, less flexible, less willing.

This doesn't necessarily mean that we are not interested in relationship. Many women speak of the week of their blood tide being the time when their relationships are at their closest. In fact, if we can imagine the nemeton to be multi layered, menstruation takes us one layer deeper. We may barricade the outer layer with spikes and electric fences, but at the same time we are consciously closer to our own core; those we do let in, we let in further.

Sharing intimacy is more poignant at this time. We are not only revealing a different degree of vulnerability, we are also closer to the source of our power, our strength. Sexual relationships, where true intimacy is shared, are either on hold or very much more intense, our awareness of self and sensation heightened. Friendships can meander to the edge of intimacy where normally they would be more superficial; truth slips into honesty where otherwise issues are blurred. We sense more poignantly and react more deeply to the emotional tides of those we encounter.

Further, we become more acutely sensitive to the natural world around us, the external environment of weather and light, electricity and sound, spirit and energy. We sense storms coming more acutely, our moods changing with the air pressure. We are less tolerant of anything that makes us uneasy, as a result often feeling a need to withdraw, particularly from human company. We find it harder to compromise, needing more distinctly to follow our instincts, to track the scents of our own desires. When we are bleeding, we feel more clearly the pull of our creativity.

Yet, needing to hide it, locking the hag away deep inside, we do our best to continue as if nothing were changed. Until something snaps. Over eighty per cent of women's crimes are committed during the four days prior to menstruation. The hag, now unchained and with resentment to offload, has no time for reason.

Some feminists do what they can to deny the reality of premenstrual syndrome; surely labelling this part of our nature, or even acknowledging it as real, confirms us to be unstable, unpredictable and unreliable, compounding our state of inequality with men. Yet for any woman who suffers the pervasive intensities and discomfort of the blood cycle, this standpoint is absurd. More poignantly, to deny the existence or relevance of premenstrual tension is to ignore this aspect of our woman nature that is humming with such potential, the wild dark red energy that is such an enormously potent source of richly positive creativity. Where such a goddess not respected and, crucially, her vital force not acknowledged and utilised, there is a significant risk of fireworks. Or all out war.

Much of the time, doing our utmost to live without the horror of failure and rejection, not wishing to look within, we immerse ourselves in distractions, evading our wild and creative soul. We keep ourselves occupied with stress, too busy to consider alternatives, forcing our focus, as the hag snarls inside. All those clever tactics that allow us to compromise - our reasoning, our sense of duty and responsibility, our compassion - we cling to with a vengeance. We stop ourselves, as we stop others, holding them back from their exploration, with emotionally explosive reasons and complex excuses about obligations and selfishness. Furthermore, any sense that our creativity doesn't fit into a conventional box that could be labelled USEFUL only adds more weight to why it should be hidden.

Studies show that the worst cases of PMS are in women who feel suppressed. This is as true where the problem is simply menstrual cramps, as it is where there is acute pain or severe depression, or where the hormones kick the woman utterly out of control. Where women are stuck in roles they don't want to be in, whether as mothers, wives, lovers, factory workers or career high flyers, the premenstrual state removes any veils that permit us to continue blindly. No longer pacified by reason, we are flooded with the urge to express what we really feel inside. What's more, if we don't express it now, allowing our powers of control still to paint the smile of acceptance across our face, our body does it for us, aching, yearning, breaking into excruciating cramps and spasms, screaming, hurling us into moods of antagonism, grief and irritability.

As such, PMS is a powerful gift. Like a sniffer dog, it zeroes in on the areas of our lives where our energy is being invested in false creativity. We may not find that comfortable, and especially not if we believe a situation to be inescapable, but being so resigned is to misjudge the power of the resource. This black sniffer dog belongs to the hag goddess of blood, and the dog has muscle. However much we hate it, premenstrual tension is an exquisite part of the raw nature of woman.

The process of easing the very real emotional and physical pain of PMS is then one of claiming our personal freedom. As we discover an honesty of self expression, the unblocked energy that begins to flow once again can be poured into the experience of actually living our creativity. Shifting our lives may create a chaos of transition, but so often such change can be achieved without harming others, and when we are doing what we want to do our path is always beneficial, both to ourselves and to those who live around us, creating a nourishing and sustainable reality. In fact, glancing back at the old tale of Sir Gawain's marriage, we might say that, in order to release the stress of menstruation, easing the pain and finding the energy of its creativity, a woman bleeding must simply have her own way.

It is no wonder that we as women fear the power of the bleeding hag. If we address the blocks that stop us from exploring our soul's creativity, we would come face to face with our dreams; we would confront the possibility of acting out our dreams, and that can be terrifying. In our vision, we see the beauty of our potential standing tall and proudly graceful beside the dreadful prospect of our falling, tumbling, crashing, failing. We see who we would wish to be, and flinch with the expectation that such a person could or would be rejected.

With her dog snarling, pulling hard at the leash, the hag holds the knife she can wield to cut us free. We try to ignore her. What happens if we don't?

Finding our bloody creativity

Our culture has spoken often of the creativity of woman peaking naturally at the point of ovulation. To acknowledge the creativity of menstruation might sound like a contradiction in terms; surely this is a time of release, destruction and negation? Yet creativity is not always about building something in a way that others can see and understand.

Creativity most often begins deep within, as an internal response to some event in the world around, a response that cannot risk the exposure of immediate expression. To reveal the tiny seedling of an idea too soon is to subject it to the winds of others' reactions before it is strong enough to stand firm by itself. It is burned by the light. Creativity, born within the darkness of the inner self, held deep in the cauldron in that silence and tenderness, gently and safely begins its journey of manifestation.

As mammals of the planet's surface it is easy to forget that some forms of life do not need light. A great many feed on its products, but don't live or thrive in it. In the same way, counter to what is most often expected some creativity is never meant to be expressed openly at all. Lingering on the edges of our consciousness, it remains within, as an internal occupation for the exploration and pleasure of our own soul. Swathed by veils, hidden beneath the canopy, we work on it alone in dreams of the imagination and journeys through otherworlds. Wild fantasies, sweet tales and complex sagas, magical relationships of the soul, symphonies never to be heard aloud, songs of the heart and of the wind, these are far from wasteful daydreams; they stretch the muscles of our desire, mixing paints upon our palette, strengthening our confidence. They are ways in which we give time to ourselves, affirming our sense of self and worth. Locked away in moments of solitude, we labour on such secret ventures, their development measured only by the glint in our eyes, or the satisfaction and serenity with which we live our lives.

If we use such dreams as landscapes into which we can escape from the limitations of our lives, our motivations need questioning; yet even here we have clues with which to break up the crass clutter and address the fears that block our creativity. If it is others, however, who judge our daydreams as escapism and evasion, it is more often than not their own fear they are expressing. So it is that, as children, we are told again and again to stop day dreaming by adults fraught with the awareness of life passing them by as yet not satisfactorily fulfilled. Yet a child's dreaming develops those deep resources within, those we need for the growing imagination, for initiative, ingenuity, innovation and intelligence, for creativity in every sense. The child, just as the adult, is playing in the dark make-believe of intensely personal creativity. Unlimited, free, the child loves the tastes of sweet potentiality.

At times, these achievements, sparkling in the darkness of our cauldron, are hard to keep to ourselves. The joy of it overflows, or in search of approval or affirmation, we reveal our work to some chosen person, stammering for words, stumbling to explain, only to have it not entirely understood, or painfully undervalued. Some projects do simply shrivel up in the light. It takes a long time, though, to learn that external approval is not necessary, that the reality of our creative process simply happening is enough, that it is OK if sometimes it is just for ourselves.

Furthermore, some creativity is not about building at all; this is another apparent contradiction that is hard to grasp or remember. Creativity that makes landscapes of wide open country, bringing clarity where there was chaos, space within which we can spin and breathe deeply, is especially powerful when crafted with the dark energy of menstruation. We create through destruction, the breaking up of old work and the wreckage of outdated patterns, the dismantling of the scaffolding that has held up the dross of our past living. Sometimes our creativity is simply the experience of demolition for the sheer freeing joy of it.

The world is spinning fast, a kaleidoscope of people, voices curling round me, faces catching me, and I shake my head to make them stop. I can't understand what's being said in the crush of noise, I don't know what I need to be doing, my feet pinned to the ground in my need to get away. Then the teacher's got my wrist and her words are digging into me, her fingers crushing my bangles into my skin, "Calm down! Now!" I stare into her eyes. It seems impossible this wrinkled bitch could ever understand what I'm feeling. My stare becomes a glare, and all the swear words I know spit venom in my mind.

She loosens her grip and immediately I pull away, turn my back and storm off down the corridor, my heart raging in my throat as she hurls her voice after me, "Detention, four o'clock, young lady!" *Screw you ...*

There's no point in trying to sleep. The moon is just above the trees, my head pounding, my body weighed down with the aching, and I'm bleeding like a veal calf hung up to drain white. Any minute now I'm sure I'll flood the sheets and I can't bear it.

Hauling my whale-like form out of bed, I plod over to the window and push it open wide, breathing in the night sky. With the only other viable option to crawl under the bed and rot, I pull on my baggiest jeans and a sweatshirt, and noisily clamber out. Though my parents' window is next to mine, being so disgustingly bloated it's hard to be quiet. I slip, losing my footing, grabbing the gutters, and gracelessly fall four feet onto the grass. I probably bloody bounce.

Lying still, tense, half breathing, I wait until I'm sure nobody is stirring: the altercation would be so tiring. The grass is cool. Any bruises don't hurt as much as the gnawing in my womb, and pulling on my shoes, I get up and tiptoe across the garden, over the low wall, across the street and away. The tedium of this small town is less oppressive at night, but it's still a relief to be past the shops, the pub, the aching stretch of suburbia, and out into the fields that stretch into forever, fields of wheat whispering pale in the moonlight, fields of freedom.

Carefully keeping to the furrows, avoiding crushing stems into a path that could be followed, I head out into the middle of absolutely nowhere, and there I collapse onto the dry mud amidst the wheat, curled up, clutching the aching of my belly, lying for a long time, just watching the stars, the self-pity stifling me into confusion.

Looking back on the day, it seems a blur of idiotic trivia, pointless moments tagged together with little bits of stupid string, moments interspersed with time sitting in smelly toilets, struggling with bloody pads and tampons. Tears sting my eyes.

Blood is flowing onto the pad between my legs. I've not brought another and I start to worry that it won't last until I've found the will to go home. I sigh and struggle to pull off my jeans, the pad and my panties, laying them carefully in the furrows. And I sit down, my bare bum on the hard mud of the ground.

I feel the blood. For ages I do nothing but feel it, this flow of blood, seeping from my body into the earth. Closing my eyes in the dark, I lay my head on my arms crossed over my knees. It's quiet, with just a faint breeze stirring the wheat, the flutter of a moth, a beetle in the dirt, and me, this girl, human being, breathing.

All the world is temporary.

As a young girl on the awkward journey into adolescence, the tides of our bleeding bring what are often the first lessons about our own mortality, lessons that can frighten us, according to where we are upon the road. What we had assumed was ours completely, unconditionally, life unlimited, is suddenly finite. It confuses, aggravating like the grain of sand in an oyster shell, an underlying and persistent stress that wears us down, shaping us through those early teenage years.

As we grow into adulthood, that reminder of our momentary existence, our fragile physicality, is with us every moon cycle with our week's menstruation. Acknowledging it as another sign of our flawed and faltering humanity, the futility of our mortality, it can add to a sense of hopelessness, bringing with it the apathy of depression, the resentful adolescent anger of feeling suddenly there is no point. Yet if we explore this part of our nature, developing an awareness of the tides of life, the brilliance of its detailed web of connections can affects us very powerfully. Recognising the blood of our own cycles as the physical manifestation of life's energy in its perpetually tidal flow can not only draw us out of that teen desolation, but deepen our sense of wonder at nature and life.

In Druidry and other Pagan religions, the absolute sanctity of blood is accepted. As a sacred force it snakes a course through our bodies, sliding through our lives, like rivers of dark water moving through landscapes of flesh and bones. Like serpent energy, blood reflects our bond with the earth, emphasising our perception of it as a power of life that holds within it the stories of our ancestors, of love and tears, strength and knowing, rage and prophecy, failure and flexibility, the wisdom of all things.

To the animist, it is important to acknowledge this, showing respect to this goddess of blood, this deity of the inside, wakefully offering our thanksgiving. In doing so, we open our souls to be receptive to that wellspring. Here, in the blood, are the tales of our ancestors' experience of life. Even if we are aware only through vague feelings and ideas that provide no more than whispers and intuitions, that source of wisdom is incomparable. In the darkness of our blood, flowing through our soul, it feeds into our creativity. Like the ancient roots of a tree, if we are awake to it, it provides a remarkable stability and nourishment.

In making an offering of thanks, expressing reverence for the source of life, the use of blood is an ancient part of so many spiritual and religious traditions. As a thanksgiving, it is another way in which we can reach again for that connection with the raw power of nature within us, accepting it, embracing it. Every drop shimmers with life's potential; the act of giving is a powerfully positive affirmation of life itself and in that action of respecting the hag goddess, her wit and wisdom touches us, inspiring our creativity.

There are many ways of doing it. Giving blood through a medical donor programme, and so sharing the opportunity of life with others, is an easy way of making such an offering (particularly in countries such as Britain where there is no payment involved). Though not useful in the same way, human to human, simply giving our menstrual blood back to the earth can be a beautiful part of our monthly spiritual practice. Returning mineral riches to the soil of our gardens and allotments, each cup emptied onto the earth affects our relationship with the earth, strengthening the connection.

Using washable blood pads may not be as secure a way of concealing the flow, but it does force us to handle our own blood on a regular basis. Washing them out, the red river energy spills over our hands, reminding us of its power, speaking to us of the precious nature of life. The blood can be collected in a jar and refrigerated or even frozen to be used as an offering. Using a menstrual cup makes the process of collecting the blood even easier.

Some women will use the blood for writing upon a candle to be lit, or a piece of paper to be burned, using this watery ink to make a sacred symbol or word. Even on the simplest level - a wavy line or an H for healing, or an 0 for an embrace, an X symbolising a gift or kiss of love - this focuses the mind into a small act of magic that can be profoundly effective. To mark anything with this almost invisible red touches it with our truth; blood cannot lie.

The simple act of bleeding onto the ground can be remarkably freeing. Our flow is for that short while unhindered, unhidden, as we relax into the truth of our nature, lying or sitting, serene in the grass, or upon the leaf mould of the forest, beneath a special tree, beside a stream. Some women create for themselves an area of their garden where, if space allows, it is understood no-one else will go. Others find some secluded place in the countryside to which they have access, and here they make a sacred place, a temple for their bleeding. In some native American traditions this is known as a moon lodge, a place that honours and reflects the cycle of the moon. It is a blood nemeton, a sanctuary within the world around us that gently reflects the nemeton of our own inner temple, the dark womb cauldron, a deeper layer of our intimate space. In many ways it is a response to the ancient call that entices us to withdraw from society when we are bleeding, to find moments of calm seclusion where the shift of focus inward is not only allowed but is positively encouraged.

Such a temple sanctuary can be an expression of our unspoiled individuality, a very personal place that we might decorate with beautiful things sacred to ourselves and our womanhood. Like the den that a child might make where she can find some solitude, a blood nemeton constructed of wood or stone, or a tree's own canopy, gives us a place in which to play, exploring in privacy the depths and the wealth of our own soul. It offers the opportunity for expressing our dark creativity, our raw truth and tenderness, within a safe space, a sanctuary out of sight.

Bringing fruit or wine, dark organic chocolate, private feastings, a journal to write in, paints, pastels, a flute or harp, whatever is the medium for our soul's creativity, here there is the sweet promise of time alone. It is a place where we can dream, meditate, laugh or cry - a moment simply to be ourselves, letting the hag free.

Blood and sacrifice

Making an offering of our blood is one thing; making a blood sacrifice is another. While the wild woman may do the former, free in the expression of herself and her nature, the reputation of the dark goddess, the hag and those who revere her, is also entangled with the latter.

There is no evasion of the fact that our ancestors made blood sacrifice, slaughtering animals for the gods, as magical petitions and payment for abundance, health and victory. There are scattered clues that human beings were also given in sacrifice; according to old Classical writers, the Druids were said to burn humans alive in constructions of wood, twigs and straw, and to inflict fatal wounds then divine by the death throes. Criminals may have been killed ritually for the protection of the community, blood feuds may have been avenged with ritually barbaric killings; it is easy enough to see such actions today in regions of the world where societies are broken by war. If human sacrifice was ever a key part of any religious practice in Britain, the evidence is now lacking.

Folk tales relate of thanksgivings made to the gods of the land at the time of the harvest, an act of appeasement, a prayer for fine weather while the crops were coming in, a sacrifice made at the start of the reaping. Blood was shed upon the field in honour of John Barleycorn, Jack of the fields, the vegetation deity whose presence had so carefully been nurtured from the sowing to the scything. Mythology speaks of a royal sacrifice, the king giving his life to the goddess of the land who had fed his people, and tales tell of villains (or, more gothically, virgins) slain in his place, and also of hares, goats and other creatures in later years. It's a tradition of blood sacrifice said to have persisted until well into the nineteenth century, a powerful act of humankind reaching to the gods who feed us. For Pagans nowadays, the sacrifice is more often made without blood, but instead with vows that reflect the nature of sacrifice in our own time: actions that irretrievably take from us that which we understand as so valuable in our modern lives - time, innocence, ignorance, comfort. However, still, for the priestess, spilling her menstrual blood upon the pale golden stubble of the newly harvested fields is perhaps the most powerful act, affirming her deep bond of connection, shimmering with the divine energy of the hag.

Like many adherents of Pagan nature religions, as a vegan I now question whether we have the right to take another life, even that of a nonhuman animal, whether for food or for ritual, but I am cautious as to how often such an attitude derives from the horror of blood that comes from a lack of familiarity. For most Westerners, bloody violence is only on television, and meat is carefully packaged, no longer dripping. Not long ago, an African-American priest of the Yoruba tradition told me clearly that animal sacrifice is an integral part of her religious practice, as it has been for millennia according to the scriptures of the Odu Ifa. For Western culture to deny her that right was, she felt, another swipe of white imperial racism, another abrogation of ancient African wisdom. Yet, the killing of animals in ritual is still done across the world. In the privacy of religious communities such as Islam and Judaism, it continues within Britain and America today, but the disinfectant-clean cultures that buy bloodless meat in plastic wrapping don't want to know. They no longer consider such rituals appropriate, necessary or acceptable.

Occult practices and some nature religions, such as Druidry and old Witchcraft, still act as a focus for the fears our culture holds around the issue of blood sacrifice. Like a scribbled note stuck by a bully onto the back of a school blazer, their fear indicts those of the old traditions with the declaration: I sacrifice babies. Fairy tales of the wildwood tell us of the hag who bewitches young children, to enslave them, to boil them and eat them with salt and bread and butter. Needless to say, this reputation is entirely superstition born of fear, but it is interesting to consider why it exists at all. The woman feared may have been a sorcerer, casting trickery with herbs, sigils and curses, but as likely she was the cunning woman, an elder woman of a community before medicine was freely available, a healer and midwife tending to the sick, the dying, the women and the insane. Her living would daily have been coloured with blood.

She was mistress of the birthing room, that den of women's magic, of dark secrets and screaming. Her hands stained with the blood of childbirth, perhaps too she took the placenta, knowing its nutritional value for a woman who'd lost blood, boiling this flesh bag for the mother to eat. She would have been called if a woman miscarried; she would have known the herbs that could induce it if a child weren't wanted. It might have been supposed that she has some dreadful power over human life. It isn't surprising that she was feared, for she dealt with that edge between death and birth. She was the witch and the scapegoat for others' insecurities.

Occultists such as Aleister Crowley, in the early 20th century, didn't help by himself speaking of the ritual art of killing babies. Yet he spoke as a provocateur: the practice he was referring to was his sexual magic of masturbation, where the spilling of his seed for his own power and pleasure would be, to a Christian moralist, tantamount of the murder of God's potential children. In using those words, he was alluding to a belief too that children developed in the womb of the blood that was lost at menstruation. The bleeding of a woman, then, in just the same way, is the loss of another of God's potential children. A woman who bled was not pregnant, and as such she was disobeying God's command to obey her husband, to submit to his carnal desires and populate the Earth. Who knows if she had used the witch's herbs to kill the child?

Every month that she bled, she washed the blood of those unborn children from her menstrual rags. The blood itself was proof enough of her hag guilt.

The frost crunches underfoot as if trying to wake me. My eyes keep closing into the darkness around me. My boots slip on the icy stones and I pull myself into balance on a bare twig of blackthorn. It punctures my finger and I suck at it, tasting blood like metal, my breath misting as I push myself on, heavy and exhausted. Each time I stop, Pridd looks up at me hopefully, pleadingly, the scents of the night enticing him almost beyond what he can bear.

At the gate, he turns and watches me, his chin high, alert, proud. Though he could slip under the fence, he waits, and as I open it he moves beside me, down paths and over the thick wet winter grass. He knows where we're heading, reaching the young oak before me and turning again to wait for me. I push my gloved fingers into his soft wet fur, crouching down before the tree. Touching the plaque, my fingers running over her name, as ever, a hundred words collide in my mind all too quickly for me to grasp each or any one of them. Instead, I breathe deeply, sighing, almost smiling, "Hello, grandma".

Protected from the wind by the other trees, a single dry leaf remains, flickering on a twig. I think of her, the old lady, so fragile and frustrated, so proudly independent, and I wonder if she'd like me to help the leaf off and into the cold wind. Yet to do so seems arrogant. An impatience of life. Tears rise in my eyes, warm on the skin of my face.

Shadows move amidst the trees. Pridd, lying on his belly, turns towards me and blinks. He lifts his nose, wondering if I might perhaps now want his attention.

From I pocket, with numb fingers, I pull out the red silk pouch and, upending it, let the little jar fall into my hands. Laying the lid on the muddy grass, I lift the jar before me, wanting to say so much and finding no words, aware instead of that flood of sensation, that deep feeling of complete connection, generation to generation, sharing stories, aching love, desolate confusion, soul to soul, century through century, for so many thousands and thousands of years. Nor am I at the head of the surge, for ahead of me somehow already present are all those generations to come.

I look up and, though the clouds, acknowledge the darkness of the universe, limitless, edgeless. A few tiny stars are glinting in that endless night, and for a moment I am filled with the peace of feeling myself to be a tiny part of the pattern.

And slowly I pour the liquid into the soil around the young oak.

"My blood," I murmur, "returned ... "

Honouring the first tides

Where the fear of blood is present, our ability to live honourably is compromised, horror looming over our ability to feel or express respect. Of course, sometimes this fear is born of trauma, but where that isn't the case, it develops with our awareness of pain and mortality, fears that are heightened with the onset of puberty. With menarche, blood becomes another loose grenade in the complexities of reality, its presence another liability that threatens our security. Primarily the issue is one too often wrapped up with shame. We must hide the flow or be discovered as dirty, gross, smelly; ugly. With puberty comes our sense of self as independent beings, separate and alone. Our growth, like human evolution, has reached that poignant moment of self-awareness. The fear of rejection is given a new dimension.

Along with shame, however, the beginning of our blood tides brings with it the heaviest burden and the most powerful gift of our womanhood: our potential fertility. For a pre-sexual girl, the concern may not be so overt, but in a society where the issue of pregnancy is increasingly spoken of, at the least such worries slide into her subconscious mind. Fertility becomes a danger, another liability that intimidates a girl's journey into womanhood.

Both these difficulties that come with the menarche are significantly reduced where a girl is taken through the transition in a way that is supportive and positive. Thankfully, this is more common amongst women born after the mid 1970s, but mostly because some layer of inhibition has been lost. Where menstrual products were before hidden away, a mother is more likely to leave them out in a bathroom now, to be surreptitiously explored by children of both genders. Television and magazine advertising is widespread. Yet though these address the concept of menstruation, they don't really touch the fear issues around blood and fertility. Furthermore, communication within families is still generally poor; most of the information a girl gets is from her peers, and is usually as erratic and spiced with fear as it is supportive or instructive.

Amongst women I have spoken to, and those I have worked with, having a mother or friends who talked about it could be enormously helpful. However, what profoundly benefits a girl moving through the transition is not chat, whether that be wrapped in giggles or in embarrassment. It is a serious acknowledgement of what the change really means. Where a girl is given some kind of a rite of passage, the change is transformed into something to be deeply proud of.

It isn't necessary, nor sometimes appropriate, to take a girl through an elaborate or formal ceremony. A girl brought up within Druidry or another Pagan tradition may be eager to be introduced to the wild goddess of blood, and eagerly invite older women who have bled for decades to share their secrets about how to manage this aspect of the hag. A religious element is not important though. The simplicity of a special evening alone with other women, family, and friends beyond their first bloods, creates a time to talk, to laugh, to share and give gifts to the one celebrating her menarche. The key importance is in the acknowledgement of the transition.

Even with such a simple act, the difference is dramatic. A girl whose menarche is honoured is likely to be freer in her personal expression, more confident in herself, her creativity unhindered by fears of her nature. She is less likely to rebel as she journeys through her adolescence, any need to assert herself as an adult now made redundant by the rite that acknowledged her growing status within the community of family and friends. As many girls start smoking and drinking, or exploring sex irresponsibly, in a bid to appear adult, the whole range of these problems are less likely to occur.

The weight of responsibility connected with fertility is also eased. Where a girl has the experience of support and empathy given with respect, she is more likely to respond with sanity to the difficult decisions she will face, staying calm, considering options, aware of possible consequences.

The menarche rite can be done retrospectively. Many women who stumbled through their first bloods are able to heal hidden layers of resentment and fear by working a rite at some later point in their lives. Though a simple gathering of friends, or a retreat alone, may be sufficient, some do choose a more elaborate ceremony, moving through the distinct parts of any rite of passage: honouring what has been, understanding the nature of the present and the doorway of the transition, accepting the challenge of the future and walking into it with integrity and respect. Within the gentle safety of that sacred space, it is possible to feel again the anxiety of the young girl within, yet this time healing the fear, recreating from that point forward, so freeing the creative energy that has been chained for so long.

Whether the rite is to be casual, unceremonious and relaxed, or one that requires careful orchestration, preparing is important; because the value is found in the process not the result, a large part of any rite's efficacy is in the preparation, in clarifying the intention and understanding all the currents of resistance and motivation. As mothers and guides, we must accept that the girl herself needs to take a key role in the conceptualisation of the rite, in its preparation and manifestation; finding the language to do this, creating a safe strong space in which to talk, is often the most healing and valuable part of the whole affair.

Sandra gets up, wincing, "Sorry, everyone," but nobody minds, faces smile around the circle, a few softening as they watch her quietly withdraw and run the few yards towards the yelling toddler. An older child is not far behind, "Sorry, mum, but I couldn't stop him, he wanted ... "

And the circle's focus leaves them; another woman has got to her feet in the circle. She gently moves, barefoot in the warm grass, to crouch before the young girl. Then groaning, she sits down suddenly, rubbing her knees. "Getting old," she murmurs, smiling.

The girl looks into her face, wide eyed. A moment before I had seen a glimpse of the woman she would become; now she's seven years old again, filled with wonder and anticipation. Taking the hands held out to her, she blinks and breathes in deeply.

"Lucy," the woman whispers.

"Auntie Meg?" she bites her lip, her eyes smiling, blinking.

"I didn't know what to bring you." Her words are just loud enough for the circle to hear, yet still they feel intimate, even here in the park under the whitebeam and rowan, children, partners, spouses, playing down by the lake. She lowers her head, a lump in her throat. Lucy's eyes haven't left her face, but now with a frown of concern that wrinkles her brow, a big tear is rolling down her cheek. Hands clasped, they sit without words, the circle of women around them watching quietly, feeling, holding the moment. I close my eyes and call a silent prayer to affirm the sanctity and safety of the space.

Sniffing, pushing her hand to her nose, searching for a handkerchief, the older woman laughs and shakes her head, "So I brought you something that I couldn't imagine letting go of, because that seems the only way of explaining how important this is". From the pocket of her dress she brings out a velvet pouch and pours out a pool of silver and darkness. "It's your gran's ruby bracelet."

The girl gasps, her eyes bigger than ever, at the treasure that now lies in the palm of her hand.

Meg, embarrassed, pushing herself through the moment, shrugs and gestures to the circle around them. "Well, other women here have probably got better advice to give you. I've hardly done brilliantly with men, divorcing and everything. But," and their eyes meet again, "I'm here if you need me. Yeah?"

Lucy nods, her face open and shining.

As Meg sits back down on the edge of the circle, her teenage daughter takes her hand and gives her kiss on the cheek. She smiles, then turns to me across the circle, with a shrug and a look of surprise on her face that says, *wow, tears, I didn't expect that.* I affirm with a smile in return, but the circle is already laughing. Another woman has got to her feet, talking, " ... So I wondered about this good advice thing. And I tried to remember what had been passed down to me: yeah, bugger all! Some of you knew my mother!" Laughter in the circle is like the burbling flow of a mountain stream. "Then I realised."

She walks back to where she'd been sitting and picks up a large square rather battered tin. And she grins. "Double chocolate brownies." Now everyone is laughing, the young girl included. "And on this special day, as we gather here to recognise you as a woman in your own right, I thought it only right to bequeath to you my mother's secret recipe!"

Walking towards me, she shrugs, "So if the Druid wants to bless them, while we've got no men and children with us, perhaps we can pass this batch round the circle ... "

CHAPTER THREE

The Virgin

The rhythms of the womb are our first physical sensations; its blood is our first taste and our first smell. In the embrace of our mother's energy, we live our first years, wrapped up within the intimacy of her heartbeat, her soul nemeton, the sanctuary of her arms. As young children we begin to explore, ever growing and pushing, discovering the boundaries of this safe space. Pushing its edges, breaking out, instinctively we are aware of the unimaginable power of nature beyond. We take cautious steps and we run wild, both with a real sense of wonder and curiosity. In our freedom we are hag-children: always seeking out experience, respectful of the web that connects all things, and entirely desperate to be doing exactly what we want to be doing.

Of course, the barricades of confusion do change that. Some are built brick by brick with poor feedback and negations, some slam down suddenly with the terror that is rejection and abuse. There are folk who barely experience that childish freedom, if at all. Yet for the child who is brought up with love, with wit and strength, the freedom of the world is limited only by her ability to explore it; in the darkness of not knowing, she plays, fearless and free.

As blood touches our lives with our own first menstrual cycles, the landscapes in which we live begin to change. Stumbling with a sense of who we are, desperate for certainty in a world that appears to be expanding by the day, coping with our changing body, clumsily we manage the precariously wobbling stack of responsibilities, most of which we barely understand. We are poignantly aware of all that we don't know. We linger on the edge of childhood, fully able to rage at what still restricts us, yet now and then slipping, running, back into the comfort that it offered us. We claim and proclaim our independence, finding power in the force of our emotions in the same way that we did when we were too young to go to school. Demanding to be loved, we demand to be set free.

And we demand that our demands are understood exactly.

Anyone watching the process of a girl's scramble into adolescence sees within her wild confusion and self determination the undeniable dark traits of the hag. Gloriously blind to the world around her, she chases the wind. The thrill is all. Whether her eyes are fixed on academic success or rebellion, on top grades, pop stars, fashion, fear or apathy, she throws everything into the moment; nothing else exists. She lives for now, not yet able to comprehend fully the possible consequences, barely willing to try and understand, riding the wild new highs of her hormonal tides, crashing with the breaking waves to scramble onto the next. To the onlooker, it is an exhausting time with very little grace.

On the inside, though, when we're in the thick of that exhilarating and dreadful journey, our focus so narrow, so intensely directed, there is barely a moment in which to pause and consider. The world is growing everyday and, with so much that is new our senses are awash with it. We glow with our own power, whether it is flowing for our own benefit or destruction.

The young adolescent is a dangerous creature. She smiles and she snarls, and she gets her own way.

As I turn from him, I see his eyes dropping down to the curve of my backside. For a moment I feel proud, and smile as I lift the gun in both hands, arms stretched out, and aim. I feel powerful, his focus warming my skin already hot in the sunshine. The shot cracks the air around me, the sudden kickback making me yelp, thrown off my cool. He laughs and clears his throat, walking towards me with a smile.

"No, no, no, you're too tense," he says. I pull away, not

wanting him to interfere, but his hands are quickly on my shoulders, big hands, swollen in the heat. They're heavy, his fingers pushing into me, massaging, and I shrug laughing, uncomfortable, trying to get him off me, but he's sticky, like a fat and overheated snake. I half point the pistol at his face wanting to spit at him, *Sick-o dick-o*, but I mumble, "Yeah, well," and drop it onto the box before he can tell me off, and I stride off over the scrub to set the tins back up on the fence posts.

"I hit this one," I yell, setting up the battered beer can.

When I turn, he's staring at my thighs. Walking back, I run my hands over my shorts, stroking the bare skin beneath as if to brush away dust or flies, and watch as he breathes in and wipes the sweat from his forehead. For a moment we stare at each other, then I pick up the gun.

"Try it like, like this," he says. He stands behind me, stammering, growling at some bug stuck in his throat. I feel his body against my back, giving off this tremendous heat. And is that his prick, like a hard rod, pushing up against me? He's breathing, wheezing, "With your arms like this ... now aim ... li-line it up and aim ... "

There are voices, the others coming back from the riverside. I push the man away, suddenly feeling strong enough to assert my space, muttering, "I can do it," and I pull on the trigger. A split second later, the bullet explodes into a dented can, and I so hope that my *father* saw it kicked from the post and into the dust.

He's smiling, walking towards me with that look of nervousness and gentle affection he so often carries, combing the mop of hair off his forehead with outstretched fingers, and he smiles at the fat man beside me, "How's she doing?"

Before long, we are joined by the others and conversations are on terrain, fires and fuel, catfish and alligators, and I've given up the pistol to somebody else. There's laughter, talking, the *tssch* of beer cans opening, and all too soon I've lost his attention. I kick over stones with the tip of my sneaker, half hunting out scorpions, the quiet of the landscape occasionally shattered by gunshot, the *tink-clink-clink* of cans falling onto the dust and sharp stones amidst the laughter and talking. It's clear I'm just a curious tag-along in this man's world.

I wander to the back of the truck and dig in a cooler of melting ice for a drink, but there's nothing but beer. I drag a water bottle from the back seat and drift off towards the river. One of the men watches me; I move my hips, feeling the sway.

A few moments later I am alone, sitting on a rock looking into the water, my toes making patterns in the gentleness of the flow. Little fish swim in the shadows, a few coming out to nibble at my toes, and I watch carefully for catfish. A song meanders through my mind, the words touching my lips, as I gaze down the river, the kingfishers diving,

"Hand to hand, give me your hand,

We shall dance round and around ... "

I wonder if it would be safe to get into the water and paddle.

"Hand to hand, follow on

Like fish in the river ... "

The words dissolve, playground songs, as I swirl my toes, watching ripples.

Was it really his prick? I feel strange, kind of sick inside, as if a slug had crawled over the bare skin of my hand ... *yeuch* ... I'm only twelve, for god's sake.

A little way off a couple of vultures are circling lower, swirling against the blue sky. I wonder what's died.

" ... give me your hand

We shall dance round and around ... "

Finding it

Though technically we may be born virgins, virginity is a state that we move into. It sneaks up very close to us; we feel its presence but aren't quite sure what it could be. Then, quite abruptly, some sweet summer's afternoon as we're watching the world go by, one of the lads who swaggers past is no longer just an irritant or a friend; inexplicably, suddenly, he's totally disarming. So near we can almost smell the gel in his hair, our cheeks flush pink and we can't say a word. We may be nine, thirteen, nineteen, but in that moment our sexuality emerges from its tight cocoon. Damp and crumpled, tentatively our wings stretch out, not yet ready to fly. Feeling the soft untouched newness of it all, we are clumsy. However much we've been told, we have no real notion of what is to come.

To the adolescent, those tender moments don't often last long. Soon enough, the energy can start to feel like a torrent of white water, carrying us down some rocky creek in a kayak with no tangible paddle. Our sense of self is developing in skids and bounds; we play in the water, showing off with every new sensation, unaware of the dangers that we ourselves are provoking, and at the same time both exquisitely and excruciatingly self-conscious. Where before we were living in a tumbling jumble of bodies, noises and emotions, now we are in a crowd of separate beings, all the time carried along on powerful undercurrents of half grasped motivations. Trust becomes consciously of paramount importance. Do we dare to get close to another human being, to reveal even a glimmer of who we think we truly are today? It's unlikely. We have puppy fat, a pimple about to explode. Does our breath smell, our armpits, and what would we say? The whole idea is a minefield of potential disasters.

We've taken the first steps away from our parents and their approval. We are starting to explore how we can achieve in our own right, probing the sensation of not even caring. Yet at the same time our hormones are kicking us around, enticing us to stare at the lad with the green eyes, pushing us to admit just how it feels when he sees us too. Curiosity leads us on, fears hold us back. Emotions draw us like magnets, filling our soul with images and dreams. The confusion is staggering. Just as we are beginning to reach out and feel our independence, our sex hormones are urging us to give it all up for one kiss.

In fact, though we may sink with weak-kneed adoration when it comes to some tousled bright-eyed pop star, in the real world it is often quite different. There is a period for most girls when they won't give an inch. As a virgin, pre-sexual, coming into our own, we are suddenly aware that there is in fact a great deal to lose. We are only just beginning to explore this sensation of freedom. It is a time of delicious discovery, emotions heightening, new drives and curiosities fuelled with a pure new energy. All we are and all we do is for ourselves. For the first years of adolescence, our selfishness is quite magnificent; and it's still, at least partially, tolerated by those around us. It won't be long before any sense of self-indulgence is stamped clearly in our minds as bitterly unacceptable.

Virginity: she is another wild goddess, another of those hags, this one drenching our soul with her carefree songs of freedom. She shrugs with that dismissive sneer of whatever, and continues her dance that both provokes attention and declares her own untouchable state of independence. Yet what allows her that confidence is not understanding; it is the blinkers of not knowing.

As any goddess, she can cause unmitigated turmoil in our lives. Unless we respect that power and start to understand her nature, that selfish nonchalance, that casual yet so determined detachment can provoke us to behave in ways that leave us utterly alone. As a teenager, it isn't an easy state to find ourselves. Innocently we stumble through the twilight of ignorance. Our naiveté might for a while allow us a freedom from affectation and inhibition, but at the same time it can draw us into tangled situations, putting our dreams in danger, trashing our creativity. Those 'white socks' set us apart as easy prey for the hungry. The most poignant beauty of the virgin is the fact that she has held a part of herself untouched; she is innocent. Both practicably and emotionally, the virgin is vulnerable.

Perhaps because of this above all, for young girls tramping through the malls of their adolescence, sexual virginity is often perceived as a weak state to be. It's an attitude most prevalent amongst kids in the turmoil of claiming their independent identity, declaring their maturity. To be a virgin is to be vulnerable, to be naive, a child, a loser. A girl who is a virgin, over a certain age or within a particular society, it is assumed, it is asserted, is that way for good reason: she is too unattractive to have been chosen. She is too ugly to be wanted. Rejected, she is the hag.

On the other hand, those who encourage youngsters not to have sex, particularly religious organisations who preach notions about saving sexual intimacy for marriage, tend to use arguments designed to reach the sensible side of the adolescent. She is told that as a sexual virgin she is clean, pure, nice, safe from the dangers of passion, lust, need, disease. She is untouched, like a new kitchen implement, shiny in its box. To lose her virginity would make her dirty. And nobody wants a dirty girl.

Either way, she risks the rejection of being the hag: frigid or soiled.

Through luck, wit or caution, many do manage to walk the blurred line that winds a path between the extremes. For some this middle way is easy: it is step by step, common sense. But with emotions and hormones rising, a great deal of inexperience, the hag whispering, laughing, inspiring us to play with our freedom, common sense isn't always to hand. Instead she finds herself in an endless game of pavement hopscotch. Acutely self-conscious, she falters, stepping forward and then backwards, in her ongoing struggle to keep her balance, always looking ahead for the next safe step. Innocence, after all, is not an effective guide. We remain fearful that the tiniest moment of distraction will send us out into the badlands of the 'unacceptable' - whether our sentence of banishment comes from our friends or society. Around us the other girls yell, at once supporting us, laughing with us, and then jeering at us with their own unstable confidence and confusion, each one as anxious to evade the horror of rejection, of being seen as that unattractive and unwanted hag.

Losing it

Unexplored, our sexuality lies like a secret, hidden carefully in a precious box tied with ribbon, kept safe just beyond the reach of prying fingers. In its darkness are words of passion whispered by our grandmothers. In that darkness it can seem vast, the dome of a starry night sky stretching out into forever, holding the enormity of our dreams of perfectly shared love. It can feel far more sane to leave such a sacred object secure and intact, unopened, unsullied, keeping it for a moment when we might feel sure it will be honoured. And though she demands absolute freedom, the goddess of virginity approves; sex is far too risky for one who so values independence.

When we do choose to open that precious box, the way we do it is just as important as the way that we've kept it closed. From an external perspective, this most critical action puts us on trial. Have we held it sacrosanct, honouring its value, and do we now gently, cautiously, offer it to an individual whom everyone agrees is good enough for such a priceless gift? Or do we lose this treasure, bequeathed to us by our grandmothers, in an act of sheer carelessness? Do we throw it away in the grimy darkness of some alley one night, our rationale thick with insolence and arrogance? What others, both peers and parents, judge to be the motivations for a girl's first forays into sexuality are likely to affect her deeply.

Inside the girl's mind is a tangle of explanations, reasons saturated in that thick brew of hormones and emotions. There may be a seeking for adventure, rebellion, or a raw curiosity driving her into the lands of the unknown; she may be looking for attention, or to avenge a mother's negligence or overprotection, or the need to find acknowledgement, the smile of approval. She may be in love, lost in the utterly private world of an intimate relationship we can't grasp or comprehend at all. She may feel her virginity to be a burden, valued more highly by others than is her own truth or happiness, more precious than her freedom. Desperate to find some sense of certainty, she might be equating sex with being grown up.

The phrase expressed by so many women throughout my research for this book was: "I don't think I realised what it was until I lost it".

There's something I'm not understanding. Maybe it's a cultural misconnection, a southern French thing. I'm used to parties where everyone is competing to see how much alcohol they can drink before we're busted or we pass out, lounging across sofas, listening to punk music or lurching wildly to its thudding noise. I walk away from the yattering girls and lean against the wall, looking around the room. They're drinking orange squash, pouring it into plastic cups from jugs on a trestle table. It's sweet and sticky in the evening heat. I'm not sure what to do with mine. I sip it and hide the flinch, and watch the dancing, trying not to frown: teddy music, these kids are dancing like they're in *Grease*! Anyone playing this music at home would be beaten to a pulp. Adèle wanders towards me and smiles awkwardly, not sure what to say to this dark moping English girl; the whole 'French Exchange' thing is a complete disaster.

With my gaze lost in my anger, I realise I'm staring. He's tall, curls of chalky blond hair falling over his face. When our eyes meet. I carry on staring, too bored and detached to feel embarrassed, too resentful to care about anything in this place I don't remotely understand.

He blinks and turns, walking through an open doorway into the garden, but somehow his gaze doesn't seem to leave me. Balancing the sticky cup on a window sill, ignoring Adèle, I stray out into the cool quiet darkness after him. He's standing on the grass beneath an old apple tree. Long slim legs in blue jeans, long fingers, he smokes a cigarette, exhaling into the moonlight.

"T'en veux un?"

I shrug and shake my head. And we stare into each other's faces again. I don't think anything, I just stare back. It's as if we are sliding closer even though we don't move ... until he lifts his hand and cups my face and, so slowly, bends down to kiss my mouth. It's like he strokes me with his smoky smooth kiss. Because he's older, maybe 22, he doesn't kiss like he's eating me like the other boys. It makes me go soft inside.

Sliding down beneath the tree, he gently brings me down with him, until I'm lying in the grass in the glow of the moonlight, with this complete stranger, and I've forgotten that I'm bored, feeling a buzz of adrenaline as he kisses my neck, his hands exploring my body, my bare legs, his fingers finding their way up the folds of my miniskirt and into my underwear. It's exciting to be the focus of his attention, to feel my body alive with his touching.

But at some point, I'm not sure I know quite when, something changes: I'm not in control. His fingers find my wetness. What felt like caring now feels invasive. I don't know how to tell him to stop. I close my eyes in the moonlight, unwilling to fight on any level, too scared of making a fuss, withdrawing inside, barely breathing, watching, as this man plays out his hunger on my body.

"T'as déjà fait ça?" he murmurs.

I think I know what he means and I look up into his face. His eyes are filled with a gentleness that startles me, and bewildered I half shake my head. Then panic, wondering if I've misunderstood him completely. He's undoing his jeans.

"I don't understand," I mumble.

He kisses my mouth and suddenly he's pushing into me. The pain slams through my body and I gasp. "Sshhh," he whispers, his fingertips touching my mouth as he begins to ride back and forth, and I watch his face, fascinated by his pleasure, watching as he seems to slide into a dream, dissolving into himself; he looks quite beautiful. I'm starting to wonder how long this will go on when suddenly he softly moans, his eyes closing as he shudders, his arm giving way so he falls down onto me. I stare up at the stars between the branches of the apple tree above, worried that my skirt will be creased or wet.

There are shouts behind us, someone calling into the garden, "Jean Luc!"

He looks up and swears, whispering, "Désolé, eh?" and in a scramble he gets to his feet, buttoning up his jeans, tucking in his shirt. I sink in the horror of his embarrassment, not moving a muscle as I listen to him strolling back to the house. I breathe, just breathe, repeating his name in the silence of my mind.

The night I lost my virginity, I spent four hours throwing up. Somewhere inside my young teenage mind I knew the transition had spun my soul into turmoil; it felt like a high price to pay. I had believed myself disadvantaged, weighed down by the not-knowing, in a world that seemed to seethe with the power of that information. Yet in the emptiness of the morning after, shaking and alone, I was all too aware that, though I may have lost a little of my ignorance, I had also lost something else, something very distinct and very precious.

The word I used in my diary at the time was 'dignity'. The secret place of my soul, the core privacy of my body, the dark hideaway that was my sanctuary, had been breached. What made it worse was that it had been found and entered so *easily*. The vulnerability that left me with was intense. I floundered, reeling with the giddy comprehension that being a woman could mean being so defencelessly invaded. Curled up on the floor, shivering and drained as the sun rose on another hot summer's day, I knew that I had lost a dignity that would be very hard to find again.

Listening to other women's stories as I prepared this book, I wasn't surprised to hear the same word used again and again. Perhaps in part it is the determination to retain or regain that dignity that provokes us to treasure our independence. Quickly do we learn that we must guard the privacy of our core, our sacred nemeton, if we are to stay strong.

Retaining it

Though the term is most often used in a biological and sexual sense, for most of us the word virgin is also a state of being.

It is an exquisite state. Perhaps most obviously, we feel it in the intimacy inspired by love. Though we may now cringe at the pouting lack of subtlety, when almost 25 years ago Madonna sang *Like a Virgin*, dressed in her raggedly provocative teenage outfits, it was a poignant expression of innocence torn away and regained. To the adult, the young pop star may have seemed painfully naive, stomping with her overly asserted independence, but I sense that only added to the poignancy of the song. However long we've been out in the brutal reality of the world, it is easy to imagine that we might never again feel that acute tenderness of being newly unwrapped.

Yet, as adults, tiptoeing into the intimacy of a particular relationship, we can feel as wholly clueless, naive and bewildered as we might have done at fifteen. We may not believe there is any overt threat, but we are all too aware of the surge of vulnerability; the experience of being undressed, of being asked to reveal a new level of nakedness, requires us to trust as if we've never before known how. Humbled by the currents of nature, we are led out into unknown territory and perhaps, somehow washed clean with the uncertainty, for a strange moment we lose the jaded visions of our expectations. Our innocence returns with a rush of effervescent wonder.

Indeed, very often this sense of virginity returned comes when the intimacy we are exploring is not sexual at all. Adding physical sexuality to the mix can in fact entirely destroy the moment, as if in doing so the limitations of touch remove the innocent beauty, clothing the nakedness of the soul in the fabric of skin and old familiar moves. In part, such times are so thrilling, so amazing and terrifying, because we are as yet untouched. We have no idea where the moment will take us. We stand in the broad open expanse that is our wonder, breathing the shimmering potential of its newness, and all we need do is experience those precious moments before anything is tacked down into decision or knowing.

The circumstances may well be those of an emotional connection with another person, but what has inspired that naked innocence may equally be a blank sheet of paper awaiting its first inky words. It may be a place, somewhere we've not yet explored, a village, a wood, an art gallery. It may a book we've been seeking that, slipping out of the shelves in the old bookstore, we hold in our hands, breathing in its dusty smell and the wealth of all that it might bring. It may be a hunk of clay, a tin of garam masala, the scent of the ocean, the whisper of wind in the trees. When our soul is open to perception and sensation, and free of the constraints of expectations, the first touch of any relationship is a touch of the virgin goddess. The more receptive our soul, the more likely it is that her touch will drench our experience, filling us with awe.

Stuck in the parameters of understanding, our creativity can be dry and unnourishing. Yet pausing to find her within our soul, her gentle wonder and mischievous freedom, that touch can show us just how to step beyond the range of our knowing, finding situations which remind us how little of nature we do in fact comprehend, breaking open our souls again beyond the cynicism of negative experience and expectation. Her innocence touches us as a gift; it is sweet cool water when we are parched by the rough roads of living.

The virgin's blessings of potential are different from those of the darkness and blood that another facet of the hag offers to us. In the depths of the cauldron, like the heart of winter, all nature is possible, yet there we curl up and dream in the peace that exists before the creativity begins. The virgin's time is early spring, with blue skies and growing light, and the first soft touches of warmth reaching into the land. Here our ideas are unproven, but they glow in the gentle sunlight with the potential for life. Instead of simply darkness, here there is freedom with a context, a world laid out before us into which we can delve, exploring, discovering and stretching with delight, utterly aware of that delight.

As a hag goddess, the virgin's self-focus is integral to her nature. Those first touches of sun inspire self consciousness; the first buds of green are only interested in their own experience of growth and presence. However, though we may become intensely frustrated with the teenage girl in all her glorious thoughtlessness of self-discovery and self-expression, we acknowledge her behaviour to be symptomatic of the phase she is moving through. Society's patience starts to fade as we slip out of our teenage years. As adults, exploring this element of our woman nature, the positivity of new horizons brings with it those dangers of innocence and selfishness. We are liable to become disconnected in our focus and attention. The naiveté of virginity compromises our ability or willingness to take responsibility.

Yet, feeling her current within us, if we learn her nature, finding her cravings, it is possible to release our chains and be with her when, where and how it is relevant and appropriate. In this way, we can find the freedom to explore those new landscapes of life without our selfishness and lack of responsibility being detrimental to others.

Indeed, the virgin's creativity isn't necessarily kept for herself.

It isn't necessarily explored in solitude. If she shares, however, or gives anything away, it is not through any trade that would allow her to be indebted. The virgin will do nothing that affects her freedom.

Bridget, the old Gaelic deity, was and to some still is a goddess of inspiration, holding the natural power that is the fire of wakeful life. So strong was devotion for her amongst the people of Scotland and Ireland that Christianity could not displace her, instead finding folk heroines through which she could be beatified. As a patron saint of Ireland, Bridget's story is one of a woman who so loathed the idea of being chained to a husband in marriage that she disfigured herself, jamming a sharp stick into her eye.

The tales of her life vary, but that which I relate to most continues by telling of her dedication to her religion. If she were to have stayed at home, albeit unwanted and unwed owing to her now frightful appearance, she would have continued to live her life for the wellbeing of her father, waiting on him as was expected within the culture. Instead she chose to enter into an abbey, a place where she could spend her time unbothered by the demands of men, in the company of women and the pursuit of creativity. Although some question her willingness to submit to the Christian (male) god, I am content to imagine a scene sufficiently isolated within a religion as yet lacking any strict conformity, where she was able to a large extent to do as she wished. To speak of community and compassion may be to meander into idealisation, but Bridget thrived, becoming abbess herself.

Indeed some versions of her tale, though not those blessed by the Catholic Church, add to the poignancy of her life story by speaking of her lovers and her sexuality as a powerful and independent lesbian of early medieval Ireland.

Some women will do anything to stay free.

A roll of belly hangs over the top of her jeans. I stare at her from where I sit, perched on a wall, flinching as I imagine her squeezing herself into them. Her t-shirt's too small as well, her breasts stretching the material to its limit. The little child in the double pushchair yells and she leans forward quickly to slap it, the hills of breast flesh bouncing as she moves. I can't stop staring. I want to touch them, feel them, in part with horror, part curiosity, and I close my eyes imagining.

The pedestrian light changes, *beep-beep*ing green, and she shouts at the child beside her. I open my eyes and watch as she crosses the road, awkwardly shoving the pushchair loaded with snivelling toddler, small baby and shopping with one hand, carrying more plastic bags and a few fingers of the other child in the other. Another dreamy little kid follows behind them. The wheels hit the curb and she swears. I look away.

I'll never do that, I think. I breathe in deep and stand up, walking along the wall. *I'll never get landed with some bloke's babies,* squashing my body into clothes that don't fit. Me? Screw that. I'm Jack fucking Dawkins. *I'll always be free ...*

Jumping down, I skip across the grass and up onto another wall, watching the tanned body of the lad in the Levi's ad as it slowly growls past on the side of a bus. I sit down again, leaning back against a concrete pillar, and put on a sullen expression to dissuade anyone from looking at me. The world slides on by.

And as usual my mind fills up with Janey and again I relive the moments I can't let go: walking past the bench where she hangs out with her mates after school. I know she's watching me, pretending she isn't, and our eyes meet and I feel every part of me aching with urgency, hiding it with cool insolence ... my body is so incredibly alive with the thrill of her just looking at me. My heart is pounding. I think I must be shining with it, as if I'm on fire and I jump to my feet and saunter along the top of the wall. I want to push my fingers through her mop of dirty-blonde hair, and hold her close to me, feeling the curves of her body, breathing her in. I can hardly breathe.

Leaning against a billboard, I bring my fingers to my lips and, in the noise of Saturday afternoon in the middle of town, alone on the wall, I kiss her, so softly, with all that I am.

Oh Janey ...

She wouldn't give me screaming babies.

Slipping the chains of childhood dependence, heading out into the world in search of a life free from other people's rules, as adolescents we can be quite sure we perfectly understand great swathes of the world. The simple action of surviving without constant supervision lends us the delusion that we know what it's all about. Of course, that can get us into trouble, the oversized shoes of our naiveté tripping us up, but is also a confidence that can be more useful than it is dangerous, for the hag encourages us to explore, learning, growing.

Yet having left behind the sanctuary of home, rejecting the old structures, the loss of that familiar, shared safe space can provoke us to effect a tough shell around ourselves - and particularly so if we feel comfortable with the virgin's current of energies. Stepping out of the family nemeton, we compensate, and our own edges can become brittle and clumsy. In the process of declaring our freedom so assertively, we dissuade others from getting close to us. As a young teenager this can be helpfully protective, but if it becomes a habitual part of how we interact, it can leave us unable to attract an intimate relationship at all. The identity of the virgin can stay too long. When the edges of our sanctuary display signs that read 'Don't Touch', and have done so for so long, it can be hard to know how to change and let someone in. It isn't easy to ask the virgin goddess to leave.

Some speak of letting go our barriers as a process of healing, but it is important not to throw out the necessary with those that aren't. We don't achieve a state of freedom by destroying the boundaries that we naturally hold around ourselves, in a bid to experience a more open and uninhibited interaction with the world. These edges provide us with our sense of self; without adequate edges we lose that cohesion, perpetually confusing our own energy, beliefs and opinions with others', constantly drained, pushed and invaded. The soul's nemeton, the sanctuary of our own individuality, establishes the boundaries of the self, naturally protecting us from stumbling in the slightest breeze.

Battered by the world, of course, the wounds of rejection and betrayal can provoke us to defend our nemeton, to the point where it loses its ease and grace, becoming self-limiting and detrimental. Afraid the hurt will be repeated, we hide inside these barricades, maintaining our independence because we are afraid. The nature of the virgin's sanctuary, however, is quite different. Though at times she may ignore others thoughtlessly, it is not fear that motivates. Her sanctuary is a place of self-discovery. Undistracted, she delves in, flaunting it with an innocent simplicity, her nemeton a den of uninhibited play.

Uncompromised by attachments, the virgin can do what she wants.

For some women that decision to remain untouched becomes key to their lifestyle and sense of self. Sexual celibacy is an increasingly common decision.

When the contraceptive pill became freely available in the 1960s, a new sexual freedom crept into our society; being able to make love without the risk of pregnancy allowed women to feel a very new kind of confidence. For my own generation, a very different kind of revolution came with AIDS. Having grown up with that earlier freedom, in the early 1980s sex suddenly became potentially deadly. Communities of friends and lovers changed as people became sick or afraid. Choosing not to have sex started to become acceptable where during the days of freedom such a stand was seen as proud or 'square'. The desolating fear of AIDS no longer looms over us like the inevitable carnage of a plague, but that old freedom is gone. Sex and health are now indivisibly connected, and for many those tangles are reason enough not to journey into the uncertain worlds of sexual intimacy.

While active celibacy was once the landscape of priests and mystics, nowadays many women are convinced by its benefits. The late nights and emotional complications of sexual relationships are incompatible with the focus needed in their demanding, secular fields of work. Such single-minded creativity can be interpreted as defensive, but it need not be. The virgin goddess shimmers through these women, not deflecting others aggressively, but expressing a dedicated attentiveness to the project in hand. Filled with enthusiasm and wonder, here is inspiration drawn from intimacy that may not be human to human, but comes through the deep appreciation of nature's patterns and flows.

Playing alone

Celibacy, however, whether a long-term decision or simply a lack of available partners, need not mean a lack of sexual pleasure. Where sexual energy rises naturally, denying that itch can be an unnecessary frustration. Indeed, for many women, celibate or not, the exquisite art of masturbation, of sexual play alone, is one that is profoundly important, inherently creative and wholly self-affirming.

For a long while I watch the fire, sitting on the hearth rug, entranced by the flames that flicker and lick around the logs that I've just put on. In part I am simply waiting to be sure the wood will take, and in part I am sliding, dissociating, losing focus as my mind surrenders to the fullness of the moment: the stillness of the house, the firelight playing in the dark, its warmth upon my bare skin, feeling everything and holding absolutely nothing at all.

The twilight song of a blackbird gives me a path, the clarity of its melody guiding me back and, blinking, sighing deeply, taking a match I light the candle on the altar of stones, smiling at the little figure of the sheela-na-gig. Her soft stone thighs spread apart, she opens her vulva towards me and stares. I sip from the fine crystal glass the sweetness of fresh apple juice, a treasure of taste, and lie back on the cushions that make a throne before the fire, dipping my finger into the juice and sucking it from my skin.

A spider moves beneath the altar, silhouetted by the firelight, her legs two inches long. She stops, hanging onto thin air with one upraised leg, spinning silk with two forelegs whirling below. I watch her as my hand slowly strokes the warm softness of my body, wondering at her creativity, and behind her the golden tongues of fire licking round the wood. The candle flame dances languidly on an invisible breath of air. Within my mind there is music, seductive, mellifluous, unconcerned. A drop of juice falls from my finger onto my skin. It rolls down my breast. The world is pausing. I lie back and close my eyes.

The taste of the juice still lingers sweet on my lips. And for a while I float in the space that is this solitude softly wrapped around me, weightless as silken veils in the breeze, deep mauve, bronze, indigo blue like a night sky above me. In the fire's glow, my hands move over my thighs, the softness of my breasts, the curve of my belly, half waking the nerves that doze in the warmth. There is nothing to do but simply be, feeling the warmth, dancing light, breath and shadows. And so do my fingers play, lingering, brushing, caressing, cool on such warm skin, until I'm stretching on velvet, on pale sunbaked sand washed lazily by gentle waves, dancing in the rhythms, unformed music pulsing through me, watching an imaginary lover watching my body move, feeling the fire's radiance, the sheela-na-gig smiling, my fingers playing, moving down into the dark heat between my thighs.

Even though we like to think of our modern Western society as being so very open and liberal, there is still a problem with masturbation. Though the majority do it, it is still barely acceptable to admit we do. Comedians throw it onto the table and we laugh, we smirk, but, for most, to confess to their own play provokes a deep embarrassment and vulnerability. What other activity is there in human society that exists within as complicated a tangle of doing and denial?

Puritanical religious teachers are clear in their judgement, perceiving any physical pleasure as play inspired by demonic forces, let alone self-pleasuring. Like shadows and spiders' webs, associated superstitions still linger around the issue, warning us that playing with own body will quash our libido, compromise our health, leaving us putrid, or even sterile. The words associated with masturbating are dirty, sinful, base. It is self-abuse. Even amongst teenagers, the wanker is weak, selfish, stupid. Sticky fingers.

Yet for a woman, masturbation can be anything from a much-needed quick physical release of stress (and as such, the very best solution for menstrual cramps), to a couple of hours or more of gently nurturing self-affirmation. With awareness, it is an important part of the journey of learning to accept ourselves: the curves of our body, the quirks of our mind, the cravings of our soul. Reaching into the depths of our own power, we assert our independence by achieving peaks of ecstatic pleasure, alone.

In many ways, this is not just the independent virgin, playing in the privacy of her own world, exquisitely aware of her own experience. The hag is here too in the form of the wild child, finding the joy of utterly uninhibited play. With no external input, and nothing shared, we stir the cauldron of our inner nemeton, spiralling into ourselves, bathing in the currents of our creativity, for ourselves alone.

Indeed, playing alone may not entail the stimulus that releases sexual energy. The sacred nature of the virgin, hag-wild and intensely aware of the sensual experience of her own living, can also guide us to explore a different response to the sexual hum. Learning how to identify its soul-deep vibration, she inspires us to develop our self-awareness, letting that sexual energy seep through into every cell, waking the spirit with its warm vibrancy. Holding it in our fingertips, we can let it spill out into words or stretch into the colours of our art. Feeling it in our lungs, our throats, we can pour it out in song. We can cook with it, make music, run, laugh and play with it, not as a mitigation of sexual frustration, but as virgin creativity. Indeed, we could simply let it slip back into the dark cauldron of our creative energy. Walking into the luxury of it, sliding, diving, drinking deeply the shimmering of its inspiration, accessing the energy of its resource, we find the womb-cauldron has never been so profoundly and intensely ours.

Lands untouched

As a child I was given the extraordinary gift of spending time in some truly wild landscapes. The story a few pages back is one of my own life: I learned to shoot in the Llanos of Venezuela, where my parents' studies of flora and fauna took us journeying through wilderness that was both beautiful and brutal. I watched as such places brought out the thug in some men, the tenderness in others. In later years, meditating on those times, the reflection between that landscape, which was so untouched by humankind, and my own wild childish soul, became very clear to me. The poignancy of the connection seemed even more acute when I considered the times I spent in the Amazon rainforest, in truly virgin forest, a landscape under the perpetual threat of being devoured by man.

Virginity seems to me to be like a ripe fruit. The virgin is the essence of nature, an abundance of vitality, sweet energy, the juices of life as yet untasted. She is wild, following still the laws of her own desires. She glows with her fertility, the energy of which she uses solely for her own pleasure and growth, her own delight. Even when she is ready to offer herself and the abundance of her body, the fruit of her glorious wildness, she may not be ready to *give* it. Standing in her independence, she is proud of who she is.

Look. But don't touch ...

To see the virgin as untouched land, as radiant and bounteous with life as the tropical rainforest, is to understand more profoundly the correlation between the power of nature and the power of woman. There is something in the psyche of our post-industrial society that infuses the notion of virgin land with a magical haze. We dream of such places, places that have not been touched by the felling, tilling, paving, civilising hand of humanity. It holds an unmistakable allure, a fascination that provokes a craving that is deeply instinctive. It is prized like a great treasure. It inspires a yearning desire to hunt it down, to explore it, to discover the nature of its depths, to conquer its challenges, to bathe in its potential. For some, the need is to claim it, to own it, whether to care for it and keep it safe from the hunger of others, or to use it, taming its dark unknown heart. Where a landscape has never been sown, its soil never been ploughed, there is a longing to know if this will be the field of gold.

The mining of metals and gems, and fossil fuels, is fired by the ardent questing of the magically elusive wealth that lies in the darkest reaches of the Earth's virgin soul. The fishing industry is driven for many by a craving to meet the power of nature that is the depth and force of the unconquerable sea. The hunting of wild creatures for sport and material gain is that same aching desire to tame and claim the ferocious innocence of nature. Poetically dramatic words, but ones that express the emotion that is provoked by the virgin. She is fit for the sacrificial slab, the bloodlust of the vampire. Her innocence betrays her. Her purity, like the wine of the Holy Grail, must be tasted.

Yet, like innocence, the wilderness is finite, as are this planet's resources. Nor is much of its earth significantly fertile. Slash and burn of the rainforest offers but a year or two of viable topsoil before it is utterly depleted - and so much so that the rainforest itself will not return. Flying low in a small aircraft over the Amazon, the extraordinary richness of the virgin forest stretches out beneath, littered with fires that blaze up into the skies, and increasing tracts of grey: the dust of land dying of exhaustion. Virgin land that is raped reacts with suicide.

The virgin is all too often an exquisite wild rose, radiant in scent and colour, in that moment of just beginning to open out into bloom. Unlike a cultivar that will flower again and again, if this wild bloom is cut and placed in a vase to be admired it will last but a short while before it wilts and dies. It is no wonder the virgin resists.

So what is it that brings her to the point where she is willing to give?

For most, there is an inevitability that at some point we shall leave that virgin land of our innocence. And most of us do. Either by our own volition, or dragged by the hand of another, we walk out of the wilderness, the landscapes of our childhood freedom. Uninhibited, barefoot with dirty fingers and toes, the adolescent still selfish in her laughter and pleasure, the girl-hag not nice enough to be chosen and swived, untamed in her freedom, sullen and exuberant, the virgin withdraws inside as we shed our naiveté and step closer to adulthood. She can slip away quietly, allowing the face of the spring maiden to come to the fore, smiling with gentle sunshine in her sweet guise of giving, or she can scream, kicking and snarling as she exits, spitting in disgust.

It is too easy to shrug and accept that how we deal with this transition is simply an expression of our own nature. There are too many factors that make a difference. It's a crucial time: the world feels new and confusing, and it seems as if nobody understands. This is as true for the journey into our sexuality as that of any virginal experience of creativity, tender with sensitivity through the process of growing understanding, whether we are thirteen or fifty six.

The most poignant and affecting gift we can be given at this time is most often the simple touch of acknowledgement. When our innocence is slipping away, our sense of self can feel dreadfully naked and raw. For it to be recognised, and gently without judgement, that we are learning, growing, changing, is both precious and rare. It is what many girls are seeking *in* sexual interaction, and to have it offered in some other way can dilute a premature urge to rush into sex.

Like the menarche rite, a rite of passage acknowledging the journey from virginity into sexual awareness or sexual experience can be done at any point throughout our lives. As a retrospective vision, its course is no different from a rite done at the time but that, where the one making the transition is older, communication is usually clearer, the sensitivities not so acute. Working with a younger girl is more powerful; we are stepping close to the bounds of her intimate space, a place that is profoundly tender, trembling as it is with self-awareness and change. To approach clumsily is not only disrespectful but can make the situation a great deal worse. ... *Nobody understands me!*

It can be as simple as sharing a bottle of wine, a quiet walk, a hug or hand offered, a mug of tea at sunset, with or without a few words of support, however direct or oblique. If the situation allows, it can be more formally and creatively put together, with friends invited, a party put together with gifts and words spoken. Either way, the key is finding a way of recognising and appreciating the young girl who is now withdrawing and the woman who is stepping forward. Flush with her fertility, still flighty with innocence, feeling the power of her independence, the growing awareness of her changing identity needs to be acknowledged. Perhaps with old clothes, photographs, stories, sharing again some sweet joy, we honour who she was and who she will become.

For some the transition can be given a name. If virginity was lost within a relationship that is ongoing, that can be honoured, so giving it a stronger foundation with support from friends and family. If we have fallen in love, it is more likely that we have lost some of that exquisite independence, albeit willingly, and this should be handled carefully, affirming strength and individuality. However, the other person may be a side issue or a source of pain; it may have been his motorbike, the gang, the security, the kudos, the wedding dress, that seemed worth the price. Looking back thirty years, we may have a sense as to whether what we paid was a mistake, or a well cut deal; if it is only a matter of weeks or months, that may not be so clear. Where we can, our decisions are acknowledged, reviewed and accepted, with laughter, rage, tears and dreams, a poignant moment of healing created and shared. With past and present considered, the rite guides our focus to the future.

Most importantly, perhaps, it is not for us to dismiss the virgin. Though we may have lost some innocence, we will always in some situations be hopelessly naive and unknowing. We don't leave her behind. We shouldn't even try to. The virgin becomes a part of our soul to emerge when she is needed, as the wit of innocence and the strength of independence, the exquisite experience of perceiving the world with wonder.

There are potions beside the basin, shaving oil, hair gel, even a deodorant in a space age grey tube that seems to have MAN written all over it. I lift an aftershave impossibly carefully, not wanting him to hear the slightest clink, breathing in the smell and putting it back, feeling the flurries of excitement inside.

Then scrabbling in my bag for a compact, my fingers come across a little pouch that isn't mine: blue padded silk and tied with a ribbon. I take it out and undo the ribbon, frowning with curiosity, imagining it's there by mistake. But then I'm sinking to sit on the closed loo seat, blushing with silent laughter: inside there are three condoms, *extra safe*, and a twenty pound note. *Mum ... !*

She'd stopped me at my bedroom door last night, hugged me in that way that only she can do, that hug which makes me feel as if the world is so huge and I've only just begun to explore it. All I'd done is ask her if I could stay over at Jim's tonight - his parents are away. I guess that was my way of saying that I thought *it* might happen, and I guess this is her way of saying ... that she trusts me.

He's standing by the open window looking out over the darkness and the quiet of the garden, his face soft in the candle light. When he hears me he turns and smiles, "OK?"

"Yeah," I nod, looking up into the starry night, feeling his energy beside me. I let my head rest on his shoulder and he puts his arms around me. He feels safe, like a warrior right there at my side; if I let myself fall, I know he would catch me. When I turn to him, he looks into my eyes.

"You OK with this? You don't want to go home?"

I shake my head, "No," and though I can feel the butterflies of my nervousness, I can also feel my mum, and my nana, her mum, and her mum before her. I know it's strange but it makes me feel strong, knowing that all these women before me have stood in this same place, in this same moment, looking into the eyes of the lad who will take their innocence.

He strokes my cheek, letting his fingertips rest for a moment on my lips. I think my heart will explode, and I blink, breathless, as he leans towards me and we kiss.

CHAPTER FOUR

The Whore

The hardest moments in life are often those of transition. Journeying from one place into another, leaving familiarity and heading through cloudy lands of change, we stumble and fall on strange ground, misinterpreting, misunderstanding, misunderhearing. Even if we are confidently walking proud and sure, we are likely to be dragging with us some baggage of the past, some now redundant belief or behaviour, weighing heavily, easily tattered, complicating life with its defiant and coarse irrelevance. So it is that, still draped in the swathes of our naiveté, we embark on the adventure of sexuality, and, like a pretty dress worn in the wild greenwood, that naiveté is all too quickly snagged and torn. Not knowing the path, we make mistakes.

No, nevertheless, means no.

Saying yes and no

Some of our mistakes are easily learned, accepted, forgotten. Some are not sketched but etched into our soul's memory, gouged deep with the acids of guilt and shame. When fear of rejection is added to that brew, such mistakes can leave us wholly bewildered, the blinds of inhibition slamming down on our sexuality, crippling our ability to see clearly enough to be able to crawl quietly out of the murk. Stumbling along, wounded, suddenly unable to express either physicality or emotion, too scared, we thwart every attempt at our life's creativity. Those blocks to our free expression can crash down at any time in our life, from our first sexual experience onwards, and they can persist indefinitely.

Sometimes we know too little to avoid the mistakes.

Yet even so, no means no.

"You better come." The urgency on her face looks undignified and childish.

"You go," I shrug, turning away from her expression and all it is saying, laying my head back on the chair as I put the bottle to my lips. The whisky spills down my throat and into my belly, glowing with its heat. I lift my foot, resting my boot on the radiator, keenly aware that the card game has been abandoned and the lads are all watching my response.

"But you're dad said midnight," Suzie whines.

"And what makes you think I give a shit?" I take another drink as the three of them cheer, laughing. Ben rolls to his feet and picks up his pack of cigarettes, lighting one slowly and looking up at her, "Stay and play, yeah? Or fuck off like a good girl, hey?" It gives me the courage to look her in the face. She turns away quickly.

Half listening through their laughter to her footfalls on the stairs, I avoid their eyes, flicking through a dog-eared copy of *Animal Farm* that was lying on the table. I sway, suddenly aware of just how drunk I am. Ben's hand touches my leg, his fingers running up and down my thigh.

"Hey, Danny," I say, trying to ignore Ben, "have you read this?"

He smiles, his eyes dozy and blurred with the whisky and dope. "Fuck the book, baby. Come sit here with me." It's a cute crooked smile and, stumbling over Dave who's lying on the floor rolling a spliff, I clamber onto the sofa. Ben turns up the music and sinks into another chair, his feet on the table. I pass him the whisky and his hand lingers on mine. My smile is dismissive, as I reach for confidence in the pounding music amidst the swell of my alcoholic haze. Somewhere in my mind I can hear Suzie's voice, warning me, judging me as stupid.

Danny turns my face towards him, kissing me on the mouth. It's a long way from what I imagined. He's too drunk and forceful to care if I'm responding. But he knows that I like him - I've not hidden it. It would be churlish to rebuff him now, just because I feel awkward with the others so close.

At first I think it's Danny's hand moving up my thigh. When I realise it's Ben, I try to kick him away. But Danny's kissing me again, smothering my words, squeezing my breast with noises of appreciation. When I push him back, he smiles, "Hey come on, what's up?"

"But Ben's - "

He puts his hand over my mouth, looking into my eyes, "But you're a party girl, yeah?" And he grins at Ben. A dozen half cut thoughts skid through my mind, not least not wanting him to think that I'm dull. My heart is thumping, and for a moment I don't know if it's just fear or exhilaration. But then Ben's hand is prying apart my thighs. I pull away from Danny, "Wait!" and bring my legs back together, but Ben looks into my face so seriously and snarls, "Don't you mess about now, missy." Suddenly I'm scared.

Again Danny turns my head to face him, his eyes blurred but shining and determined. I'm trying to find the words to say, *Wait! What's going on?! I thought maybe I wanted to be with you, but not this ... Hold on a fucking minute!* ... but all I can feel is the world turned upside down. He draws me towards him, kissing my mouth, but I push away, yelling, "Fuck off!"

In that half second pause I see Dave has sat up and is watching. He lifts a hand and runs his fingers down the length of my leg. Then Danny's mouth is on mine again, hungry and biting, his hand pushing under my shirt. I can't move an inch - each time I try the pain of hands pushing and gripping gets tighter. It's hard to know whose hand is whose. I close my eyes, sinking into a maze of confusion as someone's rough fingers are pushing up into me.

The first time I was raped, I had no doubt that it was entirely my own fault. Raping a virgin, a girl whose innocence shines in her smile, is a dreadful brutality. The same is true for any woman who is obviously vulnerable, with sex far from her mind. It's easy to condemn such acts as unforgivable. In reality, there may be a catalogue of reasons that help us fathom why a person might act that way, from drug use to emotional negligence. The seething force of nature that is lust is one of the most powerful that moves through humankind; manipulative, deceptive, both inconstant and yet persistent, that god of the wild, of the pulsating heat of sexual need, can and does so easily destroy lives. It takes just a moment's carelessness, a whisper of weakness, and we can be overcome as the force surges through us, driving us to do what we otherwise wouldn't. To acknowledge that power as deity and so hard to subdue is a Pagan perspective, and one that guides its adherents to strive to understand the nature of lust. In the secular world, however, it is far easier to declare the deed as simply *wrong*.

When it comes to provocation, however, though the fine line that delineates culpability may be drawn as clearly, the judgement is not as often against the perpetrator. If she is wearing clothes that are designed to outline the curves of her body, if she is expressing her availability, if she is displaying her sexuality, and she is raped, then very often the girl is considered to blame. She has invoked the god of lust, recklessly dancing before him. With experience and confidence we can duck and evade his grasp, but it is madness to imagine we can tame such a force.

The secular perspective can be concerned that such an attitude is too pessimistic. Whether it comes from a lack of faith in men's ability to curb what some see as an innate sexual violence, an inability to discipline their animal cravings, or if it intimates a lack of care for a woman's predicament as the victim of a crime, as the 'weaker' sex, it is an opinion that seems to display little respect for humankind in general. To the Pagan, it is not about dismissing our human strengths of reason and compassion. It merely acknowledges the power of the gods.

I was no virgin when I was raped. Preened, polished, fifteen, painted to look thoroughly desirable, I radiated sexual energy. When I strode out in my stiletto boots and miniskirt, the god of lust was watching me, and most of the time I was entirely aware of his presence. In adolescent stupidity, fear drowned in alcohol, I took bad risks - as so many girls do. But in my drunken state, unable to fight, too afraid of violence, too afraid of rejection, did I always consent? Realising I had gone too far, finding myself out of my depth, like so many girls I learned about damage limitation. Tactics such as submitting to avoid the pain or severity of force, or asking him to use a condom, have been legally identified as consent.

Statistics I came across, heaven knows where (take them as you will), stated that just a third of Western women have never been raped. A further third have agreed to sex when they really didn't want it, at least once, simply to avoid trouble - from abuse to repudiation, in all its forms: they said yes and meant no. The final third have said no and been forced into sex. Yet for each of the above, and this was clearly revealed as I spoke to women for this book, the definition of rape, of consent and of blame, varies enormously according to self esteem and cultural conditioning. A feisty soul will put up with the occasional incident where wires were crossed and she ends up giving in to physical or emotional pressure for sex even though the idea revolts her; a more tender soul might describe the same scenario as rape. However, while definitions may be disputed, what doesn't alter is the basic: no means no.

Quite sure that I was to blame, I didn't dare go to the doctor, convinced he would dismiss me as having got what I deserved. When I did go, after three days, the bruises by then black and blue, though I told him the story he wrote in my medical files 'possible' rape. The following day, my period came and I bled into my rage and shame, striding through college with a vicious pride, and with the hag-wit of PMS, and a caustic confidence, I hid my pain. In fact, around three quarters of women raped are attacked when they are premenstrual or bleeding. On some level beneath conscious awareness, the scents and pheromones we give off at this time can be both enticing and frightening: they present a challenge to be overcome.

Further, though, some women do find the last week of their cycle, the five days of premenstrual energy, to be a time when they feel a different kind of strength. Brimming with confidence, they are more likely to dress up and express the wild inside, to try the bright red lipstick and thigh boots, to snarl and spit their frustration and need. With oestrogen low, the premenstrual woman is more ready to flirt and fight: sexually active yet retaining a hag-streak of wild independence and a good deal less gentle feminine compassion.

Whore?

Hunger and shame

In the same way that I spoke of the virgin, within the wholeness of every woman there is a facet within us all that is *whore*. It's a strong word, another hag word.

The flower bud swells, bursting open in the touch of sunshine, dew-wet and delectably scented, overtly bathing in its own allure. Any creature that is fertile for short periods of time does all it can to express vividly its receptivity, with song and vibration, drenched in scent, draped in colour, blood-flushed. If a woman does the same, she is derided. Her behaviour is perceived as a lack of morality, an unwillingness or inability to control her vulgar urges. In some cultures, if she has no intention of conceiving she is judged still more harshly.

Among others, both Muslim and Christian texts declare women's sexual appetites to be the downfall of humanity. Removed from Judaeo-Christian mythology for her celebration of sexuality, Adam's first wife, Lilith, was replaced by the passive

Eve who was willing to be done to. A goddess of the old civilisations of Sumero-Babylonian tribes, fertile and pleasure-seeking, Lilith was a power of woman-nature in all her glory. Indeed, the daughters of Lilith are said to have haunted men for millennia as the succubae, the sexually hungry and sensuous spirit-women, declared demonic for they presented female power that could not be tamed.

The male force of lust is portrayed as having something vital and heroic about it, albeit at times violent. A woman's is dangerous in other ways. Perhaps because it is often so easy to bring a man to his knees with his craving for sexual release, or to the edge of the violence that comes with his sexual need, it is declared wrong for a woman to show her sensual desire, for in doing so she invokes that god of lust. The power of nature that is female libido is rather different. As a goddess, this female lust is seldom so easily invoked by a man's sexual desire; she is far more interested in her own.

Of course, this current can flow in various ways. It can be a bubbling brook, keen with its swirling fingers of exploration; it can be a wide old river that moves slowly with a confident and gentle surety; and it can be white water, surging without compromise, ever questing a course that can hold the power of its force that will give in to its craving. All these contain at least a whisper of the whore, but it is the woman who is blatantly unwilling to hide that wild flow who is declared the slapper, the tart, the slag or hussy. She is *all* whore; she's been around.

As an insult, the words all suggest a promiscuity that is unacceptable in our culture. Discussing with a group of men why it is that women who are sexually-free are still judged to be worse than men, it was agreed that the problem was because a woman's genitals are hidden. A dirty penis can be washed until it positively shines, but a cunt is always dangerously dark. A few explained to me that it was like hunger, expressing prejudices that they defended as simple human nature: if a bloke sits down to a hearty meal it's healthy and normal, but a woman's appetite should be more measured, otherwise she looks coarse and uncouth. Of course, they all concurred, she should be hungry and show her hunger - the metaphor coming into play - but there was an emphatic sense that, if she's to avoid the label of whore, this needed to be contained. Somehow that darkness was connected with the hunger.

The whore, then, is dangerous. Our culture demands (at least a front of) monogamy, yet this girl appears to ignore that shamelessly; she threatens stability, marriage, sanity and tender hearts, the sure ground of moral integrity. Brazenly independent, she seeks out and finds her pleasure, wherever. She makes a deal in order to gain just what she wants, while refusing to compromise either her freedom or her self-expression. She is hungry.

Yet at the same time she is crucial to human society. She is loved. We obsess about her, in both love and lust, and in caustic disapproval. Men dissolve at her feet in devoted adoration; women, too. We seek her out, most often in dreams and fantasies, gazing at her on the TV screen, half naked pop stars, dancing their sensuality and lust. Yet sometimes we are willing (and men in particular) to risk all we are, just for moments of her sharp caressing attention - and not just for the sake of sexual relief. There is more.

She is wild. It is her freedom we crave to touch and be touched by. Raw, animalistic, she offers us an exquisite opportunity to be ourselves, utterly. Uninhibited, soiled and flawed, naked and knowing nothing, the whore is the incredible acceptor of all that is unacceptable within us. She holds the seeping wound of our emotional shame. She guides us to explore that which we've hidden from, addressing and expressing the parts of our soul that we fear most of all.

He staggers slightly coming back to the bar stool. I reach out to catch him. He doesn't notice, continuing a conversation he's been having inside his head, slurring in his Mississippi drawl, shaking his head, " ... not sure if you've met ... it was in Shinjuki ... some sweet pussy bar," he waves a hand. I wonder what he's just taken on this last excursion to the toilets, knowing his eyes won't meet mine for a while. " ... were pissin' on the trees, man ... " He's emphatic. I take a sip from my bottle of beer.

Walking down the street, he seems to hit the ground too hard with every step. Alert for police, feeling the familiar paranoia, I try not to think of how much he's got in his pocket. Heading down into the subway I take his arm, the river of people holding us upright even though it's nearly midnight, Tokyo midnight. But he doesn't notice.

Lying on the tatami mats of his sitting room floor, he looks up at me and smiles. A moment's recognition touches him, too quickly followed by gratitude which hits too hard and tears fill his eyes. I sink to my knees beside him, my head on his shoulder, holding him, and he croons, "What are you doin' here, sugar?"

"Being with you," I murmur. Opening his shirt, button by button, I run my fingertip down the old welt of the scar, kissing it, tiny kisses, each one bursting in my mind with images of the machete blade that carved it into being. I imagine I can taste the moment, the heat of the rainforest, gun fire exploding, dripping with fear. He's told me the Vietnam stories often enough, always forgetting what he's said before, always amazed that I'm willing to hear. And when I nod because I know a part already, he reads in me an empathy that makes him yell out with wonder, "Jesus!" holding my hands tightly, his eyes glistening, "You are so damn special, sugar!"

In this room, lit by the television screen, the hum of the city around us, the familiar torrid music and screams of the horror movie turned down low, I undo his belt, unbuttoning his jeans. One of his hands rests on my head as he murmurs, and I kiss him, knowing he is too stoned to get hard. It's easier this way. I whisper, "You're beautiful." Suddenly his fingers tighten in my hair. Then the sharp bite of a blade is at my neck and my stomach sinks so fast it hits my bowels, *not again* ...

For as long as I can, I keep my eyes closed, breathing, just breathing, concentrating on breathing. Every noise seems to push up against me, voices on the video, traffic outside. I know I must stay calm, not show fear, not show him this works, not move against the knife.

When our eyes meet, his pupils are hollow black tubes bored into his soul. He snarls, staring in to me, "What are you doing here, sugar?" Gently, tenderly, I put my hand on his heart, trying not to tremble, blinking slowly, reaching for strength, his warm bare skin softened with age and drugs, his long sandy-coloured eyelashes around the redness of his eyes, the sun freckles on his cheekbones. "I like being with you, Ricki."

Prostitution is said to be the oldest profession. Conscripts in the Roman army were given brothel tokens to alleviate the frustration of being on the road so long. Around any army, any gathering of men, from stockbrokers to musicians, come a community of women willing to take their money, offering their skills in return. The image of the caring whore holding the dirty wounded warrior is poignant; and it is true not only for the man scarred in warfare, but also for those torn up by the battles of modern daily life. In her arms, he can express the vulnerability of his terrible weakness; she won't tell a soul. She offers absolute sanctuary, the perfect confessional.

Traditions of the whore stretch back far into the mists of time. Ishtar, the Great Goddess of ancient Babylonian culture, held power over most of life, from fertility to war; she was also the Sacred Whore. Questing her divine guidance, her blessing, men reached for her inspiration through her temple prostitutes. The same can be found in the history of almost every civilisation around the world, the whores acknowledged as a critical and sacred part of life. Yet throughout the centuries of Christianity, she has been condemned, demeaned and spat upon. She sees the weakness of mankind, his bawdy and animalistic, hungry ugly self. She evokes his need for her, and she retains her independence. As the value of women fell, and the taste of pleasure declared vile, the whore was dragged from the consecrated temple, down into the filth of the gutter.

In the gutter, she has no rights. So is the ancient sacred art of prostitution now riddled with the violence of any illegal trade. Whores are owned by their traders who care nothing for their wellbeing, men (most often men) who lust only after the money that their girls can bring in. In the gutter, sex is about exploitation, not pleasure, not caring.

Over the past fifty years, however, as the old traditions - the earth religions and healing arts - find a place of respect once more, gently, slowly, the whore too is finding her feet again. This is not street-dank desperation, not pimped servitude or degradation; these new prostitutes of Western culture are invoking the old vision of their craft. Proud of what they are, their work is infused with an awe for the power that is woman: the exquisite gifts of the hag as whore. Through gentleness they may simply offer the healing touch of intimacy, given within the safety of non-attachment; it may be the more brutal task of breaking a man's rigid defensive barricades, allowing him once again to *feel*, to grow and love, to live creatively, finding his own peace and satisfaction.

The whore inside us can take this role in a particular relationship and work it to mutual benefit, but it is equally possible that without sufficient skill the whore's energy damages. For the Pagan who takes the role with more dedication than within one single relationship, honing the necessary skills, the work is given as a sacred service, as offerings, sacrifice and devotion to deity, whether that be an abstract wholeness ('the goddess') or in a specific and named form: Aphrodite, Venus, Isis, Bridget, Ishtar, Sabrina. Caring for their own physical and emotional well-being is an integral part of their reverence, and essential if they are to find and maintain enough strength and positivity, caring and patience, to hold the weakness of those who come to them.

The deals we make

Like *witch*, which some believe to be derived from the Saxon word *witan* (to know), the negative implications of the word *whore* are also badly ensnared, following centuries of the suppression of women's natural sensuality. Its etymology could be sourced in the *horae*, divine maidens who danced the turning of time in Greek mythology, mellowing the souls of men with their beauty and their touch. The word is linked to the Babylonian *harine*, the Semitic *harlot*, the Persian *houri*, temple prostitutes who brought the pleasures of life to humankind. Yet far from a bringer of delight, the word now describes a woman who deals in sexuality. Used as an insult, the *whore* is definitively a woman who degrades herself. Yet does she?

Each one of us whores.

From early adolescence we are taught about the deal that is 'dinner for sex'. Neither men nor woman can pretend to be unaware of it. Even where a fellow is simply playing out the chivalric role he has been taught, he knows his actions are part of an ancient game of finding and shifting the balance of power. Some women fight it, dismissing tradition, abhorring the assumption, determined to maintain their power by ensuring they pay for themselves; others accept the deal, consenting to their part, happy to play the game even when there is an option to say no. Others fail to see what it is they are offering in this unspoken agreement, realising too late that they have unwittingly given some kind of consent, placing themselves in a situation they then don't have the courage to walk away from; youthful innocence allows the mistake, but naive hope and trust extends it. More 'enlightened' relationships may deny the deal still exists, but the undercurrent undeniably remains.

As we get older, we continue to whore, even in steady relationships. Married men tell me how their wives sell them sex, using moments of caring intimacy as a bargaining device, offering their bodies for a little more money or freedom, for a new dress, shelves fixed, a night out with the girls, a day without football. Women admit that it is so: deals spoken and deals implied. At work, just as men use their charm, their front of manly confidence, the clever woman knows how to facilitate each transaction with seduction: a long look, a passing touch, a smile given like a perfect gift. It's a power, a persuasive tool, available to each one of us to use and abuse: sexual intimacy, or a fleeting taste of it, in exchange for satisfaction, for status, for distraction, for security, for approval, for acceptance.

The hag, dressed in the guise of seductress, gets what she wants. Yet, if this is degrading - if the definition of *whore* is enveloped in self-degradation - it could equally apply to situations without sex. It is after all simply the action of selling ourselves. Certainly the word is not uncommonly used in this way. Every time the boss yells and we struggle to our feet, thinking of the pay cheque in order to get the damn thing done, we are whoring. Does it make a difference how we're dressed, or whether we are dressed at all? We have lost the reins of our life and we grasp at the edge of it, clumsily weighing up the exchange by focusing only on what we will gain. We may smile, though we're seething, and again lower our standards, frustrated and humiliated just to make the money that we need. If we are compromising who we really are for some sense of security, stability, safety, then we are degrading ourselves. Those implications so hard to disentangle from the word *whore* - of deprecation, humiliation, self-derogation - only go to emphasise the extent to which the whore is deemed unacceptable. It spells out again and again the way in which both the sacred art of pleasure and the raw nature of woman have been so profoundly and deeply devalued.

He's nervous, seeking out his confidence, tapping his fingers on the tablecloth. "So .. " he frowns, doing his utmost to look casual, "would you like to come back to my place for coffee?"

The cliché makes me smile.

"Actually, there's a place up Greek Street that has live music ... we could dance?"

For a moment his face reveals disappointment, a pale uncertainty tinged with the anxiety of rejection. He clears his throat. "Sure," he nods, trying to find his feet again, but soon he's gazing into my eyes in search of the next clue. "Up Greek Street?"

"It's a great club," I meet his eyes and smile. "And I'm told it does excellent coffee."

A waiter arrives at our table and, taking out his wallet without a word, he slips his credit card into the bill, nodding with a smile of thanks. It's almost the best part of a date: watching him pay. Then he's gazing at me again, his curiosity now overt.

I hold his gaze. It's hard not to tease.

He shrugs, finding some confidence, "Actually, you know ... I do pretty good coffee ... "

"The thing is," I smile, "I don't drink coffee."

"Ah." He looks down at his hands resting on the table, and I watch as he considers how broadly metaphorical the rejection might be: am I gently telling him that he's nice enough but not attractive, or just that I don't go that far on a first date? After taking a moment's pleasure in watching him suffer, I put my hand onto his and again our eyes meet.

"If you take me dancing, I'll come back to your place and we can fuck all night ... "

The quest for pleasure

The whore is not interested in fertility.

Still much scientific and secular thought perceives human evolution to be driven by fertility. As women, we seek out men with the best resources: strength and health in a younger man, and the alternative of wealth in an older man, ensuring good genes for our children and secure back up to protect and feed them. There is validity in that understanding. Yet in a culture where a woman is likely to sleep with more than one man before she settles down, she is also able to develop a taste for what feels good, and choose accordingly.

My sense is that this is not only true for modern Western culture, but is basic human nature. It is only comparatively recently, and most especially in politically patriarchal and monotheistic cultures, that women have been sexually suppressed to the point of marrying (vowing themselves into monogamy) before they have understood or experienced the fullness of their own sexuality. If these women had their freedom to experiment and discover pleasure, they would perhaps be less likely to accept or serve a bad lover as a husband.

The idea of human evolution weighted towards the principle of pleasure makes a great deal more sense than one weighted towards fertility. Our closest relatives, the bonobo or pygmy chimpanzees, are perhaps the most sexually expressive of all creatures; unhindered by human inhibition, they freely play with their own erogenous zones, stimulating each other's, and having sex in any combination of hetero or same sex couplings and gatherings at any given opportunity. They play, apparently, for simple physical relief, for comfort and emotional support, and for the intense pleasure they obviously derive from the contact and sensations.

As humans, our own genitals are far bigger than is necessary for effective sexual reproduction. Unlike in other mammals, the human penis is easily visible even when flaccid, allowing a woman to choose a mate on that basis alone. Size matters. Although I've known men whose sexual expertise more than overcomes any lacking in size, every woman I spoke to for this book stated a preferences for large, simply because the thicker longer penis is more likely to give pleasure if those extras are not on the cards. In a world where men are clothed, there are other ways to judge: the nose gives an idea of size when flaccid, the left hand middle finger indicates the shape, the length of the erect penis usually equalling the length from wrist to middle fingertip.

In women, breasts tend to be far bigger than is needed for lactation. They are targets for attention, for massage and play, the nipples in many women sending every erotic nerve into overdrive, particularly in women who have at some point breast-fed a baby. The clitoris is assumed to be no more than the little nub between the labia, but in fact it is some 6-7 inches long, running up each side of the vagina. As big as an erect penis, when a woman climaxes the clitoral contractions of the orgasm literally suck the semen up towards the womb. In order to create a better chance of conception, our bodies require pleasuring.

For the millennia of evolution before the link between sex and childbirth was accepted, our bodies urged us to seek to out partners that offered the greatest pleasure. As in the bonobo communities, there is no reason to imagine that our own ancestors weren't equally happy to experiment in gay, bi- or even try-sexual ("I'll try anything") unions. The suppression of all but hetero sex is, again, a male political action of Western culture, inspired by a fear of passion that engendered an asserted focus on *sex for fertility*.

I love sex.

Like the whore in every woman, I crave the pleasure of good sexuality: sex for no reason other than rich sensual delight. As a result, it saddens me to hear stories from women who have never enjoyed sex, whose experience has never allowed them the bliss of dissolving into this exquisite natural pleasure. Sometimes there is a physiological reason, or an early trauma or abuse blocking the ability or willingness; often it is not so dramatic. Many women, even those who consider themselves sexually uninhibited, admit there is a gateway that has to be broken through every time they have sex or make love. A natural protective layer, one woman I spoke to described it as a heavy velvet curtain that needed to be swept aside with anticipation and foreplay. Some women find it hard to open that curtain at all.

Sometimes, however, it is just a twist of fate that has not brought a woman together with someone skilled in the art. Most of us stumble into an understanding of sexual play, grasping various degrees of aptitude by chance along the way. One woman told me of the moment when she realised that a *blow job* was rather more about sucking than blowing ... "Instant one hundred per cent improvement in technique!" ... while others tell of the endless fiddling and twiddling they have endured with partners failing to distinguish labia from clitoris, until they give up and start the mellifluous build up to the faked climax. A great many things in life are better than poor sex, not just a hot cup of tea.

Needless to say, faking orgasm doesn't teach a partner how to do it right, but most women have faked it at some time or other. Insecurities clash as the one failing to give enough pleasure feels the failure acutely, the one failing to be stimulated claiming her own culpability. Anger can arise, relationships breaking apart under the stress of inadequacy and, most poignantly and most tragically, simple bad communication.

Though to some it might be seen to lie on the edge of the abusive, I am intrigued by stories of young men taken to whores by fathers, uncles or older friends, for the explicit purpose of being sexually initiated and taught how to pleasure women. I have met women who, though not professionals in the sex industry, have a penchant and an expertise in teaching inexperienced young men; men know the advantage this gives them.

Women talk about sex and, if a man is known to be skilled, he is much in demand.

There are books teaching techniques from the sensible to the outrageous, both the deeply serious and the playfully humorous. In order to heighten pleasure, we are encouraged to break through our inhibitions, to be adventurous, use adult toys, whipped cream, handcuffs, purple sparkly dolphin-shaped vibrating dildos. Use the kitchen floor, use the pub car park, try porn, mirrors, video cameras. We're told that revealing to our partners our sexual fantasies (emailing or text messaging can be easier than face to face) might help to propel us into new arenas of wildly erotic play; it can work or backfire badly - transferring fantasy into reality more often provokes giggles than serious orgasms.

In more dedicated sexual teachings, in workshops, books and therapy, we are taught how to share a point of focus, to avoid distractions and feel every breath. We come to be aware of the sexual energy that lies like a still pool within our body, waiting to be aroused. We can learn to feel its waking, its uncoiling, finding ways to direct it with our mind, dissolving blocks that stand in its flow, until the seething flood of erotic pleasure can pour into every part of who we are, body and mind. Such teachings also concentrate on male sexual continence: the ability of a man to hold back his ejaculation until his partner is brimming with ecstasy, nurtured and sated, ready for the final climax which they will share.

Some men can (learn to) climax without ejaculation, while some experience very acute pain if they don't; some men utterly explode, and others break open and dissolve slowly into deep pools of ecstasy. Women differ as much, some coming easily, quick and often, some only with direct clitoral stimulation, some bursting, fragmenting to the point of black out, and still others climax only by using a vibrator, or not at all, finding levels of serene bliss without the big bang. Whatever the gender mix, however high the libido, the quirks of our individuality mean that sexual play is vastly improved with a strong dose of empathy: the ability to imagine what the other is feeling. When an internal language is shared, evolving from this empathy, the slightest touch or subtle movement, a sound or breath, becomes a clear communication, allowing feedback loops of positive affirmation. In turn, these build up the expectation of pleasure rising, and so the body is better able to relax and receive.

We can use specific words that, for us, trigger associations, anchoring pleasure responses in the mind: whispering a word the moment before a partner's climax creates a connection for him or her between the word and the sensation of ecstasy. When a trigger word is fully loaded with powerful erotic association, using it at other times helps heighten arousal and expectation of bliss again.

There are so many little tricks, mind games to play, energy centres to stroke this way and stimulate that way. Yet if any *real* and profound satisfaction is going to be achieved, it doesn't matter how many body techniques or psychological/emotional theories we have up our sleeves. First there must be trust.

Sharing sanctuary

In old religious traditions from all around the world, there are teachings about sexual practice, with wisdom imparted, both as oblique suggestions and clear instructions. Some have fragmented into what we might call 'old wives' tales'; some are still wrapped up in clear spirituality or religion. We hear much about the sexual teachings of Taoism, and the tantra of Hinduism. It is said that most of this knowledge, the inner wisdom of sexual practice, was passed down through the craft of the sacred prostitutes, in temples, and later brothels, around the world.

Such old wisdom of Britain in any direct form has been lost through the moral dictates of patriarchal monotheism, yet strong clues persist, and not least within the myths that have come to us in their medieval (if Christianised) forms. The Arthurian tales, such as that of Gawain told at the start of this book, indeed the entire grail mysteries, are littered with inferences to the sexual and magical rapture that is the very real and tangible, mind-blowing taste of the sacred cup, the grail, the womb of creation. For what the cup holds is the omnipresent yet ungraspable, ordinary yet incredible, essence of life.

Druidic and Pagan teachings encourage acute consciousness of the life force, of spirit. This is no ethereal counterpart to physical form, but inherent within all of nature, shimmering as the essential vibrancy of being. The physical world around us is the creativity of spirit; our bodies, our lives, are an expression of our own spirit's creativity, as is the glory of canopy, sap and bark the art of the tree spirit; the wind hums with spirit, as do the rivers and rain. While in a secular world we are taught to reach for the tangible, the old wisdom instead teaches us to perceive the essence. We might do this with our intellect, holding it as an abstract; we might believe that we can see an energy shimmering, or a change in colour, so acknowledging it physically; we might feel it on an emotional level, through associations and memories. Yet if we perceive it with our own spirit, with the core of our being, the encounter is quite different. Spirit touching spirit, core energy touches core energy. Such perception quickly transforms into an experience of connection.

There is nothing surreal or supernatural here, and no need to believe in some ghostly reality beyond: we are simply awake to the energy of life itself. Perceiving it in another, who in turn perceives it in us, provokes us to feel the energy within ourselves. Here is the chemical response, the *rush* that so confuses and bewitches us, that strange mixture that provokes feelings of lust, inspiring a sense of deep recognition, perhaps even love. When it comes upon us suddenly, it brings those physical and emotional cravings we find so very hard to ignore or control.

" ... we knew it was wrong, but we just couldn't stop ourselves ... "

When we take such feelings into sexual play, this rush can be a tidal wave that hones and heightens every physical and emotional sensation, as if all the heavy veils that numb us in daily life had been magically removed. We are wide awake, present, utterly naked. Within such a mindset, sensitivity can be so high that touch is barely needed. Riding the crest of this bliss is an experience that overwhelms the senses utterly, a white water raft ride, free falling into a sky dive: it is exhilarating, yet at the same time - conscious of spirit - we feel ourselves safe, somehow immortal, and quite able to let go into the current that is taking us heaven knows where. Within this sexual experience, the release of full orgasm can come flooding through every cell of our being like thunder breaking, rumbling, crashing, breathless and free, changing us forever.

Connecting spirit to spirit is not easy to achieve. In search of loving sexual connection, intuitively, instinctively, we may allow somebody that close, and it may be beautiful or it may be a ghastly mistake. It can slam into us as a chemical hit, love (or lust) at first sight, but usually the rush dissipates. If we want to deepen or sustain it, we need to know how, and the only way to reach that place of touching, utterly soul-naked, and consciously, is by finding sufficient trust. After all, what we are doing is inviting someone else into our inner sanctuary, our soul's nemeton.

Actively making the choice, deliberately opening ourselves to let another in, the acute awareness can poignantly increase the sensation of closeness. We are also more likely to remain conscious of the connection, of its hum, its tides - for nature isn't constant. We are likely too to be more aware of what is their energy, what our own and when and how they blend. Further, if we've consciously invited another in, it is easier to let them out again, or kick them out should we need to.

This is the craft of the skilful whore: she creates a safe place of intimacy and trust, for the purpose of pleasure. In the play of her seduction, she reveals that inner space as a deliciously tempting haven, a paradise of bliss and affirmation. It is an elven land of music and sweet red berries: somewhere to lose yourself in utter delight. Of course, she may protect herself on whatever level is appropriate, but this she won't show. What she appears to offer is a limitless experience of sensual release.

Inviting the other into her sanctuary, the whore knows that the richest experience can only take place if we trust her, opening ourselves to her. It is her skill, then, not only to offer her own sweet sanctuary, but to entice us into opening our own, sharing with her our nakedness, ugly flaws and all. Though the experienced whore may shrug it off as a bad day, if we invite someone into our sanctuary who is still protected within their own barricades, the feelings evoked are more likely to be fear and vulnerability than deep connection. In the same way, if we remain closed and walk into the intimate space of another, we are likely to step clumsily on their tender soil, perhaps hurting them badly. When we share such soul-deep nakedness, however, open, spirit to spirit, there is wonder, empathy, and the shimmering of potential.

So how is it done? We must, first of all, be fully aware of the boundaries that define our intimate space, for only then can we consciously open it for another. It isn't a trick to be used lightly, for unless we are grounded and stable in trust, it can intensify negativity, opening wounds to bleed again. A broken bond with our father, difficult early sexual relationships, devastating love affairs, loss and abuse, all can lead us to a point where the very idea of intimacy evokes terror. Yet the process of creating a deeply intimate relationship need not be hurried. It is in itself a healing journey: it evokes profound feelings, touching memories of mother-love, our need for nurturing and complete safety, the shelter of unconditional caring.

Only when we have a sense of our own soul sanctuary and its edges, can we then begin to experience touching another's.

Aware of ourselves as independent beings, with a clarity and clear intention, with imagination, then we can take those steps, almost like outbreaths, that allow us to open to each other. Drawing aside the boundaries, two circles become one. Our skin feels alive. Our heart quickly fills as that rush of energy moves through us - the empathy of life touching life, connecting. The sensation of our spirit's innate invulnerability intertwines with the tenderness of our mortality, our emotional and physical body intensifying the moment. Sinking into another's soul, he or she, sinking into ours, we are two liquids meeting, two breaths, two stories converging, spirits stretching, gliding, languid, excited, eagerly exploring.

"Not here," he whispers, looking over his shoulder in case anyone has come through the door yet. "Wait, wait - " But still I gaze, smiling, into his eyes, not saying a thing. I don't need to undress him: even there in his high-flyer suit he is naked before me, and he knows it. The committee are just about to walk into the room.

Last night, sitting at dinner with my friends, doing his best to be polite, talking about some movie I knew he'd never seen, I couldn't help myself staring at him, allowing my energy to slide over him like the softest silk, like skin-warm water flowing over his face, down his neck, into his shirt, drops sliding so slowly and cool down his chest. He was trying desperately to stay intact, to hold the conversation and avoid my eyes, but watching him melts me, especially when he starts to lose track of what he's saying, his mind flooded with the chemicals of this fusion of our lust. He glared at me across the table, frowning, *Stop it!* and I just smiled and began to mouth the words he didn't need to hear. He forced himself to look away before I could finish the first word, clearing his throat and nodding at the words of a conversation he hadn't even heard.

Now I'm sliding through him again, and he's fidgeting with

papers on the desk before him, looking up to smile and murmur greetings as people arrive, and I know all he's thinking of is my mouth slowly shaping the words again ... *come for me* ... my lips on his skin, the heat in his prick, and his mind is utterly blank, swirling in the storm of yearning, lost so deep inside. He won't look at me.

Then suddenly the meeting is all around us, skidding past us, and I try to engage, as does he, stumbling over words, making suggestions, scribbling notes I don't understand, as conversation strides through a world that seems just beyond my grasp. And then it's over, and he's fussing with his papers and his briefcase until he's quite sure the room is empty. He breathes deeply and looks up. I'm standing by the door. Smiling, I push it closed and walk towards him. I can feel his pulse racing.

"You know," he murmurs, "we really can't work together ... "

I shake my head, still smiling, sitting on the edge of the desk. And alone, undisturbed, my smooth charm falls away, and I gaze at the powerful dignity and tenderness that is this man I long for. And I wait as he closes his eyes, breathing deeply, reaching for his own centred strength, his calm, such beauty. When our eyes meet again, it's like falling through a window you'd assumed was glazed. And we do fall, tumbling right into each other's souls, plummeting through stillness, diving, barely moving ... then riding invisible currents, not even touching, we glide an inch apart, our spirits drenched, still entwined. He lifts his head, the change sending ripples spilling over my body, caressing exquisitely tenderly, silently. He opens his mouth, as if to breathe, surfacing for a moment.

I lift my hand and, slowly enough to feel every subtle layer of resistance dissolving, I bring it towards his heart, closing my eyes, pouring through my fingers all the love that I am feeling.

I have described the edge of our intimate space as if it was only one layer thick but, in reality, the poetry of the image allows us to remove layer after layer after layer. Like a dance of seven veils, the whore plays with the colours, the quality, the sensation of each one, before letting it drift to the ground at her feet. Each time we let one fall, we reveal more of our core, our truth, naked and wild. Our awareness widens, our sensitivity increases. Sharing energy at these deeper levels, through intimate play, allows a brilliance of inspiration to stream into the core of our being, affirming and strengthening our very foundations, bringing us a clearer awareness of the invulnerability of our essence: it is exhilarating empowerment.

Though such soul adventures do change us, the shift in how we express our creativity doesn't come of simply having experienced and shared this level of intimate sanctuary; the truths we have experienced must now be grounded, integrated into our everyday interactions, or it will remain a magical dream, the source of that dream becoming an obsession. We must instead accept and use our greater freedom.

Within our sanctuary, we are beneath the guises we might use in daily life. Unclothed, we can feel as naked as it is conceivable to be. It is possible to share more deeply, however, stepping into the twilit places and the darkness beyond.

Even the less sensitive amongst us can usually intuitively pick up who someone is behind the screens of their peripheral protection; yet the deeper we go into somebody's intimate space the more unfamiliar a person can become. Though we may well know and love them, as we journey into their innermost cauldron we can start to wonder who they are. Specific energies are intensified, priorities quite altered, and these we feel acutely. We tread in lands where demons of denial and suppression lurk. We face unpredictable defences, even where the person is longing and eager for our presence. The usual mirrors that exist within relationships are here too, both intensifying and confusing our needs and our fears, yet in the twilight they are dim and easily mislead us, threatening to send us down muddy paths of delusion and dread.

Beyond the shadows, however, is the darkness where the self slips away. When we come to the edge of all that is familiar, and step beyond into the darkness of total potentiality, it is easy to feel that we are losing our last fingerhold of control, sliding into the unmapped land of insanity. Overcoming the fear of these black depths of the cauldron is a powerful journey in itself. Coming to understand who our playmate is on this deeper level, and how we can engage, connecting, arousing and giving pleasure when every nerve is so wide awake is a beautiful task. Whether the adventure is purely emotional, or if it is physical and sexual, we learn how to release our grasp for control, letting the flood of sensations become all that we are. Indeed, at times, all that is left is the shimmering essence that is the thrill of touch that is life itself. In this wild limitless place, it is the essence of the whore within us, hag-wise, who guides and holds our being.

In fact, those who have journeyed into this dark inner place of their own accord, those who have shared on this level in beautiful relationship, exude a confidence that is intriguing. It can be utterly bewitching. Some recognise it as a sparkle that is both light and darkness in the eyes.

The gift of weakness
Old tales of many cultures speak of the woman as dangerous. She is, we are told, best kept covered, worked hard, tired and servile. If given the opportunity, she will entrap a man and, with her power, she will destroy him. Her terrible weapon is her cavernous great black cauldron, within which she carries the storm of her inner darkness. With it, she overwhelms, she engulfs and encloses; with her cunt, she devours him, consuming his strength, draining him of his life's purpose and his vitality.

Stealing his soul, she is said to reveal to him a magical world of ecstasy, of touch softer than warm fur, of love that is both angelic yet also demonic, filling his mind with the knowledge of moments brimming with exquisite pleasure and perfect peace, then leaving him bewitched, obsessed, a spectre wandering the land of the dark, the land of faerie, in search of that love again, in search of certainty.

It is the ability to manipulate that is often stated as woman's most terrible vice, and certainly the more we understand our nature, the more we are able to use those inherent skills to *get what we want*. After all, the hag's power is sourced deep within our nature, and as we explore our being, healing the wounds and clearing the blocks to our creativity and freedom, we increasingly have access to that power. If our intentions are negative, then our manipulative strategies will bring chaos and destruction: we do have the power to bring men down. But with clarity, generosity, caring, those same forces can shift mountains, creating beautiful change.

Any ethics as to how we should use the power are not a part of the hag's nature, though. The more we know of her, the more we realise she is as merciless (and nourishing) as darkness, as deep water, as ice and fire: as nature. It isn't nature that informs us as to how we might live responsibly, but our relationships with and within nature.

So, to be the whore where there is no strength to give or not give consent is not fair play. The woman who rapes, whether her victim is male or female, might do so for many reasons; the energy that drives her comes of the wild storm that tears through her cauldron. Spitting rage through the wounds of abuse or suppression, her view is distorted, her empathy wrecked. She may be craving the inner touch of intimacy yet have no ability to reach it but through trauma; she may have no experience of true connection but where it is spun out on the intensity of adrenaline and fear. She may still be working with the whore-hag within herself, but without a whisper of respect.

Consent is a powerful notion. Sometimes we know just what we are agreeing to, but often our consent is based on faith, on trust, and again this is something the skilled whore knows well. It is crucial when she is taking another into the intimacy of her sanctuary, into the depths of raw nakedness. Here, she offers that most powerful gift of allowing, accepting and even provoking in another the relief of expressing, through trust, the extent of their weakness.

Of course, we can do this gently, playing with the ideas and possibilities, just as we can play around the edges of her energy, revealing little hints of the whore in a glance, a comment, a sway of the hips. So too we can explore the whore's power and her sanctuary in a way that is more about fun than transformative danger. Bondage toys are available now in novelty stores, furry handcuffs and 'naughty' lingerie, tempting the average woman to suggest or agree to a little spice in sexual play. Such games do need consent: to be cuffed to a bed is not an easy decision to make when trust is in any way dubitable. Yet when trust is affirmed through an exquisite session of sex, with one partner restrained, the intimacy shared can be deeper, the relationship stronger. Where such games break through layers of inhibition and fear, the effect can be significant, but often it is simply play.

For some, the yearning for intimacy is never truly sated unless they are able to share energy on much deeper levels. It is with more serious bondage, agreed roles of dominance and submission, or through sadomasochism that many find their path into these depths. Again, these are skills of the whore. Such acts can be unquestionably abusive when they are not wholly consensual; consent can be a blurred line if our self-esteem is so low that we don't believe we are worth more, that we only deserve pain. Yet freely given and informed consent is common, and given from a sure calm grounding, even where the decision is to submerse in a situation that to others would be an undiluted nightmare. In such adventures, when the soul is shocked into losing its reference points, hurled into the darkness, we can find ourselves deep within the inner cauldron - and when, far from abandoned and alone in that space, we are held powerfully, sharing those extreme moments as they skid-slide around and through each other, the experience can be extraordinary. We may feel we have no control, but protected by consent and intention, the knowledge that we are safe within her sanctuary allows us again and again to extend our act of surrender to the whore.

We meander here into what many term the perversions of sexuality, a sweet topic if we are considering the parameters of what is *acceptable*. Indisputably, there are some things that are over the boundary line. Sexuality with prepubescent children, close family members, with animals and the dead, are prohibited in almost every culture worldwide; where this is *not* visibly non-consensual, it is feasible to doubt the level of education or under-standing within the culture with regards to basic human society, emotional development, disease and so on. Educated consent is always the first check point.

However, uneducated prejudice must be the next. Are we judging something to be unacceptable because of our own fear? Until fairly recently masturbation was considered a dangerous perversion, liable to cause infertility, blindness, not to mention a free ticket on the fast train to some god-blessed inferno. The judgement on homosexuality was even worse.

He is naked, on his knees before me. I run my fingers through his hair. The chink of the buckle is the only noise in the stillness of the candlelight. He doesn't look up - he knows not to - and slowly, carefully, I secure the leather collar around his neck, my fingertips lingering on the tender-soft skin at the base of his throat. The energy between us changes tangibly, almost immediately, and I close my eyes, breathing, exhaling deeply, relaxing, reaching down into the well of darkness within me, until I can feel it rising through me, filling my mind. I stretch my fingers, tingling with the surge of energy. I lift his chin so he faces me. Our eyes meet.

Who do you belong to? I no longer need say the words aloud.

"You, mistress," he whispers, and I feel so profoundly his devotion, not to me but to the power of woman, to the goddess of the cauldron, and through that perfect devotion I feel her energy even more acutely, curling up through me, seeping through my body, my blood, my soul, like the smoke of a musky rose oil. I murmur my instructions and, bowing his head, he complies, with perfect respect.

In the twilight of the room, naked but for the collar, he breathes to calm his pulse, his hands softly touching the wall. I lean against it to watch his face, the anticipation flooding his mind with presence. And as I cuff his wrist with the wide leather strap, binding it to the wall ring with a length of cord, he feels every touch, hears each whisper of skin on skin. Running my fingertips down the soft inner skin to his armpit, I cuff the other wrist and pulling it up, carefully quietly tying it tight. I feel every quiver of resistance in his soul, and the absolute surrender of his every muscle as I move his limbs, slowly pushing his legs apart, one by one, cuffing his ankles with the leather and securing them with the cord.

His vulnerability is exquisite.

"Close your eyes," I murmur, and for a while I just watch him, feeling the tides of his emotion as they swell and subside and swell again with expectation, as I wonder at the beauty of all that he is. Then, in the silence and the flickering light, I lift the cat, letting my fingers move through the weight of its eight leather 'tails' ...

The level of trust required in a bondage scene like that is far greater than that needed to sustain a sexual or intimate relationship where we aren't playing with the balance of the power. Some do give themselves in profound submission to individuals they barely know: the process of surrendering to another can be as thrilling as any high adrenaline activity. Without assured trust, however, such games can feed a negative belief system, affirming our lack of self-worth. Where the stranger is skilled and respectful, our consciousness is poignantly focused on our deepest intimate space and, where there is trust, a holding and caring sense of support, the demons of self-negation can be confronted and even slain. Who better to help us than the whore.

As hag in the guise of *femme fatale*, she needs both to feel trust and to elicit it. For many, though, the key subconscious memory of sharing intimate space is that given by their mother, the complete caring, the unconditional love, yet the whore doesn't give for free. She offers us the power of her dark sanctuary, but she demands payment for her services. She requires her own needs satisfied, and the chances are that she will only give if she trusts she will be - or has already been - paid in return.

In dark alleys, in the night, in secret places of our heart and mind, we trust her, yet what we offer into her keeping is specific: our flaws and our weakness, our cravings and perversions, all that we feel is unacceptable within ourselves. Somehow, perhaps we trust that she will not reject us for our failings.

Or do we trust her because she is unacceptable too?

No woman is all *whore,* whatever her character, her profession or situation. Yet within every woman, there is a whore, whether that hag of her nature is expressing herself in exquisite creative abandon, lingering in the shadows wondering, or locked in a cellar not quite out of earshot. In the conventional undercurrents of our Western culture, she is still unacceptably powerful: powerfully unacceptable.

Accepting her natural wisdom of freedom and autonomy, enjoying her wild and sensual desires, can only make us richer.

CHAPTER FIVE

The Mother

Being brought up for the most part in Latin culture, both in Spain and the Americas, I learned at a young age the crucial difference between *la princesa* and *la puta*. The princess: she was a woman who loved her man unconditionally. She never let her interest stray to anybody else. She dressed for him, cared for him, creating the perfect glossy home and sweet smiling family. Unfailingly attentive to his needs, she was exquisitely gracious to his guests but only in order to please him. She bathed in his pride in her and worked on that tirelessly. Though she might have a life of her own, filling the moments when he didn't need her, it was of no real importance compared to her devotion for him. The *puta*, however, the whore, was bound to no one.

A Venezuelan boyfriend once lifted his hand as if to slap my face, an instinctive and immediate reaction fuelled by a sudden rage, and a sense of his own humiliation, as he snarled at me, "You even look at the girls, goddamnit!" My focus had drifted momentarily away from him, to a good-looking girl across the bar who was laughing with a deliciously contagious abandon.

Though I got up in horror and walked away from him that night, our relationship did continue. It was significantly changed though. My real appreciation of another human being had been the last straw for him. He loved (or wanted) me with a passion, but at that moment he made the decision that I was no longer the sort of girl he would introduce to his mother. With relief, the next day, he took my hand in his; he no longer spoke to me gently, trying to impress me with his money and his knowledge of the world, playing the dark romantic lover. Instead I became his confidante. We had sex without inhibition. And, even though he was sleeping with me, he resumed that most essential quest for his *princesa*.

His acute jealousy was, of course, unhealthy, but it came from a very real and globally widespread social conditioning that had guided him to polarise our female nature. In effect, he was acknowledging two powerful faces of woman, categorising in an attempt to simplify what he had been taught was so complex. The whore holds those parts of us which we feel are unacceptable, the flaws in our nature, the deeds and desires that we are ashamed of. She doesn't judge us to be wrong or weak or stupid, because her experience of life has taught her a different measure of honour, of wit and courage. Her world is a twilight of self discovery and inner creativity.

The princess, on the other hand, is the virgin girl who grows up to become the perfect *mother*.

Mother goddess and mothering

The entirety of creation upon this blue-green planet is commonly called Mother Earth; it's an idiom used even within religions that claim the sole source and parent to be one male god. In some strands of Western Paganism, and particularly those that emerged through American feminism in the 1970s and 80s, that which is most devoutly revered is the 'mother goddess'; she is the origin, the provider and the one who holds us through the transitions of death. She is a foundation: the principle of life. Further, in the ubiquitous undefined spiritualities of Western culture, where there is but a vague sense of some guiding or creative force, and life's complex patterns are acknowledged through simple science and philosophy, nature is still most often seen as 'mother'. Even in wholly secular culture, we hear the phrase 'mother nature', referring to the universality that creates and embraces life, reclaiming its remains when it comes to an end.

However, most commonly where the term is used it implies a gently nurturing entity. It celebrates nature as a wholly benevolent being, one who tirelessly cares and provides for the countless creatures dependent upon it. Such sentimentality is incomprehensible within the old animistic traditions, for not only does nature destroy, but its modes of regeneration are more often than not neither pretty nor comfortable.

Nonetheless, and justifiably, there is awe at this power. We are amazed by the tiny flowers of an oak, its swollen hard acorn nut that, with moisture and time, can grow into such a glorious tree. There is sheer wonder at the process of new life birthed in any species, from bumble bees to buffalo, and in human beings that is no less. It may be natural, but it seems still to be almost beyond comprehension. We gaze at the mother, her round belly and doe eyes, as if in her hands she were holding a smidgen of glinting stardust, a glimpse of forever.

Yet, it is nature that is so amazing, not the mother. Though *mother* shines, her light is the glow of that natural force of reproductive creativity, which flows through her like a wild river, rushing and tumbling from horizon on to distant horizon. In a secular world, we might speak of the drive to reproduce that is a part of our human nature, generation through generation, linking each of us together in the journey of evolution. But to the animist, that force is a deity, moving with its own purpose. So powerful and single-minded is it in its flow, it can break a woman into a thousand pieces without a glimmer of caring. In the old religions, those are unmistakable qualities of a goddess, and this one is as ancient as nature itself.

She is brutal. Like any goddess, she demands respect. If we aren't awake to her presence, her purpose, her power, we are at risk of being overwhelmed, smothered, thrown into chaos. In her desire to create, that force can destroy our lives, for what she is powering into being may not be in harmony with what already exists.

She creeps up on us, she leaps at us. She can flood our lives with too much, at times drenching us with entirely irrational longings, such as the crippling *need* to have a baby of our own. Even when reason is not lost and we've no desire for a child, she can pull at our souls, dragging at our animal instincts, making us grieve for the loss of children we never wanted, making us broody and miserable when having children is not sensible or possible. Indeed, she plays with us, proffering 'babies' in the form of any project that inundates and saturates, leaving us unable to deal with anything else.

Then there are times when she abandons us, leaving us in a drought of wanting. She lingers just out of reach, like a scent in the air we can't quite catch, like a thirst we just can't quench, drawing us on, inspiring us to keep exploring, following ideas until we start to grasp something tangible - or break. For it is when we find her current that we find our creativity once more. Yet, like any goddess, any attempt to control her is entirely in vain; and should we stumble into submission, she may just overwhelm us, surging through our lives destroying or subsuming anything in her path, like an ancient river once more claiming sovereignty of its floodplain.

Though we may call her a mother goddess, for she is the force that perpetuates that essential regenerating creativity of nature, this force is no goddess of mothering. When she moves through us, we are no more than the medium of her own creativity and desire. If she moves with too much brutality, leaving us beaten, bruised, broken, barren, she simply moves on, without a care.

She is there when inspiration fuels us into selfishness, when we know our choices are hurting those we love, but our passion to achieve some goal is too strong to allow us to turn away. She is there, wild and merciless, and so very ancient, dragging each infant from the womb, bloody and bewildered.

She touches his hand, "Are you ok?"

He bites his lip, saying something about the neighbours, but another one's rising, right on the back on the last, and I can't help but holler, this time my shriek beginning with, "I don't give a fuck about the fucking neighbours - " before my words blur into the noise my whole soul now needs to vent. They're both talking to me again, telling me to what I should be doing, as if I had any choice or could give a shit. I shriek again, panting, pushing, trying to hold onto the elusive handles of this bloody speedboat no one's bloody driving.

Then I'm not sure. About anything. All I was was pain and terrifying pressure, as if someone where pulling my head down through my body and out between my legs, but now there's an emptiness. The pain that tears through my body appears to have torn me somehow free of it. I don't know what they're saying to me. I smile at him, wanting to comfort him in this moment of quiet, to reassure him.

But then I'm crashing back down onto the hard bottom of this boat, surging on such high seas, and I appear to be yelling, gulping tears, and I realise I probably didn't smile at him at all. I think I'm telling them to "Shut up, shut the fuck up!", but he's holding my hand urging me on, saying, "Yes, you can, you *can* do it". And for a fleeting moment, I'm amazed at how much anger this is drawing out of me. If I could I'd smash his face in and kick the fucking midwife out of my house - I'd run away down the street, shedding this pain and blood like clothes in the wind.

And I'm shrieking again as another one hits me, this demon that's pulling my soul out through my cunt, and I'm quite sure I can't survive it. But again something breaks - and there's the silence again, the soft light of the room, the darkness shimmering, as if there is suddenly all the space I need to close my eyes and breathe in slowly, deeply. The woman at the bottom of the bed is mouthing something at me, urgently, encouraging me, her face wet with tears, a smile almost breaking, but I've no thoughts anymore, no idea ...

His voice comes closer, his hand crushing mine, suddenly,

"Almost there, one more, come on, baby, come on, you can do it!" And I'm aware of this enormous wave, lifting my body, higher and higher, then crashing down bringing all I am with it, and I'm shrieking in fear, and rage, and because there is nothing else I can do but come crashing down with the wave and *push* ...

Like many women, had it not been for modern medicine, surgery, anaesthesia, I would have died at my son's birth, taking him with me. Even with all the preparation I'd done, getting involved in every way I could, reading natural birthing books, adjusting my diet and exercise routine so I was as healthy as I could possibly be, when it came to the crunch I failed: too petite to birth a child with Scots Viking blood. In years gone by, such limitations were no doubt a naturally efficient way of helping to keep a population stable.

Nowadays, however, even for those who *could* give birth without the tongs, drugs and blades, uncertainty is poured in. Chemicals are offered to dull her mind, and what follows is a complicating flurry of intervention, disempowering her at her most vulnerable, giving her the easy way out by removing from her the little autonomy she does have. So is she denied one of the key initiatory rites of her gender, with all its pain and confusion and ancient glory, a rite that awakens within most women an incredible strength.

Certainly, it is not her miracle; a woman doesn't give birth because she has honed particular skills or is in some other way special. It is a marvel of nature. As a force of nature, the mother goddess surges through the woman's body in an expression of her own creativity. To the techno-medical profession, however, it is a situation on the edge of chaos that they believe only they can manage safely, and all too often mothers are treated as if they were the obstacle to easy childbirth. Indeed, the medical industry lays heavy bets that the woman is likely to screw up.

Yet, giving birth is about her relationship with that mother goddess. If as women we submit, cowering in fear, she may crush us. She may simply ignore us, in which case we risk learning nothing, gaining nothing, from the encounter. If we hide from her, the same is true: we sidestep the possibility of real creativity. But if we face her, becoming conscious of how it feels when she is near us, when she's with us and within us, and screaming through us, we have a chance to learn how to ride those wild seas - not just in childbirth, but in the birthing of any creativity. Nurturing that relationship, we find both the inspiration and the fuel we need for the full expression of our soul. We have a chance to experience the deep pleasure of achievement which that brings.

The distinction between that mother goddess and a goddess of mothering, however, is fundamental. When we mother, it is not that wild storm of creativity that we are feeling, that we are so acutely aware of in the process of giving birth. The mother goddess seethes within the currents of every creative act in the way that water exists within so much of this planet's nature. But mothering, like whoring, is a far more specific aspect within the wholeness of the female being.

Just as conception, gestation and birthing are not the results of wit and skill neither is motherhood. Women with no interest in children, no knowledge of physiology, with poor health and minimal emotional maturity, can conceive and bring new human beings into the world. With social security systems that hold overlarge, uneducated and underemployed populations just this side of tenable, our society continues to support inadequate parenting. Where there is the money to hand children over into the care of nannies, minders, nurseries and schools, the issue is the same: women have children they don't really want and don't know how to care for. It is only the exceptional degree of human adaptability that in itself has brought our species to this point in its evolution that allows children to survive the most frightening levels of incompetent parenting. It can be seen in every social and economic context; though children may grow to be emotionally and intellectually disabled, even physically compromised, they can survive nevertheless to have children themselves, to abuse through ignorance, negligence or malevolence.

Being a mother doesn't need intelligence. It takes incredible patience, care and wisdom to do it well, but a halfwit can be a mother. It's a powerful reason why woman as *mother* is no longer much respected.

Mothering is hard. Many women who have tried it have headed back to work with relief, freely admitting that full time committed parenting is just too demanding, both emotionally and physically, not least because it can numb the brain into a blur of domesticity and baby talk. Those women who don't run from it back into the workplace are nowadays considered peculiar, or sufficiently devoid of intellect not to notice the stupor. To those who avoid children in adult society, the dedicated mother is seen as desperately tedious, her mind addled by the hormones and sleepless nights; she is unable to speak of anything but washing liquids and food shopping, and her fat little child. Too tired to go out, to dress up or make love, she is observed at a distance by the women not mothering; they watch her and wait, and wonder when she'll get 'herself' back together.

However, like virgin and whore, *mother* is not simply the active parent, struggling with children, domestic appliances and self-identity. As a part of women's nature, she might well find expression young, as a little girl running across the playroom for the toy pram and baby doll; some, later in life, are more than happy to abandon their position in an aggressive and ambitious world, not questioning their decision until the children have grown up and long gone. Some are compliant, giving into it yet ever remaining a little bewildered, wondering where and when their old self disappeared. Within others, the mother silently hovers in the wings, never comfortably showing her face but in emergencies or private intimacies. For some, *mother* can be as appalling as, to others, *whore* is startling.

So who is this creature, this being of our soul?

Mother as sanctuary and caring

Mother is the facet of woman that seems the most obvious.

Indeed, in many ways it is in her very nature to be obvious. She lives in the daylight that balances the whore's night. She appears to be approachable and amenable, acceptable. Lovingly, she cares, nurturing the beauty in all things. Just as she holds the newborn infant, so does she hold our own nascent creativity, providing safe space for our first words, our first steps, our first colours tentatively painted in the light. She nourishes us and all that we long to have acknowledged, recognising the tender aspirations before they are affirmed: the part of our self expression that so aches to be accepted. Even when she is firm, she is gentle with our innocence and our vulnerability. She holds our hand, compassionately guiding us into play.

It is more than a physical gesture. Intuitively, we can sense when the mother is at the fore of a woman's soul. Our reaction is instinctive, revealing our own experience of mother energy. It can evoke in us a sense of sweet relief, or it can provoke real fear, for what she gives is very specific.

The mother offers her sanctuary for another to use. It's a unique gift: setting aside her own creativity, she devotes her cauldron of creativity to someone else's venture. Deriving her strength and pleasure from the holding, caring and nurturing required, this *extra*ordinary, very ordinary behaviour is what defines her as mother.

As a parent, such apparently selfless caring may come naturally. Most often, a woman finds the mother within her invoked as a response to the presence of that primal force of creativity; it can take a while, but it comes. A foetus grows into a baby held within that physical manifestation of the sacred cauldron, the womb, and when the infant emerges, it is the mother within that continues to hold that child within her nemeton, bathing it in the vibrant energy of her spirit, suckling body and soul.

Pondering potential pregnancy, we might imagine, consciously or subconsciously, that having a baby is in some way a product of our own creativity, but it doesn't take long to realise such a notion is delusion. Even in the first months after conception, throwing up and exhausted, our bodies know that what is growing inside us is alien. At some point, usually just into the second trimester, it is as if there is a truce, an holistic acceptance that we are in fact not the artist. We are the carer, the nurse, cook, cleaner, teacher. We are the home maker: the one who offers that safe space in which another human being can grow.

It isn't only her own children that the mother holds. She offers her sanctuary to anyone who might need a protective and nurturing environment, whether that be a friend, a colleague or a partner. They may need it for healing, for a moment's dissolution into tears, a place to find confidence and affirmation or courage; there she enfolds them in warmth, giving absolutely the certainty of her embrace. It may be an integral part of a relationship, where the other is struggling with insecurity and unable to access their own spirit's strength, or it may be a momentary sharing for one who has temporarily lost the haven of their own sanctuary. Either way, her creative energy is channelled as support, as encouragement and nourishment: she mothers.

She sets the teapot on the table amidst the mess of daily living and, as if the prosaic nature of the action were the last straw, she breaks, the empty mugs clattering from her other hand as her legs give way and she falls into the chair. As her priest, I pause, letting her decide what she needs. There is a moment when she waivers, but when she looks up her eyes make it clear and I move to the chair beside her, wrapping my arms around her. With no more hesitation or pretence, she surrenders into my care as the tears start to pour.

Between wet sniffs and tearful gulps, she relates what has happened, and I listen, half hearing a tale that's been told by women for thousands of years, half hearing the specific details of her own desolation. And all round us is the chaos of her temporarily neglected home, knowing that right now she has no sense of home at all.

Drawn by the noise, her little daughter has wandered in on soft footsteps. She looks up at me with big eyes. "Come here," I whisper, offering a hand, and the child tiptoes forward. She pushes up against me, and I lift her onto my lap. Slowly she finds the trust to lay her head on my shoulder, a big silent tear rolling down her cheek as she watches her mother sobbing with deep bellyaching pain. "Daddy's gone," the little one whispers, then looks into my face, as if searching for the enormity of what has been lost. I kiss her forehead, feeling the vast emptiness. There is nothing, no solution, no pacification, no words to be said.

After a while, the little one and I find a rug and together we tuck it around her mum on the sofa. At four years old, with a serious face and sweet dedication, she explores this feeling of caring for the one who has always cared for her. We make a fresh pot of tea, the first one having gone cold untouched, and pour her a mug, leaving her to rest alone. Standing in the doorway, the girl gazes at her, without judgement, taking in the picture of this human being who has now nothing to give. And for the few hours that pass, she sticks to my side, holding my hand as we move from room to room, clearing, cleaning, tidying up. She lets me know where things go, quietly, softly touching her sense of home.

We are sitting at the kitchen table, she drinking juice, colouring in flowers I've sketched in a notebook, when her mother emerges. The little one looks up, momentarily cautious, but immediately she sees the change. Leaping from her chair she runs into the arms of this woman who has again found strength enough to be her mother, a flood of relief drenching her little form.

Lifting her, kissing her face, she holds her daughter tight.

Nothing needs to be said between us, but as I get up to leave she whispers, "Thank you".

"Call me."

As I walk out into the street I am poignantly aware of having set down the souls I was carrying. It fills me with a moment's sweet solitude, a lightness and freedom, tinged with a sadness: the rich blend of feelings I've learned are part of the priesthood.

Not a goddess of creativity, this current that inspires the powerful drive to mother is well worth exploring. To the animist, the quest is to find that force of nature, to understand it, to craft a relationship with it; only then can we ensure that we won't unnecessarily stumble, hurting and being hurt by it, clumsy in our blindness. We learn to find the current within and around us, accessing it when we need it, respectfully acknowledging its essential nature.

Honouring that force as deity the immediate sense is that she is a goddess whose primary intention is *giving*. Inspiring us to set aside our own creative goals, she encourages us to provide for others, fulfilling their needs, feeding them from our store. She is a goddess of generosity, of hospitality and benevolence, calling us to care for others before we look to ourselves. She can evoke an altruism that is expressed as a fleeting moment or a life's vocation. She is the wellspring of strength for that mythically perfect *princesa*.

Yet, like any goddess of nature, she issues no limits or warnings with her gift. She offers no advice. A Pagan goddess, after all, doesn't care if we kill or are killed in her service, for all she is is that flood of specific intention. Consequently, this force of nature can inspire us as women to give too much. As nurse, carer, teacher or parent, mothering can deplete us. Subsumed by her, the mother can become the self-determined martyr. In giving away her energy, allowing another (or others) to use her cauldron and her haven, she has nothing left for herself.

Indeed, by clinging to the role longer than is needed, inflating its demands, hiding within its obligations, the mother can evade the need to face her own creativity, with its crises of failure and rejection. She helps others in order to escape from herself and her own fears, in order to affirm that she has no right to joy or satisfaction. Self-negation a steadily flowing undercurrent, she is drained. When she whines in complaint, her audience is usually bored and uncaring. Where this is the norm in a relationship, women can be insidiously manipulative, doing all they can to keep the other person dependent on their caring, their cooking, washing, 'loving'.

This may sound like the behaviour of the *hag*: another aspect of the unacceptable nature of woman. However, it is not the skilled mother who plays such deceitful games, but the mother who has given in to the power of that goddess. She isn't riding the divine currents, she is letting herself be dragged under, kicking out as she gasps, choking for breath. Yet to understand why so many women do go under, I suggest there is more to this mothering goddess than that force of giving.

Opening her sanctuary, *mother* invites another in. She provides not only the space, the container for creativity, but the sense of safety needed for that other soul to explore and create: she holds them. They may be closed, may barely even notice who it is that she is, but wide open, she feels their presence acutely. Within her drive to give, then, is the profound desire to be close to another.

During pregnancy and the parenting of a child, for some women this is the closest they will ever get to another human being. It can be hard to let go. As the child grows and finds his own feet, eager to explore the world alone, the prospect of releasing him from that intimate space is tantamount to losing him altogether. Yet where she holds him in a way that is no longer consensual, the intimacy of her mothering becomes dreadful smothering, the cauldron suffocating the child's experience of freedom and growth. So can any relationship be compromised or destroyed, the mother within us unable to let go: the creativity in her care becomes stifled, stunted, stagnant, never quite finding its place in the world.

Here the mother isn't overwhelmed so much as overwhelming, refusing to step away when her care is no long needed or wanted. Her sanctuary becomes not a haven but a prison. She is determined to *get her own way*.

The mother's exchange

Fuelled by her love and enthusiasm, a woman mothering may well feel she is giving without any need for return. In human culture, a mother is supposed to give unconditionally. Either purely on account of her gender, or because she has been blessed with the divine gift of children, it is somehow assumed that her limitless and altruistic giving fully provides its own reward. It doesn't. Everyone knows that it doesn't. But for a mother to let slip this essential fact is to show the hag-face of her role in all its ghastly glory.

What she asks for in return is not complex. As she pours her energy into holding and nurturing another's creativity, the mother's needs are simple and specific: caring for another, she requires that other (or an other) to *care for her*. Through acknowledgement, appreciation, consideration, through love, respect and trust, perhaps a home, shelter or security, through hugs and assurance of unfaltering commitment, the mother seeks caring.

Where nature is tenable, there is always a receiving in harmony with the giving. It may not be obvious, nor in the form of direct reciprocity, but often that exchange is built in as an underlying current or pattern that provides viability. With the mother, the underlying force of nature that inspires her to provide sanctuary, to give and to feel close to another, is empathy. It's a fundamental drive. She cares for another because she relates to their predicament: as alone, vulnerable and unsupported. Through her sensitivity, she needs to ease the other's pain because she feels or fears that pain herself.

So humanity works; the whore gives pleasure to receive pleasure, the mother cares to be cared for. The whore's payment is immediate; it must be so in order for her to give and receive her pleasure while retaining her freedom and independence. The very nature of the mother's exchange leaves her in a very different situation, however. Commonly the timeframe may be so long or the transaction so indirect that any notion of exchange becomes obscured. More often than not, the reason why she is providing sanctuary for another is because that individual has not the ability to stand alone. They may be too young, debilitated by stress, traumatised, ignorant or simply incompetent: they are in need. In giving as she does, the mother forfeits her independence.

Dependency: the word sets off screaming bells and flashing lights in the minds of many women. Yet, this is a warning system that is not integral to the mother within us. The single woman with kids, heart broken and cynical, may shriek an assertion of her independence, but it is not *mother* yelling (the warrior side of *bitch*, perhaps - explored in the next chapter). For the mother is by nature dependent. It is a side effect of her gift, and a part of the exchange - she is willing to wait for payment.

The ability to be dependent gracefully is an exceptional skill. It is all too easy to feel disempowered and lose our confidence in the process, defences kicking in as we attempt to adjust the balance of power to mitigate our vulnerability. If we are to be successful, we must be sure that the relationship we are mothering sufficiently enhances our own strength: the nurturing we give must heighten our sense of our cauldron's worth and potential. If each time we mother, we learn to feel more acutely the boundaries of our sanctuary, we become clearer as to what we can give, in quality and quantity, and we learn only to give that which truly strengthens the soul whom we hold, neither scrimping nor squandering our resources, nor smothering our charge.

It is a risk each time. What we give may never be fully acknowledged. As women, we are often encouraged to achieve *inter*dependence instead, but in many ways that dilutes the gift the mother gives. Symbiosis is an exquisite part of nature's viability and reason, but a deal crafted which requires immediate reciprocity is not one made by the mother. To reject or belittle the hag of dependence, and its inevitable vulnerability, is to deny the true power of the mother, her immense courage, her faith, strength and caring. Her success, and her dignity, is based on her ability to nurture in a way that facilitates her charge's growth towards independence, when the child can run free, and once again so can she.

Not only is she dependent, the mother is often in part also disconnected from the wider community. Attentive only to the safety and growth of that which is in her care, her interest in the world around her is significantly reduced. At times she fails to honour other relationships, her focus is so specific. She may be alert, and acutely so, but only in order to protect that which is in her care. These blinkers only add to her vulnerability. It is easy to see how mother has lost her autonomy, and with it her status in the evolution of society.

Mother as a resource

After hundreds of millennia of hunting, gathering, scavenging, it was just fifteen thousand years ago that our ancestors began to experiment with agriculture. It is now thought that the provocation was necessity; a warming climate collapsed into another icy freeze, possibly due to melting glaciers disrupting ocean currents. The resulting severe conditions led to famine for what had been a growing population, and human ingenuity had to kick in. Around ten thousand years ago, new ideas about cultivation began to seep through human societies in what was perhaps the most dramatic shift in our species' story.

In Britain the resulting changes become evident when, around 3000 BCE, the focus of religious practice appears to alter dramatically. Instead of tomb shrines used to reach to the powers of regeneration, round barrows were erected as burial mounds for individuals, implying settled tribal cultures where hierarchies were developing. As cultivation became effective, a tribe's excess of produce could be used to support a ruling family and its defending warriors. Possibilities for trade grew, both within a tribe - where craftsmen evolved into a class creating innovations, improving technologies - and for trade between tribes, stimulating the spread of inspiration and ideas. A complex social structure emerged, and one increasingly dependent on the success of its resource. So came about what appears to be the focus of this era's religious practice: fertility.

Circular bank and ditch earthworks were created, great wooden posts erected, followed in later years by standing stones laid out in lines and circles, with increasingly complicated alignments to the setting and rising of the sun, the moon and key visible stars. At a time when science and religion were interwoven, these were calendars, temples to the cyclicity of nature, to time and the seasons, to the gods of the wide clear skies above and the divine fertility that was the response of the land beneath their feet.

The effects were dramatic. Where a tribe settled, investing its vital energy into the earth's fertility and cultivation, it claimed ownership of that land. Equally, animals herded upon that land, both wild and domesticated, were claimed as owned. So did the women become yet another resource, giving children to the tribe that in turn could work the land in what was a far more labour intensive lifestyle than had previously been known. Where wealth passed down patriarchal lines, women became objects to be controlled to ensure the right children received the right inheritance. Women, like land and cattle, were now claimed, owned and traded.

The changes must have had both severe and subtle consequences on the emotional health of a tribe. Physically, whereas hunter-gatherer women would have been giving birth every four or five years, retaining their infertility through extended breast-feeding and cold hungry winters, carrying the infant with them as they worked and journeyed, the cycle of birthing changed for settled women. With work that didn't allow an infant to stay at the breast, women had more pregnancies, perhaps every two years, providing more children to work the fields. Forced weaning and separation from the mother both tend to trigger higher levels of aggression in a child's development, aggression that was no longer channelled into the perpetual need to hunt. With the domestication of goats and cattle, not only were human beings now in permanently close contact with animals, but for the first time infants were given nonhuman milk to supplement their mother's. So did some of the most tenacious diseases cross the species divide into humankind, including tuberculosis, smallpox and measles.

It was the beginning of what we call 'civilisation'. Accumulation became feasible, and desirable. Fertility became a source of that wealth. And wealth, definitively, belongs to someone.

"What a'you doin'?" He's yelling above the noise, his arms folded as he jerks his broad square chin out at me, glaring. We hadn't seen him come through the crowd. She panics.

"Jez, don't. She was just - " she tries to smile. "Only, her bloke's just asked her to marry 'im, and - " He doesn't take his eyes off me. I glare back, unwilling to be crushed by his obtuse brute force. "Jez, leave 'er alone."

"Shut the fuck up." Still he stares at me, unblinking, waiting for an answer.

I breathe in and sigh. A thousand words fall into my mind, and yet I know each one would provoke him in a way that she would feel later on the back of his hand. As calmly as I can through the music, I say, "Let it go, Jez. She isn't doing anything to dishonour you."

"And what the fuck d'you know about honour, ya fuckin' whore," he snarls, stepping towards me, his chin high, distaste souring his face. But underneath, it's so easy to see the lost little boy, the playground bully. So I shrug, "Jez ... "

Immediately he lifts his fat hand, a rigid finger pointing into my face. "I don' want you puttin' ideas into 'er fuckin' head, alrigh'? She'll do what I tell 'er. Is that clear?"

"Please, Jez," she's stumbling onto her high heels, clumsily getting out from behind the table, gathering up her coat and little patent leather bag, "Let's go, Jez, yeah?"

I turn to her, feeling his anger like whisky-breath on my face, feeling my deluded notion of twenty first century women's liberation slipping away. "You don't have to leave, Mandy. I can have him thrown out - "

She looks into my face, with resignation so deep it leaves an emptiness across her face. "It's easier this way."

And I watch as they push their way through the crowd.

One of the barmaids strides over and sits down beside me. Leaning over to talk above the noise, she yells, "Dan says you're getting married! You can't run a club and get married! I mean," she looks over at the dance floor, a seething mass of sweating bodies in the darkness of this city basement, the music pounding, "you'd get tempted every bloody day to taste some new delight, eh?"

"In here?!"

An explosion of laughter hits the bar and we both turn together: three rugby players so drunk they are almost dribbling.

In animistic traditions, ownership is a barely comprehensible notion. All of nature hums with soul, and every soul has its own purpose, its own path of life. Every creature - every part of nature's ongoing creativity - craves simply to thrive as what it is, held within the fabric of life. Accordingly, every interaction must be based upon relationship, soul to soul, subject to subject. Where, however, most of nature is perceived as inanimate, we find ourselves surrounded by objects, things we can use to fulfil our own needs. When something or someone is seen as an object it can be owned, and when ownership creeps into any relationship, the level of respect tumbles. We can value what we own, prize it, even adore it, but we don't acknowledge it as having any rights of personal freedom.

What makes a man perceive a wife as a *woman owned* is long millennia of evolution. In part it is based on instinctive male competition, wealth measured in grain, slaves, cattle, women and children, greater wealth allowing him to stand more securely above and beyond the line of peer aggression: a man owns a woman in order to display her and so raise his status in the tribe. Yet ownership of a woman is also about controlling her, and that is based on the fear of her nature: too much of a woman's nature is wild, irrational, unacceptable. Further, though woman is declared unfathomable, dark with potential, *mother* can be worse, for she ensnares the unwitting soul in her prison-sanctuary, and keeps his children like an unholy ransom.

In the fourth century BCE, as Greek culture moved into the later Hellenistic era, the power of the nation state finding its brawn, women became little more than domestic slaves. It's a culture into which is rooted so much Western and Christian philosophy. History documents that a husband must be a good deal older, better educated, of higher status and so on, in order to ensure that his wife submit to his dominance in total obedience. Contemporary Greeks wrote about neighbouring peoples, judging them barbaric for the way in which they allowed women freedom, choice, land and love. In early Christianity, the purpose of marriage was to condone the sinful act of sexual interaction. It was only in the sixteenth century that marriage became a Christian rite, taking into its liturgy and law all it could to affirm the subservience of women.

In twenty first century Western culture, fewer people are getting married. Divorce statistics are lower as a result, but the number of single parent families is higher than ever and fast rising. There is no doubt that marriage glues a couple together through hard times, where cohabiting allows them more easily to separate. While the misery of an awful marriage may be worth abandoning, there is value in the commitment a marriage inspires.

In Paganism, marriage or handfasting is still favoured, indeed treasured. Whether a couple declare their vows before a legal registrar or simply their family, their community, their gods and ancestors, the foundation of a Pagan marriage is not just honour (with its basis of respect and responsibility) but also freedom. It is a freedom recognised as crucial if each individual is to grow and change, continuing to explore their own truth, their sense of self, and their ability to live fully. An unvowed relationship can require constant affirmation, particularly when moving through periods of change, but when vows have been proclaimed, witnessed and accepted, vows written by the individuals involved after long consideration, the commitment allows for a wealth of freedom.

Those wedding vows craft the initial edges of the sanctuary a couple will share, but marriage itself, however unfashionable it is to acknowledge, is a skill of *mother* - and not just because a man can be so domestically inept, caring for a house as if he were a puppy or a teenager (some women are no better)! Giving of herself fully, it is the mother within us who creates the sanctuary of home, the haven within which that love can thrive and grow. It need not be the *princesa*'s four bedroom celebration of suburbia. Home may be no more than the safe space that holds a moment in gentle certainty. It's never absolutely permanent in terms of bricks and carpet, but knowing where the boundaries are of that precious sanctuary allows for a surety, providing grounded nourishment for our creativity. Well done, just as a child well-mothered is barely aware of any limitations around his journeys of discovery, finding at the edges instead the affirmation of love and sound support for his growing freedom, the same is true of a good marriage.

Further, because life changes us, a Pagan marriage is often based upon more than one initial handfasting rite, the couple updating their vows now and then in witnessed ritual to ensure they remain relevant, each time securing the foundations of respect for the other's soul freedom. Nor is there any sense in modern Paganism that a marriage should be between just two people, one of each gender. The pluralism of its tradition, the acknowledgement of nature's quirks and rich diversity, all of which add so crucially to its health and sustainability, are welcomed within the parameters of marriage. It doesn't matter what gender the partners are, nor indeed whether there are more than two individuals involved, the important element is that dedicated and witnessed commitment, and the sanctuary of home which is created upon those secure foundations. It couldn't be further from ownership.

Mother as a sexual being

In the same way that she holds the sanctuary of home, mother can also offer her nemeton in a sexual relationship. Here, the mother holds and nurtures her partner, and where this is consensual the sharing can be just exquisite. Creating a wholly safe and loving place, she allows him (or her) to express a more profound and sensitive vulnerability: a fuller truth. Potentially strengthening trust, such mother energy can deepen a relationship remarkably.

His shoulders are slightly hunched in that self-protective way of slim young men. He fidgets on the bar stool, picking up his beer and drinking, glancing at me, all self-conscious as I watch him, his half smile wary, wondering, wondering what I see in him. The gap in our ages is less than a decade, but they seem poignant years. He pulls on the thin roll-up, barely exhaling. I can't take my eyes off him.

"I know you don't like me smoking," he murmurs.

You'll grow out of it, I want to say, but instead I just smile, and hope. He doesn't want my dog-eared advice, my patronising opinion; he simply wants to know that I care. It hurts to see him smoke and I let it show in my eyes. His expression softens, almost to vulnerability, and he rubs the soft stubble of his half grown beard and crushes the cigarette into the ashtray. And gently he looks up, his face breaking into a smile that is all carefree and mock innocence, yet the expression is such a dilute hue upon his genuine innocence.

His every move pulls at my heart so.

"What?" he laughs, and blinks in shy surprise.

Lying in the half light of the bedroom, later, he sleeps, his body sated, an arm draped across me. His cheek is squashed against the pillow, his mouth slightly open, his breathing so gentle, his sleeping effortless. It's been a while since I've lain beside a sleeping man this quiet.

My fingers lift from the covers in an undying curiosity simply to feel the warmth of his skin, sliding over the curves of his muscles, the smoothness fascinating, enthralling me utterly. I can do this for hours, loathe to sleep and miss a moment's opportunity, completely focused on his soft and flawless skin.

He breathes in more deeply, now vaguely aware of me, and contentment touches his lips as he shifts his arm off me and he turns onto his side. His shoulder blade moves, the skin stretching so easily, and he murmurs a little sound as I kiss him, my lips against the silky warmth of his back. I close my eyes, that feeling washing through me, the most extraordinary tenderness that only he has evoked in me. In all his youthful perfection, he seems so terribly mortal.

"Hold me?" he whispers, and as I curl myself around him he slides gently back into his dreamless sleep.

We don't automatically think of mother as a sexual being. Yet a woman as mother can be the most generous and attentive lover, devoted to fulfilling her lover's every need. Offering the beauty of her soul, offering her body for the other's pleasure, the mother wishes only to fulfil their desires, because she cares. She is not the hungry and demanding lover; she is the woman who creates a safe space, bathed in trust, giving gently, with absolute patience. Her pleasure comes from every sweet gasp of pleasure her lover makes.

Of course, as in other areas of her life, a woman can mother in her sexuality through fear, using her generosity to avoid the expected pain of her love or lust not being reciprocated. Her lover may not notice, continuing instead to take all she gives, failing to see that she receives too little in return. And in her anxious uncertainty, she can smother, afraid that she may lose the one she is holding and, no longer needed, face what she believes to be the inevitability of rejection.

There are good reasons, though, why mother is not principally associated with sex. Not unusually, when her life is filled with mothering, a woman may well have a low sex drive. Whether the offering of her cauldron has led her to be wrapped up in nappies and baby talk, or the demands of some other project, the full-time mother may well be too tired or single-minded to engage intimately with anyone other than her charge.

Not infrequently, however, the lack of libido is due to a lack of good communication; her sexual needs can be specific. As a woman, having cared for another all day, she may need to be, and long to be, drawn out of the mother role; yet, all too often, those around her fail to see she can be anything else. On the other hand, still mother, she may simply crave the careful handling that is in her mother nature. She wants to be cared for.

Mother as the soil

When I was pregnant, the most poignant advice I was given came from a friend whose wife was to give birth to their second child around same time that mine was due. He said, "Beware of the demon inside you". I smiled, "Oh yeah?" When my new baby was but a few months old, I discovered what he meant. My son hadn't slept for more than a few hours without waking for very many weeks; my body was still healing after the disastrous process of giving birth and I was completely and absolutely shattered; the tyke fed, again, positing up the lot again, and cried with all the confusion of his frustrated soul. He cried and he cried. I tried everything to help him but all my love and every trick in the book didn't make a hint of difference. Then, quite suddenly, my patience expired. And for a stark moment I understood just how it is possible to hurl a tiny baby at a cold hard wall. I put him down on his sheepskin fleece, making sure he was safe, and with defined steps I left the room. Sitting on the stairs in shock, I breathed myself into calm. For a moment, I had lost *mother*.

Mother's love is extraordinary. Of any love, it has within it the treasure that is pure nourishment, body and soul. It gives the sweet scents of breast and milk, the magic of skin-soft intimacy. Built into it are layers of magical patience and instinctive trust. Though our own mothers were each flawed human beings, throughout our human lives we long for such connection, ever seeking in an uncertain world what we perceived as a bond of absolute trust, unconditional love and uncomplicated intimacy.

In our relationship with the earth, with mother nature, we seek the same - and we make the same mistakes. As infants crying out for food and love, we assume her resources are endless, we fail to reciprocate her care, and thoughtlessly we express a persistent lack of respect and appreciation. In other words, we use the earth, as we use the mother, bewildered and enraged when she doesn't give us *everything* and for free.

In very many of the old myths of our heritage, the power of mother is denoted as a goddess of the land. Most often, these tales are lessons about the way in which we treat her, warnings woven in as an underlying thread to the tale. When we *use* the land, taking without respect, through greed beyond need, assuming that she does give to us unconditionally, we soon find that we are wrong.

In British and Gaelic heritage, religious and folkloric traditions tell rich stories of the relationship between the people and the land. The understanding is of the tribal king forging an agreement with this goddess of creation, regeneration and abundance in order that his people may thrive. Where the deal is not met, where the king disappoints or reneges upon the agreement, the goddess simply, quickly, withdraws fertility. She no longer supports his people, leaving the land barren with drought, flood, famine, devastation. The belief that a king's power is dependent on his sexual potency, through his ability to please the goddess, is played out in our history where kings have made choices about whom they marry, believing the queen to symbolise the land and its potential fertility, the world soul; if he marries well, he ensures the success of his reign. Sovereignty, in other words, cannot be claimed: it is a gift given by the goddess when the king's bond with her is good.

Rhiannon, a goddess of Dyfed in south Wales, is symbolically associated with a white horse. Her influence may well have spread into southwest England, or perhaps local English deities with different names shared some of her qualities: either way, many feel the ancient chalk figure of the horse at Uffington in Wiltshire, as other horse figures in chalk and clay, remain an invocation of some ancient celebration, proclamation or source of sovereignty.

The mare, as power of the land, suggests not only her strength but also the need for perfect co-operation. In the tales of The Mabinogi, Pwyll, Lord of Dyfed, sees Rhiannon riding upon her white horse and is immediately enchanted. Even with the fastest mounts in his kingdom his men fail to catch up with her; only when he rides himself and calls out to her does she turn, coming to him of her own accord. Though in time they do marry, trickery, rivalry and doubts about her fertility and loyalty to Pwyll pepper the tale, showing how hard it is to keep the bond clear and strong. As ever, the tanist (the chosen successor) is always present, poised in the shadows, waiting for the moment when the queen happens to turn her gaze upon him, giving him permission to remove the king and take his place beside her.

In Ireland, the link between marriage and kingship was overt, the inauguration being the *feis*, sometimes translated as 'feast' but more accurately meaning the lovemaking. The tale described by Giraldus Cambrensis of twelfth century Irish kingmaking beautifully links with the myths of the goddess Rhiannon. At the time of the inauguration, in the midst of the assembled gathering, the king had sexual intercourse with a white mare, after which the horse was slaughtered, cut into pieces and boiled in water. Bathing in the broth, drinking it, eating the meat and sharing it with his people, the king had proved his sexual vitality (and power to control) and so his viability as king and husband to the land.

Perhaps the most famous of all Irish mythic queens was Medbh of Connaught, Queen Mab, the Fairy Queen. As goddess of the land, her name suggests the mead or honey wine that is the essence of sweetness and abundance. Though she took a series of husbands, she offered sovereignty at a high price. In the Irish medieval text, The Tain, she says, 'If I married a mean man our union would be wrong, because I'm so full of grace and giving. It would be an insult if I were more generous than my husband, but not if the two of us were equal in this. If my husband was a timid man our union would be just as wrong because I thrive, myself, on all kinds of trouble. It is an insult for a wife to be more spirited than her husband, but not if the two are equally spirited. If I married a jealous man that would be wrong too: I never had one man without another waiting in his shadow'.

She is the landscape of Ireland: an extraordinary wild woman.

The easiest way is simply to sit on my butt in the mud. Tipping out another square of soft wet crumbly earth, carefully holding the little seedling in my already muddy hands, I push a finger into the soil, making an indentation, then place the fragile creature into it, easing the earth around.

The scent of it fills me. It hums with last night's rain, rich with the compost we've dug in year after year, rich with the memories of every harvest that has fed my family and my community. For a moment I close my eyes and breathe it in. Slowly, magically, my perception shifts, and I find myself aware of my outbreath being so much an integral part of this garden. The apple tree behind me, the hedge, holding me, breathing me. I can't help but whisper my thanks, my fingers outstretched on the earth, this beautiful generous earth.

I tip another tiny seedling into my hand and slip it into the next hole along the line, then another, as one tray is emptied and I start on the next, shifting myself along, getting muddier and muddier.

A robin, singing in the hawthorn of the hedge, halts his song of sovereignty to fly down, landing on a little tump of turned earth, and our eyes meet. He listens to me, and I realise I too am singing, humming. I smile, and he tilts his head, a sparkle in his little black eyes.

As virgin, the goddess of the land has no pact with the people; still wild, she has no interest in making deals with humanity. If men do tread upon her, she doesn't notice, or if she does it doesn't disturb her. She retains her independence, laughing, wild and free. If, however, she is abused, she withdraws completely, leaving a landscape that is increasingly lifeless.

In our Western society we no longer have an all-powerful chieftain or king, but there are many whose decisions affect the landscapes we live within. Developers, corporations that mine, quarry and build, farmers and fishermen, those of us who tend to gardens, each and every consumer who gives money into the system, we all are a part of our people's relationship with the land. If that bond is good, she offers herself to us as mother. She holds the people. Where she is disappointed through lack of care and attention, she steps back - and we feel that in the vibrancy of a place, in the mud and the trees, in the air we breathe. Where she is raped, the toxicity of her anger sickens the land, together with those who live upon her.

Perhaps because the mother's skill is to give seemingly unconditionally, never demanding immediate reciprocity, it is excruciatingly easy to take her for granted. Yet perhaps too when we have experience of a woman as mother, we can forget that mother is not all she is. Without exception, complacency is dangerous.

CHAPTER SIX

The Bitch

Suddenly I am wide awake, staring at the ceiling, the monochrome gloom above me, my face cold, my hands sweating. It takes a moment for the catatonia to lift. And I stare, barely breathing, until the last thoughts of my half-dreaming emerge from the shadows of my mind, like a pack of hungry wolves, drooling saliva from their moonlit teeth.

I can't be ...

Falling from my bed, I stumble into the bathroom and lean over the basin in the dark.

The world seems silent and still, as if every person, every creature, every thing were poised, waiting.

I'm only three days late ...

I pull on the light, tugging at it harder than I need to, shutting my eyes to the glare as it fills the room, and I sink to the cold floor, curling up against the bath.

I can't tell him. Though he's always been clear he's not interested, into his soul will fall pictures he can't resist: the warm bundle in his arms, looking up into his eyes, making *da-da* sounds he'd interpret as recognition, and he'd murmur softly words of a love that's all-protecting. And when I say I can't do it, when I say I don't want this child, *I don't want to be pregnant,* it'll be murder so specific, blood hurled across those perfect pictures right before his face.

I want to cry, but I'm too scared.

It's like a noose around my ankle, where I sit here huddled on the floor. Wherever I walk now, that noose will hold me, and even when this fear is gone I'll still feel its grip cutting into my flesh. Some vile she-demon has ensnared my body for her unconscionable purpose, her monstrous bloody hunger for human propagation. And caught like this, I know the only way out is to slash myself free, so fucking clumsily I'll pour with blood and tears like an old battlefield, heavy with the stench of guilt, wreaking pain that'll linger about me forever.

I can't be ...

I lift my fingers to touch the face of my gentle free-spirited lover as if he were there in the empty air before me, his beautiful face, feeling the doubt in his eyes, the bewilderment, a grief muddled with such brutal uncertainty.

Please, no ...

Not all little girls grow up to be *mother*. For some women, the idea of having children is simply abhorrent. It may be a phase, or it may last throughout her life. For her, the exquisite natural gift of her fertility is nothing but a bloody curse.

The Buddhist belief that a woman can never attain enlightenment purely because of her physiology - because she can have children - is an idea that is shared in less specific and differing forms amongst many dualist theologies and philosophies around the world. How can she focus on spirit when she is so caught up with matter? It's a misogynistic perspective that would make many women seethe with rage, not least the mother whose experience of birth and the self-sacrifice of nurturing is often so profoundly spiritual; she's invested her energy in the very essence of life, after all. Yet on a practical level, some women would agree. It need not be a matter of spiritual purity, for even in a religious tradition of animistic integration, children can be no more than a damned effective disturbance.

In Arabic, Hebrew and other Semitic languages, the word 'dam' translates as blood. It's found throughout Indo-European languages in words such as *madame* and *damsel*, and the swearword, *damn*. Menstruation brings us our power of fertility, yet with it comes the curse of physically perilous childbearing and emotionally perilous motherhood. Avoiding the risk altogether requires surgery or celibacy; the alternative is the revolting taste and indignity of slippy rubber condoms, constant attention to dates, vaginal mucous and temperature, with frustrating days of abstinence, or the butt-expanding contraceptive pill, the muddle of cap or coil, and those amplified stress levels as we head towards our blood-due date, worrying that this month will be the month it just won't come.

That 'children? no bloody way!' response to our fertility is a good introduction to another side of woman's nature. Say hello (and duck): here is the *bitch*.

The bitch's goddess

It's an aggressive word. It implies a spiteful woman, one who is malicious, uncompassionate, offensive. She is a female dog (a fox, an otter, a wolf), licentious, selfish, acquisitive and sly. Looking back through our heritage in search of the word's root, she is linked with old Pagan goddesses of hunting and death, their prodigious hunger, their vicious hounds. Through time, the bitch has been and still is a woman who's retained enough of her wild energy to be banefully anarchic. She has her own set of rules, and they don't necessarily comply with social conventions or expectations.

As with so many forces of nature, seldom do we carefully consider and decide to open ourselves to her flood. There are times when the bitch sits within us for days. There are people, places and circumstances that seem to evoke her, causing us to behave cruelly again and again. Some women appear unable to be anything else, everything in life provoking bitchy behaviour, snide remarks, judgemental, callous disregard. The constant expression of anger can be exhausting. The resulting friendless isolation can creep up, glaring as an emptiness when suddenly we find ourselves desperate for company, for love, for help or support. Nobody trusts the bitch.

Seeking the patterns of nature, looking to forge relationships with the gods whose currents of intention course through our lives, the Pagan will always be drawn to those forces that are the most destructive, hoping to find understanding and avoid any unnecessary devastation. As a result, the goddess who inspires the bitch in us is an important deity with which to craft a working bond; for she can be the most brutally, irrationally and relentlessly ruinous force within us. Even where a woman's warmth and loving gentleness can be discerned through the barbed wire and machine gun rounds spitting off, few can be bothered to take the punishment required to reach that tender soul within.

But it isn't only a powerful force of nature; it is a fascinating part of our human nature. In her most basic form, this goddess is simply one of *reaction*. A natural current, she is not thoughtful, considerate, patient or just. She has no capacity to judge what is immediately appropriate or proportionate, nor does she care. She is that instant kick of energy that drives the ball back across the net, the defensive reaction to an anticipated blow that throws a fist straight back at the perpetrator, the eruptive rage at an insult or injury that fuels the retaliation.

She may provoke us to run or hide, but never to cower. She is a comprehensively active force, whether whispering or screeching, driven by the expression of what Newton described in his third Law of Motion: when we are pushed off balance, it's the bitch inside us who pushes right back.

The bitch's sanctuary

Bitch may not be the most difficult aspect of woman to understand, but she is often the least knowable. Not only is she often too spiky to get close to, but she can also be almost impossible to see into.

The virgin, having shared the intimate sanctuary of her soul with no one since her own mother's embrace, retains an innocence and naiveté that shimmer about her. Untouched by human hands, she glows like a wilderness bathed in spring sunshine. She protects that space with feisty determination, but also with her precocious arrogance which simply does not register the presence or validity of a potential threat. The bitch is as protective of her space. Unlike the virgin, however, she sees and reacts to every threat, every potential threat, and everything that looks vaguely as if it might just, at some point, become somehow close to being threatening.

She's been hurt, and she's determined it won't happen again.

It may have been the kind of brutal abuse that would be considered horrific in any culture or era, but what provokes a woman to express the bitch is far more likely, and more commonly, the simple mess of having been badly parented. A child who has felt neglected by a parent too busy with other children, absent at work, emotionally remote, feels that pain deep within. The effects can make it hard for her to believe that she is or will ever be loved; equally, it can leave her with an inability or unwillingness to love. In the same way, a parent who can't or doesn't control their temper will leave marks on a child's tender soul, each sharp word screamed leaving welts that heal very slowly, becoming tight angry scars if the blows keep coming. The younger the child, the more open she is to that parent, reaching out through the craving of her natural dependence, and as a result the deeper is the pain of that absence or violence. Such a child may grow to find it hard to trust or believe she is trusted, throughout her life.

The same kind of pain may be sustained later in life; when someone who has been invited into the intimate haven of our sanctuary then turns on us, the damage can cause chaotic and profound uncertainty within our core, shattering what was our soul's inner safe haven. A lover's betrayal is the most common example: when we are hurt by someone we have trusted enough to be fully open, that wound can be very difficult to recover from. If the one inflicting the wound has intruded upon our intimacy uninvited, whether through violence or deceit, the problems are often worse. Our sanctuary has been breached. The foundations have been shaken and the whole world suddenly becomes unstable and dangerous. It is the experience of such intrusive hurt that evokes the bitch within us to react, her declared intention being now to keep that sacred inner space very much for herself.

The bitch does not share her sanctuary.

Carefully negotiating how and to whom she offers sovereignty of her rich and fertile lands, the mother knows the exquisite power of submission; the whore teaches it so that others may surrender to her touch, sinking into the ecstasy of her cauldron. The bitch, on the other hand, feels she's been forced into it. She won't now submit to anyone. She rages against any glimmer of pressure or suppression. Having been overcome before, she has no intention of allowing the possibility again; the edges of her sanctuary, the edges of her cauldron of creativity, are now seriously reinforced.

Yet, how others perceive our soul sanctuary affects how they respond to us, and so how we relate to them. Our struggles and fears are reflected in the boundaries, anger and confusion sculpting their form, painting their colour. If we cause them to be opaque, these boundaries allow us to hide, making us seem aloof, mysterious, impenetrable, the workings of our mind remaining incomprehensible to those around us. On the other hand, defensive barricades hastily erected might be brittle, easily shattered, expressing a fragility that creates a poignant sense of vulnerability or instability. We might encircle ourselves with an energy like barbed wire or electric fences, signalling to those around us that intimacy is off limits; if we are conscious of what we are doing, the consequent isolation may be welcome, but if not we may feel lonely, and confused as to why it is we consistently fail to make close relationships.

Sometimes a person's sense of self is so damaged by

aggression and abuse that the boundaries of their soul are cracked and broken, draining energy, integrity and confidence. Or they may be intact but so loose and porous as to be useless and, barely perceptible, allow others to wander in, intruding, violating, interfering: 'feel free to walk all over me'. The craven need to ensure that she doesn't provoke any trouble, face criticism or rejection, can inspire a woman to be so flexible, she may as well have no edges or *self* of her own. And with no safe haven within her soul, she is unlikely to manifest safety around her.

In some cases, the woman who incites anger or violence in her partner does so because her own boundaries are so severely damaged, usually by previous abuse; with no sanctuary, her sense of self is distorted and vague, confusing her ability to feel. Partially numb simply because she is so open all the time, and consequently perpetually pushed and pulled, her connections misfire. She is soul-naked, her boundaries shattered, a state that can rouse a fury sourced in the fear of uncertainty, confusion and frustration, for she is hard to reach or hold. It can also entice fascination, provoking attention, which in turn can generate the sort of unfounded jealous rage that so often underlies such violence. Yet, wrapped in the impotence of her constant vulnerability, her sense of self crippled, she aches to feel the touch of life once more, soul against soul, edge to edge.

Every cell of my body is tingling, warm. I used to cower, trying to get away, but now I just stand before him. It's like I imagine it would feel to be in a wind tunnel, the speed rising and falling just as the force of his voice does, bellowing then threatening, accusing me then hating me, hurling his vilification about things I've never done. I feel naked in front of him, as if his wind-words have stripped me bare, my hair blowing out behind me, my eyes half closed in the storm.

When he lifts his arm to strike again, I half expect the blow to go straight through me, his hand finding no resistance on my skin, my body without substance, his rage moving right through my soul. But it doesn't; it hits me and then I hit the wall. Then the floor. And again I realise that, if I had remembered I was solid, I could perhaps have fought back. As it is, being solid only means that I'm capable of taking the blows, and feeling them.

The noises change when she arrives, however many moments later, her voice shrieking as she kicks the door open. And somewhere inside my soul I smile as I watch him losing control before her, storming across the room towards her, barking with his anger like a stupid dog, anger quite different from that he shows me. He swears, and she just curses back at him. I creep away, closing my eyes, not wanting to be seen.

Then there's a *smash*. I think she's broken a bottle over his head. I look up to see the laboured crash as his great lump of a body hits the floor. Then she's beside me.

"Oh poppet, are you alrigh'? Bastard, fuckin' bastard! What did he do to you this time? I could fuckin' kill 'im. And he's no fuckin' right to call me a bitch, I'll tell you!" She puts her hands under my arms, "Come on, love, he'll be out cold for a while". She lifts me to my feet, helping me stagger towards the door.

I'm afraid to speak in case it breaks the cap on my tears, but I manage to whisper, "I don't think he sees me, Trisha."

"He can't see you, love. He's out cold. You don't need to worry for a while." But that's not what I meant.

As with rape, the man or woman who perpetrates such violence is the one our society must bring to account, not the victim of such abuse, but my interest here is in those sides of our nature that we recoil from as shameful, as unhelpful, as unacceptable - not who else we can judge as culpable when things go wrong. Every incident, every horror of human brutality, rides a current of reasons and emotions, the various forces of nature crafting the storms and turbulence that are just beyond our control. Yet it is our most foundational paradigms that create the boundaries of our inner sanctuary. And these are the bases of how we react to the world around us.

When those beliefs are positive and constructive, our soul's edges naturally express a strength and flexibility. The healthy individual doesn't need to proclaim the boundaries of her intimate space; they are clear, gently adapting to each new situation, at times withdrawing in protective tension and then relaxing with ease, allowing her to live her freedom and grow into the person she can become. Where our beliefs are self-negating, however, we express that lack of worth by diminishing the integrity of our sanctuary. If we have no doubt that we are unlovable, worthless, in some way soiled, unwanted and good for nothing, that will affect not only how we present ourselves to the world, but how safe we feel we are within. So it is that, with all the injustice of nature, the broken nemeton, such as that of a soul badly abused, tends to invite only further abuse.

The bitch's response to pain is quite the opposite. Declared with defensive aggression and held with an irrational emotional tenacity, her edges are reinforced with every word she speaks, every movement of her body, tense and alert. In securing her sanctuary so forcibly, though, the price can be high. Such rigid edges keep her isolated. The bitch can't afford to get close to anyone, let alone risk the merest flicker of dependence.

Bad bitch

When that sacred inner space has been closed off for years, we forget what it feels like to be open and free. Perhaps we have memories of childhood, of jumping in piles of fallen leaves and watching trails of ants, of stomping in puddles, of endless afternoons. Perhaps we remember when, as teenagers, we made love on the beach, went out dancing in the rain, sleeping in the back of cars, exploring, always exploring. Or perhaps we have no memory, no vision, of what it is to be free, yet still a suspicion lingers in the shadows of our mind that *there must be more than this.*

Losing our freedom, we tend to become stupefied, our motivation to explore waning along with our ability to be innovative or take the initiative. We complain. Living in a socially acceptable inertia, the energy of our creativity stagnates; we forget how to be creative. We forget how to play. Alcohol or drugs help us not to care, allowing us to retain that tame state of apathy.

Or the bitch may emerge.

As a natural force of *reaction*, the bitch is not always explosive. She may creep out, at first quietly simply slipping scathing comments into a conversation. She judges the world to be as worthless, useless and tedious as she fears herself to be: little is worth her while, nowhere is sufficiently interesting to warrant her attention, and every step along the way is almost unendurably pointless. She sulks in a way that brings her inaction into the limelight as if it were through indignation that she is failing to contribute positively. She undermines as if to provoke in those around her the anger that she herself would like to vent. She is so closed off, separated from the world within her inflexibly defended soul, that she fails to empathise with anyone or truly hear another's story, her complaints being caustic and devoid of patience, compassion or care. Thoughtless in her independence, she gripes and dismisses any notion of co-operation. She hisses and snarls, and walks on alone, criticising others as beneath her, as incompetent and witless, angry that she is always having to do the work alone.

At times, though, that reactionary force is not simply snide and moody. The bitch can come storming out of the shadows, frustration forcing our natural soul energy to shudder under the pressure of its suppression, and suddenly she is exploding like a machine gun in a fit of rage, kicking off in bitterness and resentful destructiveness. Holding within her a store of anguish from many years of isolation and self-negation, the bitch is more than capable of reacting entirely out of proportion to the circumstance, completely irrational and out of control. She can be terrifying.

Whether it is alcohol, hormones, or some last-straw that has softly found a place to land, the bitch's violence is pure hag-fury, deemed to be wholly unacceptable within our culture. Quite unlike the man who loses his temper and ends up in a scuffle or a fist fight, the woman who lets rip, spitting wrath as she scratches, thumps and screams is a sight that leaves many an onlooker nervous and bewildered. Not so long ago, such behaviour was cause enough for a woman to be removed to a lunatic asylum. Hysteria was not just a disease of the womb; it was believed to be incurable.

As human beings we have a *powerful* need to be creative - a need that is powered or fuelled by our very nature. Our species' survival has been driven by our ability to think creatively around problems, crafting solutions however much they require us to adapt. It isn't about aesthetics: that creativity is the lateral thinking, the playful exploration and curiosity, the reckless decisions that lead us to innovation, the trying out of ideas and making various tiny adjustments or radical changes. The aesthetics shine through when our thinking manifests into something we've created which brings a deeply intuitive satisfaction. That visceral sensation and appreciation of beauty comes when we behold something that *works* - and the more exquisitely it works, the more beautiful it seems.

Our ancestors may have had a more acute awareness than we do of our human dependence on finding exactly what does work, solving problems that were more immediately and directly connected with their own survival, just as so many human beings in less economically developed nations still are. In our twenty first century Western culture our need to be creative is no less. Where it is unfettered in our nature, we may express it through our work and play, whether we are teachers, lawyers, administrators or writers. We may daily play it out in simple tasks such as how we dress, prepare food, or even write a list. Yet if we are so wounded that we can't appreciate any small act of our creativity, or indeed are incapable of expressing creativity at all, instead functioning solely upon habit and others' direction, that fuel within our nature is going to sour. It becomes bitter, and the bitch steps in to express that bitterness through us.

The same is true of intimacy. For the vast majority of human beings, there are long periods of our lives when we crave the experience of being close to another soul, as friend or lover, as confidante, as co-creator. We long to open our sanctuary, to stretch, relaxed and safe enough to touch another soul. In that intimate connection, with trust and support shared, our sense of self is nourished and affirmed, healing our soul and allowing the edges we present to soften.

Surrounded in our culture by billboards, commercials, movies and magazines, each declaring how easy it is to find that intense connection, where we lack it, unable to find the trust to open to another soul, anger and resentment can build like a toxic gas, sporadically igniting. Again the bitch steps in, leaving showers of shrapnel around her. Of course, what is being advertised all around us is actually just sex, given a lens-perfect gloss of plastic commercialism; it is usually quite devoid of genuine intimacy. Yet still it provokes, reminding us that it is the touch, soul to soul, of shared sanctuary that makes the difference to a life.

That shared sanctuary is exactly what the bitch doesn't do.

Good bitch
Being conscious of the way in which we present and express ourselves, then choosing to use our boundaries for our own benefit is an important skill. When she is strong in her own power, the whore opens hers with a sensuality, inspiring her partner to do the same, that they might both share the depths of

intimate pleasure; the conscious mother opens hers in order that she might hold her charge within the complete safety of her intimate haven, blessed with deep caring. The bitch shares that sanctuary with nobody. But she knows her boundaries, absolutely, and she uses them.

Out of control, the bitch can cast her rage thoughtlessly, carelessly hurting others, provoking chaos. However, if we consider the current that moves her as a goddess of reaction, being a destructive bitch isn't the only way to work with that force of nature. Certainly, the bitch asserts herself. She has an opinion and she doesn't shirk at expressing it, however much it may question or oppose the *status quo*. She's been hurt, and where she perceives injustice she simply has to respond, albeit at times irrationally, inappropriately, unacceptably wild.

Yet she need not do it straight away. The specific skill of *bitch* is her ability to express her truth, undiluted and without compromise, and life offers so many situations when we need that distinct ability in order to shake a situation by the roots and stop whatever it is that we feel to be *wrong*. Centred within her sanctuary, standing clear and strong, glowing with her own vitality, and roused by an acute sense of what is justice, the bitch uses her edges as if they were a weapon. She is keenly aware of the power of her own soul riding the divine currents of reaction; she understands the rich character and force of the emotion provoked within her; and consciously, carefully, she allows its energy to flood her sanctuary until she can feel her soul humming, saturated and tight. And she holds it, and holds it, until the time comes to let it go. When she does, a minute later, a month later, ten years on, releasing that energy upon the trajectory of her sharply honed intent, the bitch can move mountains. She is an unshakeable force.

If she can make her point better by holding the edges of her soul a shimmering scarlet, or pushing those edges out so that she stands twelve feet wide and as high, then she does. If in her expression it would be valuable to break open her soul, she does so, but only when and because it amplifies the effect; she lets no one close.

This is the wild force of woman, untamed by society, unashamed in her own capacity to hurl a stone into still water, generating chaos just where she wants it, challenging face to face without deference to any notion of authority. Humming with the pure energy of the emotion that has drenched her soul, yet *responding* in a measured and thoughtful way (as opposed to angrily, too quickly reacting), she can be perceived as dreadfully cold, calculating, manipulative and conniving. A woman who has the ability to use the vital energy of anger to fuel a carefully considered, effective and perhaps brutal response to any situation is justifiably perceived as dangerous. Here we find vengeance. Indeed, whether her protest is sound or irrational, whether her cause personal or on behalf of another, whether she is yelling in defiance or quietly manoeuvring, the bitch who knows how to work with this divine power glows with the stench of the hag: her undilute objective is to get her own way.

Crucially, the difference between the bitch who is overwhelmed by that goddess of reaction, and the bitch who rides that dark and sacred current, fully aware of what she does, is that the latter genuinely *cares*. She fights tooth and nail, with every skill at her disposal, with intelligence and force, because she cares. Her own experience of pain may have led her to close her nemeton to everyone, disallowing her from sharing intimately the haven of her soul, but where her empathy kicks in it is because she sees another soul who has been wounded as she has. When she is driven to campaign on behalf of others, it is those whose hurt she too feels, the abused and the downtrodden, those whose sense of self and worth has been cracked or shattered.

Those wounded that evoke her care may not be human; her indignant rage may be incited in defence of the nonhuman world, the animals our species tortures and slaughters for food, science and entertainment. It may be the landscape itself, the environment of forests, oceans and wilderness. It may be the beech tree on the corner which some development company wants to cut down in their plans to build yet another bloody supermarket.

When I first came to discover the Pagan traditions of Britain, one of the images that imprinted on my mind was that of the Roman invasion of Ynys Môn, the island of Anglesey. The Roman forces had already taken occupation of much of southern Britain, destroying those tribes who had not surrendered their sovereignty; many of the Druids who were still opposing the Empire were said to have retreated to the wealthy island on the northern coast of Wales. Tacitus wrote of the British resistance gathered upon that island's shores, 'with its dense array of armed warriors, while between the ranks dashed women, in black attire like the Furies, with hair dishevelled, waving brands'.

The fascination these ancient tales had at first evoked in me intensified over the years of my studying Druidry. By the time I had dedicated into the tradition as a priest, the feelings had grown into a rage like an ancient floodplain in my soul, the waters ready to surge forward in defence of that very Pagan understanding of *home*: the sanctuary of not just one person but of a whole people, utterly integrated with their environment.

Across that wide stretch of shallow water, the tiny lights of their fires transfix us. No one has seen so many fires before. It would have been hard to imagine - it is as if the skies have dropped their stars upon the earth, littering the ground at the base of the mountains.

No one moves, no one talks; we stand there on the sand, listening to the song of the wind and the water, the gentle ripples of waves washing up onto the shore, watching as the first light of day begins to seep into the skies. The light is a pallid grey, that early light that comes before the colours wake, and the stillness of the night is given its measure by it, the weight of our souls in our damp and heavy robes. One of the priests begins to sing, drawing the silent anguish of these moments into sound, as soft as the rays of that light on the water. For a while there is nothing but the song, its tones lifting and reflecting every footstep on soil and sand, every loaf of bread broken, every vow made and witnessed, every cup shared, each drop of blood, each tear shed upon this sacred Island of the Mother. There is an aching in the song that whispers of these memories, a whisper that silhouettes my frame against the rising sun as if it were already a memory of all that will be lost, its notes crying out in desolation, calling me home to the lands of the dead. I close my eyes to the fires of the enemy across the water, the flames now losing their sparkle in the dawn's grey light, and I breathe in the darkness of my inner night as if to step back in time.

Feeling the hard cold of the pavement's kerb beneath me, I open my eyes to the noise of the city and the shuffling, tramping, stamping of feet as the march carries on past where I've paused, sitting down to catch my breath. A group of young Muslims, chanting in Arabic, then some quiet chatter amongst those that follow them, banners declaiming the war illegal, banners calling for peace, for honesty, a couple of families with children, one blowing bubbles from a plastic gun, a community group with drums, dressed up and dancing, a group of Buddhist monks, barefoot and silent, traffic rumbling, sirens, and the constant unintelligible yelling through tinny megaphones ... for a while I watch them passing, reading the banners, one showing a child, dead or dying, bloody in her parent's arms, and slowly through my exhaustion the bewilderment slips into frustration, then irritation and the anger begins to build once again. So tired I breathe it in, letting it seep through my soul, until I can feel it tightening in my fingers, its sharp tingling energy moving down my legs, into my toes, bringing me the strength I need. The friend who's stayed with me reaches down his hand to help me to my feet, "OK?"

I nod, feeling in my heart the weight of those ancestral memories - standing on the shores of Ynys Môn, watching as the first flat bottomed boats pull out towards us, the Roman soldiers moving into the waters with the returning light of day, as if wading into my very soul, and in my mouth I can already taste the slaughter to come. And I am angry.

The bitch is woman as warrior.

One of the most potent and inspiring figures of our heritage is Boudicca, queen of the pre-Roman Iceni tribe of Britain. As *bitch*, she was a powerful force, and wholly justified in the way she used it. After the Roman invasion of Britain under the emperor Claudius, her weak and cowardly husband, Prasutagus, became a tributary for the occupying regime, on his deathbed bequeathing half his territory to Rome, the other half to be shared amongst his daughters; needless to say, the Romans took it all. When Boudicca objected she was publicly flogged, her daughters raped before her eyes.

She didn't bow in defeat. Instead, now head of her tribe, she raised a vast army, inciting most of southeast England into revolt, and, with much of the invading force pushing into Wales, she sacked the Roman towns of London and Colchester. Confronting the all-male brawn of Rome, flaming and glorious in her victory, the tales tell of her making it clear that, although it wasn't uncommon for a woman to rule in Britain, she was fighting not as a leader of her people but as a woman, bruised and angry, a woman whose freedom and honour had been bitterly defiled. The impression she made was sufficient for Roman writers to document her presence and her actions in fine detail, her harsh voice, the golden torc she wore around her neck, her waist-long wild red hair.

The tales tell that the main body of the conquering army returned from the west, all too quickly they vanquished her vast but comparatively disorganised rebellion. Boudicca herself took her own life, the poison chosen in preference to Roman authority. Yet to this day she remains an archetypal figure, an icon of the woman who stands against injustice. She is the woman who defends herself, the one who steps forward out of the crowd, willing to fight. She is the single parent, the suppressed wife, the worker facing prejudice or inequality, the woman abused or unable to stomach the abuse she is witnessing, the one who speaks up.

Sometimes she holds her dignity, sometimes she just kicks someone's head in.

Though it may not be unusual, physical violence it is seldom the easiest, most effective or efficient way of communicating in mainstream modern Western culture. The bitch who is serenely in control of her energy doesn't now take up the axe and cudgel to get what she wants. She will, nevertheless, use her personal strengths without hesitation, from rhetoric to intellect, grace to sexuality.

Using our bodies

The woman who uses sexual enchantment to entice someone into a particular action is consistently viewed as unscrupulous. It's considered doubtful whether she could ever be trusted. Whether sweetly subtle or blatantly overt, sexual manipulation can be so utterly irresistible to the average human male, it could be said that using it is on every occasion wholly unjust. For the bitch who knows how, it is the easiest and most brutal weapon. It's a skill she shares with the whore, but the whore's goal is all pleasure; for the bitch, the purpose is quite a different kind of satisfaction.

Would you use sex to get what you want?

It's a question often asked in circles where ambition is an

integral part of the lifestyle. Some women defend their right to use their sexuality by declaring that they are simply using their strengths and resources, their best qualities. Feminists have riled at women who they see flaunting their gender's assets to achieve their aims, declaring it to be degrading, but far more women see it simply as a true expression of very real and very female power. There isn't really a moral difference between fighting with the wit of your intellect or the curve of your breasts, for both tacks can be obvious, both can be deceptive. The intellect may deploy the craft of reason, but not necessarily with wisdom, compassion or understanding. Sex is a more potent force, triggering deeper reactions, and as such it can be the more effective lever. Used unethically, it can cause the greater damage.

Regarding the whore, those who feel sex is dirty consider those who use it to be dirty too; if the purpose is pleasure, then there is a moral highground some might stride up onto to dismiss the senseless vulgarity of her Bacchanalian lack of inhibition, and so hold her sexual expression as unacceptable. The bitch, however, is a very different exposition of sexuality. Because she doesn't allow anyone close, recoiling from intimacy, the bitch is more likely to play someone along than fulfil the suggested promise of touch. Because the bitch's sexuality is more obviously manipulation, it is rejected as unacceptable on the grounds of being sly. If she lowers her eyelids, bats her lashes, moving with an acute awareness of her effect on the audience, it's because she's looking for the power to take something or someone apart at the seams.

Where her pheromones are glowing too, the bitch's game is intensified. It barely matters what she looks like; nature is doing its job, the goddess of lust playing her lyre, whispering delicious scents and intimations into the breeze. But that goddess is hard to bid leave. Winding someone up and not following through can be dangerous; if her ploy is not justified, not honourable, if she is fighting for selfish needs and not common justice, if she got into trouble we might shrug and say she had it coming.

However, if *bitch* has beauty on her side instead, she is more likely to maintain her control. Indeed, some swear that a woman's beauty is the most potent force in the world. Beauty sells success. It sells cars, cat food, chocolate: anything at all. The beauty of the bride sells us a vision of her future happiness. A beautiful woman, they say, can *literally* get away with murder. Beautiful women, it is imagined, don't need to try; they glide through life quite unaware of the normal frustrations and struggle, the world at their command.

If a woman is both beautiful and intelligent, she is immediately proclaimed dangerous: she has all that she needs to be the perfect bitch.

Yet physical beauty, like any power of nature, is not easy to tame. It is a part of nature's wild heart, devoid of justice and compassion. In talking to women for this book, the really beautiful women all told me that their looks were far from helpful in finding or sustaining intimate relationships. Indeed, often their appearance made it much harder, for beauty acts like a double perimeter fence around the soul, keeping people at a distance. Usually when we communicate with someone, naturally we look into their eyes, but with a beautiful woman it is hard not to look *at* her rather than engage with her. Our behaviour may be subconscious but those tiny movements are felt. Beauty provokes awe which can leave a woman isolated.

Unless a man's confidence is sufficiently boosted by his own good looks, wealth or talent, he is likely to feel uncertain about being close to a beautiful woman; why would she be interested in an ordinary man? Most men find it hard to trust a beautiful woman; knowing that she is wanted by so many others, it can be difficult to believe that she won't take up another offer that's at hand. The need to compete for her attention or commitment never seems to go away. It is altogether safer, easier, less effort, to commit to a woman who is plain. For the beautiful woman, it too often becomes clear that people are with her only because of her looks. She is a trinket, a trophy, as friend or lover. As a result, she herself finds it hard to trust that anyone's feelings or motivation are any deeper. A beautiful woman can struggle to believe she is liked or loved.

While some beautiful women manage to kick away the pedestal, some continue to live with the distance that has naturally developed along with their beauty. For some, that lack of trust and connection inspires the bitch within: she makes it official, setting sleek diamond-collared Dobermans on patrol between the double fence that surrounds her soul. She uses her beauty to manipulate, distance and control.

Further, being beautiful can be dangerous. For some women, their beauty has brought nothing but pain and abuse, from dishonesty to rape, the mere glimpse of appreciation triggering fear in her soul. Some respond by going to great lengths to disguise or destroy that beauty, with funereal make up and shapeless clothes, with drugs and self-harming, by not eating and, emaciated, becoming utterly asexual. Because there *are* some advantages to being beautiful, if you have it and complain about it, or lose it on purpose, the response is incomprehension, bewilderment, resentment. To those who can only witness it in others, beauty's power is intoxicating. It seems sacrilegious self-sabotage to throw it away. But when a woman has been hurt by it, it is easy to see why she might choose to discard it, ignore it, or let it become a weapon of the bitch inside.

Relying on it, however, can be desperately stressful. The beautiful woman has a great deal to lose, and losing it is inevitable. The power of beauty is advertised everywhere we look, together with all we might need to enhance our own, to reach up and capture or hold onto a little for ourselves. With coloured pastes, creams and powders, we change the texture, light and hues of our skin and hair; with the trickeries of modern fabrics and corsets, we pull in this bit of flesh and push out that, changing the shapes of our bodies when dressed; with the possibilities of plastic surgery, we change who we are naked. Concealing the flaws of our genes and age, we can be gloriously creative in who we present ourselves to be, and we can be wholly deceitful. If our beauty depends upon the paint and clothes we're wearing, when we take off the glamour we remove the power that beauty brings. We can't afford to let anyone get close. Indeed, we can destroy our lives trying to grasp it, desperate to be touched by it, and losing in the process the treasure of our own soul.

Hating our bodies

Too many women talk about sex as the excruciating nightmare that requires them to reveal their naked bodies. Some women won't undress or make love but in complete darkness, simply because they are too embarrassed, too scared of rejection and humiliation, even when their partner has clearly expressed a sincere love and acceptance of all they are. Bellies sag and breasts loll, deep wrinkles and cellulite crimple our skin, muscles gently softening as our bodies change over time, and with every new day the shame and insecurity deepen. *We aren't perfect and that's not good enough*: what a tragic paradigm to live with.

It's an issue for which the bitch has her own sturdy soap box. That there are women in our culture for whom life is unbearable, their freedom completely disabled by a desperate crisis of body image, is an idea so riddled with bewildering injustice that the bitch couldn't possibly disregard it.

Most heterosexual men and lesbian women like female curves. Every one I spoke to for this book expressed real appreciation of the soft lines of a woman's body, each one dismissing the fashion model as bony and plastic, unripe and ungiving. The glamour or porn model on the other extreme may be sexually alluring to male fantasy, but she is no closer to the average female form, with breasts too big for her thighs and belly. In films we are increasingly offered images of more ordinarily shaped women, yet these don't help our self-esteem: the actress is simply a woman paid to reveal her dreadful flaws terribly publicly.

It doesn't matter what we look like. The statement is like that other pacifying deceit, 'It will be alright'. It may turn out fine, whatever *it* may be, but nature is not fair and there is always a chance that the situation will get worse. We may assert that what counts is not what we look like but how we feel, but our society does tend to favour the beautiful. Nature is merciless. There is nevertheless real value in addressing the complex tangle that perverts our perspective, of both ourselves and others. It shouldn't matter *what* we look like, but it always matters what we *feel* we look like. For every woman lives through times when she feels herself to be horrendously overweight and unattractive. When such feelings provoke the bitch within us, we use our negative body image to manipulate, distance and control those around us. We use it to maintain the closed integrity of our soul sanctuary, isolated and safe from hurt.

The origin of our self-negation may be a fundamental paradigm about life, sourced in a moment that loiters persistently and maliciously in our memory. As a youngster, a dismissive comment may have landed a machete blow to the waking awareness of self. A critical observation can devastate a pubescent girl as she starts to perceive herself as a sexual being. The heart-breaking collapse of a relationship can leave us vulnerable and open to believe those caustic denunciations hurled in anguish and defensive aggression. However beautiful we do look, however often we are told, there can be a part of us that simply can't accept it to be true.

For a good many women that body self-negation happens for a week or more in every month. With the water retention of PMS bloating bellies and thighs, the extra grease and sweat that comes with menstruation's raised body temperatures, the tiredness of riding those hormonal high seas, it's hard to see ourselves as anything but a shabby wreck. After a day of aching, blood and tears, we slump into the ragged soft folds of our body. We're meant to look pretty, but we feel like shit. The bitch shrugs, and kicking her shoes across the room, in baggy clothes and no make up, she curls up on the sofa with the tub of chocolate chip.

If she has no responsibilities beyond herself, that she closes down her willingness to engage with the world is no doubt sensible, allowing her recovery time, ideally in rest, solitude, and self-reflection. But often we don't have that luxury: barely coping, we kick others away in our need for space and quiet, the goddess of reaction spitting her sacred energy through our soul, causing us to express ourselves in resentful and angry self-protection. Such bitchy behaviour is unkind and, in the long run, usually completely unhelpful.

When this is how we live, we need to address the problems, rationally making changes to ensure that our life is tenable, nourishing and worthwhile. However, there is seldom a need to slip into mother-giving or compromise ourselves just because we really should be *nice*. Where *bitch* is itching to scream inside us, she is unlikely to be pacified by a little distraction. Kept tied and gagged deep inside, she quietly drains energy from everything that we do. Like creeping buttercup or bindweed, she spreads in the ground beneath our awareness, sending out roots and runners, always seeking opportunities for a snide remark or bitter retort.

Yet in the bitch there is such rich creative energy. When she is given space to express herself, she fuels exquisite responses. Because she plays with reaction, bitch is a wonderfully provocative energy to ride when we are considering the creativity of how we present ourselves. When we cast off social expectations about body shape and style, and begin to present ourselves as we would like to, we find a confidence that allows us to ignore the plastic perfection we've been struggling and failing to emulate for so long. I don't underestimate the weight of pressure that we may feel to conform. It can be hard to break away from what is expected. However, if we don't, we are not only colluding, but also reinforcing the pressure on ourselves and exerting it on others. But step by little step, with a pair of red shoes, a dark purple lipstick, a flood of magenta silk, we start to find our freedom.

We're in that place, standing a foot from the bed, having made our way through the house, shedding clothes along the way, barely able to go a moment before our lips are drawn together again, drinking in the passion of our lust. I push the shirt unbuttoned from his shoulders, so it slips to the floor, and as he lifts my arms to pull the t-shirt over my head, I feel a part of me tense. Though I breathe softly, hiding it as best I can, for a split second I am no longer the pliable sensuous lover; I am ready to break him.

His eyes register surprise, and he breathes in deep, swearing under his breath, and when his mouth comes to mine again it is with a passion more uninhibited than before, an urgency that makes me smile deep inside, as his fingers move up to explore the soft downy hairs under my arms, followed by his mouth as he breathes me in and bites. My barriers soften, then fall to the floor.

Since the time I found myself on the edge of the Japanese porn industry, the models allowed no body hair whatsoever, the most popular girls looking distinctly prepubescent, I've felt uncomfortable about removing mine: the soft hairs feel to me a glorious sign of sexual maturity. They allow a sensitivity to touch that is delicious. They hold the scent of the wild wind, of lust and love. When a girl starts to shave her legs at the age of eleven, it is with a desperation to be acknowledged as growing up, yet in doing so she is denuding herself of one of the keys of that process.

In our culture, the unshaven women is perceived to be the perfect hag. Indeed, altering our bodies in any way to conform to the demands of a society's fashion is, to the hag-bitch, sickeningly tedious.

Being creative with our bodies out of personal choice is quite different. Waxing our pubic hair into shapes, shaving our heads into patterns, dying, cutting, piercing, tattooing, are all expressions of creativity that lie deep within our heritage and the ancient traditions of our people. The word 'Britain' is said to derive from the name given to the ancient inhabitants of these islands, the Pretanni, or painted people. Most famously our ancestors decorated their bodies with woad, certainly for battle but no doubt for many other reasons, not least the free expression of individual identity.

To the bitch, this personal creativity is a powerful expression of truth. Just as she will adapt the colours and textures of her sanctuary boundary to get what she wants, she will explore the possibilities of free expression, discarding the constraints, and present herself according to her own rules.

When the bitch cares, with that creativity comes a more acute awareness of our health. We realise how much cleaner, clearer, brighter we can be, and that independent reactive energy propels us to act, making changes in order to improve what we've got. At its simplest, a good kick of confident self-expression can radically improve our energy, fuelling our motivation and that baseline of self-esteem. And there is nothing more beautiful that the shining of life in someone's eyes. We all have our own unique individuality: the bitch encourages us to show it, to use it, and to the full.

Forging the bitch's trust

Just as the bitch finds her empathy, and caring, through witnessing in another a pain that she can relate to, so does this empathy help to guide her ability to trust. Whether *bitch* is predominant within us, or simply flickers across our consciousness with the occasional emotional reaction, a good deal of our healing (our ability to feel at peace) is achieved through easing this force within us.

Not only will she not share her sanctuary with another, but others are reluctant to get close to her. Her hag-energy is not just that she can explode into unacceptable violence, but that when she has perfect control of her emotion she can be extraordinarily powerful. We know we can't ignore or suppress her; instead, we must learn how to ride her current, finding a sensitivity to the fuel of her emotions and responding in a way that does not assume there is always a threat.

The first step is trusting ourselves - not to fly off the handle and destroy what is before us, not to close down and shut the world out, not to react badly. Awareness of how that goddess moves through us allows us then to see ourselves reflected in others. Slowly, we learn to trust others.

Lesbian relationships can, of course, be as abusive, physically and emotionally, as those between heterosexuals, but where they work one of the crucial and nourishing layers of foundation is a strand of deep empathy that just can't be found between different genders.

Men and women do function differently; to proclaim otherwise has been fashionable, but is clearly delusional, not least in the ways that we seek out trust in order to open our soul sanctuary to share intimacy. Men, except the particularly sensitive, *tend* to secure this through having sex; they need to know that a women will accept them and give fully even when they have exposed the vulnerability of their virility. Women, on the other hand, *tend* to need confirmation of trust *before* they have sex. Whether consciously or not, a woman feels that if he can't manage to control the itch of his lust, it would be folly to trust him to manage or control anything else (his anger, his hunger, his bank account). In each relationship one or the other has to break the deadlock and compromise. Even in our modern, open and free Western culture it is the woman who *tends* to appease the man,

The Bitch

consummating a relationship before she feels comfortable in her trust.

Asking women why we do, the answers were both self-affirming and resigned. While the male soul is so often complicated by a lack of emotional literacy, generally a woman's ability to cope better with the seas of emotion means that she is often more willing to accept emotional uncertainty, at least in the immediacy of decision-making. She may tire of it, crying out for the stability of commitment, but her initial strength allows her to step forward without trust before her partner. It's easy to see how this is evolutionarily useful, albeit hard to live with.

Talking to women about same-sex relationships, it was an issue that came up again and again.

Research into mammal behaviour suggests that, while homosexuality is a perpetual undercurrent in most species, a group's acceptance of it rises significantly where there is overpopulation, naturally stabilising viable numbers. In our crowded world, such growing acceptance (and the fanatics' fearful opposition to it) is certainly evident within many human cultures today. Where homosexuality is the inherent drive, the individual following her natural desires, there is no moral justification for declaring it unacceptable.

However, as it becomes more acceptable, an increasing number of women are finding it emotionally and socially possible to explore same-sex relationships. They may have felt the occasional glimmer of attraction for another woman, but have spent their lives walking the more conventional and expected path of heterosexual relationships, perhaps even marriage with children. Hurt, again and again, tired of perpetually misunderstanding and being misunderstood, for some women there comes a point where the idea of entangling themselves in the complications of the male psyche, with its penetrative sexuality, loses its appeal completely.

In that she is riding a current of reaction, here is a little of the

195

bitch. She may be angry and hurt, and so closed herself to the possibility of further danger, but as ever there is a source of energy and creativity offered by this goddess. With awareness, it is that sacred force of reaction that can provide the momentum and courage to take a new direction.

Breaking through such barricades in terms of sexuality has far-reaching effects; for, more often than not, a woman finds depths of creativity within herself which, until then, she has felt hidden or beyond her reach. She strides into new landscapes, experiencing both the strength and vulnerability that comes with exploring and expressing the unconventional and idiosyncratic sides of her nature. She catches a broader sense of personal freedom and grasps the courage to use it.

For the woman whose sanctuary has been closed by life's crises and pain, same sex relationships can be a beautiful way of making intimate connections that don't penetrate so roughly. Such relationships can teach trust, healing wounds of old battle grounds, allowing the bitch to dismantle the tensions and complications of her life in order to find a clear sweet path ahead.

"Do you know what I love about being with you?"

She bends her head and licks slowly the dark circle of my areola, looking up with a wide and beautiful smile, "What's that?"

I whisper, "It's like making love to myself, only ... "

"I know," she murmurs, and we gaze at each other, seeing ourselves in reflection in the silk-muted lamplight. I lift a lock of hair, moving it from her face, my fingertips touching the line of her cheek, then slipping down slowly to the curve of her breast; I hold its weight, moving my thumb back and forth across the nipple, in a long sensuous moment of effortless quiet. Her face glows with pleasure and I close my eyes to hover on its intensity, wings softly spread out upon the thermal. She breathes in. And suddenly we're tumbling again, down into the flood of craving, mouth to mouth, entangled in this fluent sweet scented moment. And into that kiss, like every other, every detail of our lives, our loving and crying, is somehow confided. All that we are we've always shared: nothing needs to be explained.

And when we lie back, our hands clasped together in that deep bond of friendship, and I'm gazing through the open window, moonshine painting light and shadow on the maple leaves, I wonder how I ever manage to make relationships with men. The fissure between the sexes seems suddenly too wide to bridge. Whatever could I know about being a man, about what a man could want or feel? Vague memories of trust spanning the divide, the thrill of the journey, glint somewhere in my mind, but the warmth of her body beside me is gently scrambling my thoughts. She squeezes my hand and sighs, wandering through her own dreamy thinking, and I turn towards her, the intense softness of her thigh sliding across mine, the warmth of skin on skin filling my mind.

Above me, she moves slowly so that her nipples tickle my breasts, the heat of her vulva on mine spreading through me, and I'm lost in this fusion of gentleness and lust. Her hair falls forward onto my shoulder and I lift it from her face, her beautiful face, aware of my own breathing, the rise and fall of my chest, and I run my fingertip along the lines that radiate from her eyes, the journeys of her life etched by laughter and pain. And she smiles, watching me, her mouth slightly open. My heart aches with the tenderness of this moment so full of love, empathy, silence. And she leans down as passion breaks over us in another moonlit wave.

CHAPTER SEVEN

The Witch

It's not that she's a good-looking woman. There's just something about her that makes everybody stare: baskets in gloved hands and coats buttoned high, each soul's gaze is drawn towards her, following her every move as, with inexorable poise, she glides in and walks straight to the front of the queue.

Serene in her purpose, as if directing a play from stage-front without the knowledge of the audience, she lays her hands softly on the counter and for a moment holds the hush that has followed her in. Then she smiles, and addresses the young fellow who, despite the momentary quiet, has not yet found the words he would need to object.

She isn't disregarding the other women, patiently waiting as they do in their dishevelled but clearly ordered line; far from it. She radiates an imperious calm that, I begin to see, is a silent communication with each and every one of them.

Nobody says a word. Yet they aren't quiet in order to overhear her conversation, which, for some odd reason, is neither low nor clearly audible; it is simply that they are, for a moment, overwhelmed. Enchanted.

Nor are her clothes so remarkable, but for an idiosyncratically tilted hat. She carries no bag, seeming to hold all she needs in the pockets of her coat and the certainty of her voice. I can't help but notice her fingers though, which seem implausibly long, pointing, pondering, always directing.

When, her business complete, she turns, she smiles. It's a smile that says simply, *well, I've done what I had to do.* What the waiting women do next is obviously, to her, of absolutely no concern. And she disappears through the doorway, leaving the crowded little shop suddenly strangely empty. I find myself breathing in, as if to catch the drift of a scent that I sense she has left in the air.

Then the chatter begins in a hasty surge of noise, as each woman adds her clattering pennyworth into the communal tin of outrage, wonder and indignation.

Wicked witch, white witch

It is a fabulous word. Without the 'b' bite of *bitch*, the negativity that seems to saturate it is even more insipid; indeed, the 'w' seems to hold an inherent implication of misguidance, a directive whisper of bedevilment, a surreptitious undercurrent that seeps out, threatening to bring with it only rank misfortune.

It's a perfect insult: to call a woman a witch is to accuse her of being thoroughly dishonest, disloyal, a troublemaker and dishonourable in her every action. She is deceptive, untrustworthy. The witch, we are brought up to believe, is a woman without empathy or compassion. She uses her innate and honed powers for manipulation, for malevolence, free from the normal constraints of human conscience. She glowers out from the pages of children's stories, isolated and alone, threateningly ugly, deformed in her wickedness, a caricature of all that is deemed wholly unacceptable in womankind.

Where Western culture is still hung upon the framework of monotheistic perspectives, the word sketches a woman who clearly has no relationship with God, and as a result she has lost touch with decency, with Truth. Where secularism is the stronger force, the witch is as much the outsider, for she has rejected the looming singular vision of Reason, of all that is asserted to be just, right and true. Dismissing patriarchal authority, with its social bindings of paternal control, like every other aspect of the dark goddess the witch is lawless in her freedom, living according to her own rules; and for it she is feared and despised without restriction.

The claim that nine million women were accused of witchcraft in late medieval Europe, to be unjustly tried and executed, is thankfully now accepted by most to be nonsense. The myth was propagated in the second half of the last century, alongside the feminist assertion that all the world's ills are caused by men and their innate distrust and hatred of women. Many thousands were brutally murdered, particularly around the turn of the seventeenth century, but this was not about men slaughtering innocent women, whether they were witches or not. The provocation was the fear of difference, the xenophobic intolerance of anyone who did not toe the line through an era when long-held fundamental assumptions about nature were beginning to slip into doubt. Jews, gypsies, visionaries, innovators, healers, scientists, heretics and individualists, the disabled, the unfamiliar: these were the people killed by the forces of authority. They were individuals who had knowledge, understanding, ideas, or an appearance or instinctive wisdom that lay somehow outside the norm, who expressed their truth and lived in their own way, beyond the bounds of convention.

Certainly women were killed. In the historical records of the trials, there can be found confessions made by women deranged by terror and torture, documented in the most glorious contemporary language of diabolic infatuation. Yet, the feminist proponents of the mythic persecution claimed those accused of witchcraft and murdered by the various bodies of the Inquisition were not the wild seers of seething magical ecstasy. They were the kind of witch that so many in twentieth and twenty first century Western culture aspire to be: the altruistic devotees of a loving goddess whose care holds a community. Nurturing their intuitive connections with the natural world, retaining an inner peace where others have lost their souls to the rapacious speed of industrial progress and civilisation, this romantic image of the witch is of a spiritual healer, a woman who knows the medicines and poisons of herbal lore, who can read the weather, the wind, the tides of growth and decay, who helps with the birthing and dying of those in her care. For the mythic witch of medieval society, such wisdom was both intuitive and had been handed down by word of mouth, mother to daughter, through countless generations, perpetuating the vision of a natural divinity. Inevitably and brutally she suffered at the hands of the Inquisition because her goddess was not acceptable to the male monotheist authority; as the religions of one-god spread, their intolerance, like a harsh bleach-washed brush, had swept the old tradition of women's magic into the shadows.

In terms of historical accuracy, this is as idealised and unhelpful as that which attributes fact to the myth of an ancient golden age of matriarchal peace and abundance. In reality, the witches of our heritage were a mix of sorcerers and cunning folk, using astrology, tools of divination and suggestion, heightened intuition, sensitivity and perception, with not a little trickery and deception where necessary, their main aim being simply to make an honest or dishonest living. They would tell fortunes, some working to ease the soul of the one paying, while others benefited only themselves, threatening evil where they were not paid to prevent it. Dependence upon herbs, potions, icons and charms made them unpopular with the church, and where their skills provoked disquiet or disharmony a neighbour's accusation of witchcraft provided the possibility that the authorities would remove them. Indeed, historians point out that often it was other women who came together, then as now, against the one they felt to be the troublemaker, the one who was upsetting the carefully balanced apple cart.

Sometimes, of course, what alienates an individual, stopping them from following a conventional path in life, is an acute sensitivity or instability, and it may be that some of those accused of witchcraft had what would now be diagnosed as mental illness: the madness of a psychopathic or a sociopathic disorder, for example, or schizophrenia, or manic depression. Some of these are chemical imbalances that horribly cripple us, but some are caused or not helped by the society within which we live: when the soul is awash with visions, when we are acutely sensitive to the energies and intentions that surround us, when we hear voices, sense the presence of the dead or departed, when we have premonitions of the future, and the culture has no language that explains or supports what is happening, it is easy to descend into isolating madness. It is more likely to have been women like these who found themselves labelled as witches and, indicted through a community's fear, became victims of the Inquisition.

Perhaps I am too harsh in the picture I paint. Some would object to my words, with the assured assertion that 'real' witches have indeed been persecuted throughout the last millennium and before; but what is a *real* witch? The question is not one for which I am seeking a definitive answer in these pages.

Witchcraft is one of the core traditions of modern Western Paganism and the one that attracts the largest numbers. Those who now identify themselves as witches claim this potent word as one rich with both mystery and positivity. Expressed as an ageless, beautiful and intuitive religion, its focus is the magical power of nature, and in particular (for many) the power of woman as mother, healer and lover. Like any other Pagan tradition, it draws seekers of all genders, each soul questing understanding of these powers, within both themselves and the world around them.

The word is increasingly synonymous with Wicca. Largely crafted in the mid twentieth century, drawing on aspects of occultism and mysticism, Classical and other Mediterranean Paganisms, together with more local myth, poetry and folklore, Wicca has tended to be a more formal and structured religion than old witchcraft. With a disciplined training system, its rites include written prayers and invocations, various consecrated tools and rules of behaviour. For many it is a dualist religion, honouring a mother goddess and her consort, these two principal powers creating the world in perpetual cycles, represented within a temple group or coven by the high priestess and her devoted priest. The distinction between Wicca and witchcraft used to be stronger, but over the past decade, particularly in North America, modern witches are using the term Wicca, in some cases to dissociate themselves from the problems that still hum like flies around *witch*. Indeed, Wiccans are also using the term witch, often to discard the more directive formality and embrace the wilder connotations offered by the older word.

Over the past fifteen years, this once hidden religion has stepped out of the shadows, stretching in the light. As a result it has become an even more eclectic mix of ideas and practice. In the process, it has also been besieged by a flood of popular interest; television programmes such as *Buffy the Vampire Slayer*, various teen movies, and even the archetypally English magical hero, *Harry Potter*, have all drawn youngsters in. Countless websites give implausible histories of the tradition, and definitions that sparkle with stardust and secrecy, interspersed with recipes for scented bath oils and love potions. There are dozens of books available now, providing spells for success in love, giving ingredients for incense and herbal tea, and tips on how to *magic up* your life (wear black, buy a cat). For a while, witchcraft became an adolescent fashion, spawning teenagers in black velvet with kohled eyes, dripping with silver pentagrams and talking about the Goddess.

As we head towards the end of the first decade of this millennium, witchcraft is just starting to shed this awful reputation given it by the glossy commercialism that so eagerly ran alongside in order to make money; business and fashion are thankfully fickle. For the serious student of the old tradition, the replacement of connotations of evil and scandal with those of plastic and glitter was not progress. As a result, for those modern Wiccans and witches keen to present their tradition as entirely positive, there is still work to do. The term 'white witch' can now and then be read in the media, but only where the journalist is ill-informed or ignorant. People within the tradition never use it, for it does not describe some acceptable antithesis of the evil witch practising black magic; historically the words only imply that the witch's inherent darkness has been superficially whitewashed over.

Using neither paint nor gloss, many expend a great deal of energy transforming the word witch into something acceptable, emphasising the tradition's spiritual focus on healing and personal development, self-reflection and the exploration of human nature. In some quarters, the idea of gods and spirits is explained using the language of myth and Jungian psychology, ensuring there is no mistaking the practitioner for a primitive polytheist.

Yet, it is that apparently definitive wickedness that, for the purposes of this book, is so fascinating.

The heart of witchery

Acknowledging that the practice of Wicca and witchcraft is now a modern interpretation, drawing in a good deal from other Paganisms and present-day culture, including a focus on environ-mental and social ethics, I would here like to set it aside. In the remainder of this chapter then, by *witch* what I shall be referring to is not the twenty first century practitioner exploring her own understanding and celebrating her own spirituality. My witch, instead, will be the essential archetype of *witch*, only a part of which feeds into modern witchcraft - how much or how little depending entirely upon the individual.

Witchcraft has, after all, been an integral part of human culture for many thousands of years, all over the world. Its definitions are varied: the gentle, altruistic and responsible healer promoted in an attempt to sanitise and civilise the face of the tradition in Western society is no more than an occasional and flickering part of it.

Where nature is understood not only to be sacred but as the source of wisdom and order, any nature-based Pagan will reach to those forces that are battering and shaping her world. In some traditions the desire is simply to comprehend the patterns, the tides and cycles; where she can make out nature's currents and intentions, she has the opportunity to adapt in order to live with efficacy, with sufficiency, with peace. In witchcraft the desire is a little different: rather than adapting, the witch seeks to provoke or cause a specific change in nature, one that she believes will make life better - for herself or others.

Modern science does just the same thing. Studying in order to grasp understanding, the scientist justifies his action with reason, laying out his proofs with a guise of objectivity, asserting that what he does is wholly rational. Shifting the course of nature in each distinct field from medicine to meteorology, individuals craft ways which they assert will improve human life - their own or others.

When modern science was in its infancy, through the sixteenth and seventeenth centuries, the distinctions between magic, religion and science were blurred; it took powerful characters like Francis Bacon to push the current towards the latter and invest it with the power of authority. Needless to say, since that shift, where a knowledge base or worldview differs from the determined perspective of accepted science, any work that seeks to describe, to direct or alter nature is seen as dangerously invalid. Whether in jest or not, such work is at times declared to be witchcraft, implying a lack of academic form and delusory ideas. Indeed, scientists weren't the first to denounce those whose worldview they disliked. Before this new science, it was the church or some other authority that decreed whether such work was acceptable, useful, safe, valid, worthwhile, or not. Throughout our history, great strides in human understanding have been sidelined or lost because the religious or philosophical context was not deemed acceptable.

Equally, though the witch may be using the biochemistry of herbs and minerals, or the power of thought, suggestion and intention, and other tools of psychology, without scientific proofs or academia's self-referential framework, her work is judged to be irrational, subjective and so of no value. What the witch does that provokes disquiet is not her desire or her ability to create change, but that she does so without the benediction of the authority that is rational law - nor does she seek it. When she succeeds, under scrutiny her achievement is often wholly incomprehensible. She works magic.

Magic: a simple definition is the act of creating change by the force of one's own will. An adept in the craft may enhance that to include the ability to harness the powers of nature in order to manifest some change; such ideas tend to be seen as alchemical and occultic, somewhat outside the bounds of modern Paganism, the word now spelled with a *k* as magick. However, as a simple foundation it is this ingenuity of creativity that is at the heart of old witchcraft.

Most Pagan religious traditions are not all *nice*. Waking the soul to the power of nature reveals to us how fragile our own existence is, showing us how much life itself teeters on a knife edge of viability. Perceiving nature's implausibility, the witch is inspired to believe that anything is possible. If she is to practise her magic, such an attitude is essential.

Acknowledging the darkness, most Pagan and animistic traditions accept how dirty, muddy, scary and bloody difficult life can be. I recall the amazement I felt when I began to study Druidry, finding places where I could feel the power of nature seething, singing, roaring, where I could touch that power and feel it within myself. It made me acknowledge beyond doubt that there is no justice in nature. Indeed, nature is merciless a good deal more often than embracing. To the witch, this power is not just a source of wonder; it is a wellspring that she dips into in order to find her own.

Furthermore, where belief in a single creator god is not a part of the picture, what allows life is the web of connections, intention touching intention, relationships touching relationships, each flow affecting and influenced by numerous others, inspiring, providing opportunities, shifting and changing, giving, taking, receiving: each part of nature constantly involved in the perpetual movement of creation. The witch is acutely aware that she is a part of that web of life; with every thought and word, with the slightest action, she is making a difference. Even when she is not aware of her intentions, assumptions and beliefs, what she creates will be fuelled by those energies. So is the art and the craft of magic the ability to create with the poignancy and potency of total consciousness. Where the witch has powers beyond normal understanding, it is because she uses her consciousness to make happen what she wishes to happen.

She is the perfect hag: she gets what she wants.

The witch and the wanting

Like any aspect of the hag, the witch is a part of woman's nature. The average woman won't light incense and chant spells in order to change the weather, but where she sees something could or should be changed, she feels that tug inside, and before long she is drawing upon her resources to manifest the necessary changes. Indeed, the woman who finds herself unable to let things be, who is irrepressibly involved and often naturally skilled at stepping in and sorting out a situation to her own satisfaction, is tapping into the witch within her soul. Whether with subtlety or overtly she uses reason and emotion freely and as appropriate to her cause, manipulating relationships, adjusting attitudes, until the job is done.

As a fundamental part of female nature, it is exquisitely useful to explore this side of who and how we are. Once again, the Pagan way is to understand those currents of nature that affect us so that we can live honourably, respectfully and responsibly, instead of allowing them to flood through us, overwhelming sense and taking us over. When it comes to the witch, the force of nature she rides is in many ways simply the power of creativity, yet as that broad energy is inspired within us what the witch does is take control. It may not be fear or anger that provokes her so finely to manage a situation; most importantly for the witch, it is the desire to ensure that what happens is exactly what she wants to happen. Infused and enthused by this energy, in simple terms, she is the control freak that resides within us all.

The bitch knows what it is she does not want. Given the slightest opportunity, she is more than willing to use all her wit and resources to destroy or remove it. She screams and rages, manipulates, gossiping venom and disregard; she tears up what is wrong to find a freedom beyond threat within the bounds and surrounds of her own precious sanctuary. The witch is equally concerned with change, but she is busy carefully controlling the creation of what it is that she *does* want.

As children, some girls have a natural ability to bewitch, to lay shimmering moments like spells upon a situation, turning it around so that it lies within their favour. Storming with rage, her soul filled with desire for a particular this or that, stamping her feet in indignation, she may learn how to force others to do as she wishes, but here she is flooded with that dark goddess of control. It is only when such a child does it without anyone noticing, with silence and sleight of hand, that she is finding the scents and sense of her *witch* within. It is a skill that is often admired as intelligence and wit in a very young girl, but soon such actions are slammed as deceitful, as manipulative and dishonest. Once she starts to menstruate, such behaviour is declared wholly undesirable. She is directed to be open about her intentions, to lay herself bare in what is dubbed honesty, selfless and responsible consideration. The dark places of her nature, she learns, are out of bounds and best ignored.

This imposed fear is enough to cause some girls to discard the witch's skill; if the social feedback from her actions is always negative, she may let go of the ability, convinced that it always wrong to use it. Other girls never lose the talent to take control, creating space in which they can express their soul's rich creativity, even (perhaps, especially) in the most unaccommodating and difficult situations. As women, we may use the powers of the virgin, whore, mother, bitch, each aspect of our nature engaging in a different way, but it is the witch of our being who explores what we want, and manifests that reality where there seems no hope. Where she has skill, she does so without yelling demands, without any sign of trade or bribery, achieving her goal with subtlety and apparent simplicity. The clever witch knows that the less others realise what she is doing, the more she can get away with guiding a situation entirely towards her own advantage.

Yet, just as the bitch can cause mass destruction, her emotional energy uncontrolled, anger ricocheting like bullets off plate metal, as she tears down the whole house to find her freedom in one room, and just as the mother can smother with all her caring, holding her charge without allowing it to breathe or grow, so can the witch create devastation.

First, if she is deranged by some dreadful experience, some kick that has left her stumbling with bitter revenge or delusion, it need not mean that her power to manifest is compromised. The witch who is working with hate can wreak apocalyptic havoc. Without compassion or consideration sufficient to make her think twice, controlling a situation with precision and conviction, the witch can be as dangerous as the fairytales relate.

Secondly, she knows what she wants. Or rather, she *thinks* she knows what she wants.

Although most who are taught the tools of magic in witchcraft and Wicca never quite grasp it sufficiently to be effective, there are usually moments when the power seems to flow from their fingertips like ethereal liquid electricity, intention sliding seamlessly into sweet manifestation. The same happens to folk playing with New Age healing, empowerment ideas, change management or politics, or simply the energy of wishes and dreams. Sometimes it really works, and it can be alarming and exhilarating, leaving a deep warmth of satisfaction and sense of real personal power. Yet, so often, after it has worked, when we have before us what it was that we so deeply wished for, we realise we didn't really want it at all. And sometimes what we've manifested isn't so easy to throw away.

How *do* we know what we really want? It is one of the hardest questions we face in life. Evolution has been taking the human soul from a focus on the past, on experience and memory, into the ability to conceive the future, to abstract ideas, imagination and innovation. Though we may have no end of grand ideas and dreams, when it comes to working out what will actually nourish us, as a species we are still not that accomplished.

If our ability to perceive for ourselves is flawed, when it comes to seeing for others our vision can be even worse. We may feel sure what someone else needs or wants, but most of us have experienced and witnessed when that goes dreadfully wrong. If the other knows of our wish to help, we are dependent on them communicating their needs with perfect clarity; if they don't know, all too often we are juggling with assumptions, too often based upon our own projected needs, our own fears and desires. For the witch conscious of what she is doing, the ethics of her magic become horribly tangled; seldom is there the certainty of irrefutable consent. If things were left to develop upon their own sweet course, the result would be an expression of every influence on a situation, but the witch forces the issue, ensuring that *her* influence is the strongest, and consequently what is created may be out of synch with its environment. Where dramatic change is necessary, that may be a perfect outcome; where it isn't, the result can produce friction, causing more pain and confusion than the pleasure that was so hoped for.

If she happens to be an exceptional woman, with a wit and wisdom that allows her to perceive the widest scope of potential ramifications, reactions, consequences, it is possible that she will look around at what she has guided into being, without having made a mistake or three. If she is lucky, and her wisdom extends a little further, she might know what next she might do. This is the witch that knows her power and just how best to place it. She can be a *wonder*fully powerful and positive force within us, shining in her own presence and clarity, glorious in her creativity, with a poignant sense of responsibility both to herself and to the world around her.

Most of us, however, aren't that exceptional. Life's potholes, thunderstorms and mad drivers have made the road bumpy and the driving hard, and though we've learned from some crises there are others that have left us both scarred and afraid, all too willing to be blinkered and selectively deaf. We forget to consider all that will be affected by what we create. We forget to look inside ourselves as well as around us. Where the dark goddess of control is tugging at our soul, her current calling us to stride in and affect some change, the result can be a blend of complicating and desolating disrespect.

For many, however, the witch is not so active. She is a part of us that, like the old hags of persecution tales, spends her time in the darkness of hiding. Pushed down with suppression, or even further into denial, the clues to her existence flicker as the shuddering resentment and resignation that lie within the soul: the weight of never having crafted the opportunity to have, do or be what we really want. Such feelings can soak deep into our adult mentality, limiting the reach of our lives, our creativity, and even our dreams. Cowering or sulking, a witch suppressed is seldom seen but in anger, when she explodes with bitterness, often clumsily forcing the change she desires. Biding her time in the shadows, she waits for a moment which may only exist in her dreams, all that power of control, its sharp edges and desires, being used not for creativity but to stall the flow.

Acknowledging these forces of nature within and around us, there is seldom any value in laying culpability for our lack of creative expression upon someone or something else. For most women, admitting what it is that we really want provokes the unendurable pain of not achieving it; far easier, then, if we were simply to continue in the blur of not acknowledging our desire. After all, the idea that we could achieve it lies somewhere beyond the barbed wire and mined fields of potential failure, and that is a journey that is obviously much safer to avoid. Failure is too dangerous a risk to take; it is ever too closely allied with annihilating rejection.

The women who do find a way through the mines are often felt to be a threat to those who don't. The witch, as a woman who grasps her dream, is often one who must also learn how to avoid the vicious rage of bitching snipers. She must know how to stay centred and focused on her goal, even in the face of wild storms and civil war.

In reality, it usually takes maturity to find that place.

Though I assert that every aspect of woman exists within us all, if the chapters of this book were laid out as a chronology of our lives, beginning at pre-puberty and the first bloods of menarche, the virgin and whore would perhaps describe our teens and twenties; the mother and bitch are aspects we explore in our thirties and forties; perhaps the witch is a side of us that naturally emerges through our midlife, if or when we find the strength proffered us in our fifties and sixties. The fashion for witchcraft amongst youngsters of our society may poignantly express the sense of disempowerment they feel, together with some lost sense of life's mystery, but their flittery spells are quite different from the clear magical intentions of the older woman. The witch, striding into the second half of her life, is a woman beginning to take responsibility for her own life and her soul's dreams. At that age, we are ready to dismiss the patronising tedium of male authority, instead of having to fight it.

Our bodies are changing, and with that comes a shifting that begins as a seeping flow under the floor boards of our lives, rising slowly and surely until suddenly it arrives as a flood of change. Priorities turn around, back to front, inside out. And through it, a new sense of self is emerging. We start to let go of all we've worked so hard for, any sense of ambition palpably easing as we wonder what now is really worth the effort. The extra years of living have given us the courage to relax, to let someone else do the work - so that now we can spend our time doing what *we* want.

Age has another advantage. Over the years, deep within us the skills of the witch have been honed. No longer do we need to yell and stamp and demand; the dark goddess of control is an ally that need not overwhelm us. If we can access the witch within us, now it is easier to walk through the uncertainties and criticisms, quietly and calmly, to claim and craft what it is we want. Certainly, the experience we have gained means there is not so much likelihood of making those dreadful mistakes that crushed our pride as younger women, but also the witch provides us with a confidence that assures us we don't have so much to lose: now we can afford to make mistakes anyway.

With a good chunk of life behind us, we can let the witch out to play.

He turns away for the briefest moment, lifting his eyes in thought: how I love to watch the human face when the mind is lost in thought. His fingers gently touch his mouth - as if to ensure the precision of his words - and when he talks, looking back at the other man, every nuance of his thinking flickers over his face. I can feel his enthusiasm, the clarity of his ideas, even though he's quite beyond my hearing. And I feel the response within myself - a swirling mix of appreciation and curiosity, and at the very centre a lust that is deep and dark and silent, like the heart of a night cyclone, an ancient lust.

A hand touches my arm. "You're very quiet."

She almost startles me. I take a breath and smile, "I'm fine," pulling my gaze away from the lad by the window. He must be almost twenty years younger than I am. I should behave myself.

But she smiles at me, noticing, "He is pretty damned sweet. Certainly brightens up these dismal gatherings. Too young for us, though, darling," and again her hand rests on my arm. Manicured nails and expensive rings, and she whispers as she moves away, "Although the idea is quite lush ... " And I'm left once again in the silence of my own space, surrounded by conversations I've nothing to do with, my gaze again drawn to him.

I sip from the glass in my hand and smile inside. Yes, it is *lush*. And what would happen if it were more than just an idea? I close my eyes for a second, remembering my world and considering for a moment how such a reality might land within it - but I find nothing there to stop me. Of course, he may think me too ancient, but even if he does, there is nothing I would lose by the act of gently enquiring.

I breathe in again, this time dissolving my mind into that dark, deep power of my wanting, finding the edges of my soul, finding the control, my roots deep in the earth beneath me, feeling the endless night of the skies above, that perfect connection. And wordlessly I acknowledge nature's forces, my prayers intensifying with my focus, filling my soul with their energy, silently humming.

When I open my eyes I am looking straight at him.

And he turns to me -

The witch's craft

Talking of magic is all very easy, but understanding how it works is fascinating, and crucial if the witch is to be successful.

She isn't just baking cookies, stitching outfits, penning sketches, drafting stories, alone in her sanctuary, in some isolated bubble of creativity. The witch's work is more than simply personal expression. She is fully involved in and conscious of the ongoing creation of the wider world in which she lives. As such, her work affects others, as is she affected by others' presence; and it is because others are involved that she asserts such control over every task. Yet that control is not imposed upon her; whatever she is expressing, the skilled witch does so with complete freedom. Without the freedom to act as she wants or needs to, her magical art is entirely compromised.

There are two basic keys that allow her this freedom.

The first is a profound understanding of her emotional self. In this she is similar to the bitch. Needless to say, however, like any hag, neither are interested in how they might suppress the power of their emotion in order to behave decently, nor in the process of healing to maintain a state of balance or to live in a way that is conventional, asserting sanity through an apparent social normality. They both know that their power is dependent on an ability not just to feel emotions as they rise within or around them, but to manage those forces of their human nature.

After all, emotion is simply nature's energy animated with the consciousness or intention of a belief, an assumption, an idea. It is our human response to stimulus, providing us with the energy and the direction we need to make our next move. As such, emotion can be seen as the fuel of the bitch's goddess, for the world around us is constantly provoking a *reaction* from within us, and it is our beliefs about the nature of reality that effect the form of that reaction; so are we filled with rage, timidity, jealousy, and so on.

Because the bitch uses the energy of emotion as fuel for her own cause, it is useful for her to know what energy she is playing with, and just how deep that well runs: she lets the power of it fill her until the moment when she needs to let it go. At that point she may explode with destruction, or extend its moment of expression like the slow exhalation of a note softly whistled. The more she knows of the force that fuels her, the more likely her reaction will be as she desires it to be. However, in many ways all she is doing is reacting.

The witch seeks to do more. Her undiluted remit is a specific creativity, and so she needs an acute control. Like the bitch, she may dive into each emotional current, not allowing the force to overwhelm her, but she uses the flow for the dance of her own clear creativity. As a result, she needs to know exactly what those emotions are, and ideally too the beliefs that provoke and sustain them.

The majority of emotions are triggered by beliefs that exist beneath our awareness, ideas that are stored in our subconscious but nonetheless still activate particular reactions. If we believe fire to be hot, dogs to be dangerous, the law courts unjust, a gang of lads a threat, we will respond in whatever way we feel the most relevant, any necessary action fuelled appropriately by the energy of that emotion. Where we are unaware of a belief system, though, an emotional response can be confusing, causing things to happen that we don't want or understand. I could, for example, get angry when I hear someone practising 'Frère Jacques' on the piano, not realising my association with the sound is from the loneliness of childhood; the anger makes no sense to me, so I might express it as a general irritation and aggression, my mood suddenly changing in a way that could sabotage whatever it is I'm doing at the time: the bitch reacts. If, however, I am aware of the association, I can adjust it. The witch, needing absolute clarity as to her source of emotional energy, will use all the information she can access in order to finely tune her ability.

While someone studying the art of magic might gently yet thoroughly become aware of each potential stumbling block that remains in their soul, the witch within us all may not learn how to do this with such discipline or studied attention. It is simply the passing of years and the roads of experience that, with luck and a fair wind, allow us as women to know ourselves better, acknowledging and accepting who it is we are. We grow more *emotionally* intelligent: the ability to identify an emotional energy when it is triggered, with a sense of where and why it was sourced, allows the witch to understand its force, its reason, its craving and direction. It doesn't overwhelm her or take the ground from beneath her, but instead she contains it without a struggle, pausing to consider the wisdom of any action she might take, pausing until her view is extended in every direction. Nor does holding the emotion for a moment, a day, a year, dissipate that energy; when she is ready, the witch has the ability to direct that emotional energy, with all its force intact, in a perfect vibrant stream of creativity.

It takes practice. The natural witch has an instinct for it, but most have to work at it, an important hurdle being the feeling of personal insignificance in a world that is so vast. Instead of the impotence of believing she can't help, a well of grief may be used to fuel a gathering that celebrates community, a burst of irritation fuels the implementation of a more effective system, a flood of respect provides the undercurrent for the creation of a support network, the desperate pain of unrequited love generates what is needed to transform another's opportunity for life, a relentless tide of rage allows her to set up a business that addresses the issues involved. She doesn't complain, make a few suggestions and hope someone will do the work. She gets things done. The witch makes a difference.

Yet, like every aspect of woman, she is simply a power of nature, and nature is not always *nice*. Although the good witch inside us knows how to do these things, the wicked witch knows too. Nature's drive is to express itself; and within the self-consciousness of human nature that need is only amplified.

The magic of connection

I said that there are two keys that allow the witch to work with freedom, the first being her understanding of the forces of emotion: not overwhelmed by her emotions, her creativity is fuelled yet not compromised. The second is her ability to make extraordinary connections. Yet, bear with me if I approach the idea from a tangent: sex.

As human beings we are erratic creatures. Because emotions are so often rooted deeply within the soul, maintaining control can be hard, particularly where there are beliefs and connotations crackling with detrimental energy. For the witch who is ever seeking rich sources of creative energy, sexual intimacy can be one of her most valuable springs of both inspiration and energy. If she plays it right, that energy can be an ecstatic high not complicated by the tangles of thought, providing her with a purity of emotional energy that can be used for any purpose she might choose.

Knowing just what it is she quests, the witch may dip into that well of energy without any emotional interaction, finding her ecstasy in the mere physicality of sex. Again, let's not confuse her with someone definitively ethical: the hag and her dark goddess are aspects of nature that can be as productive as they can be destructive. The witch may seek a purely physical encounter even where it may not benefit the other. She may know, however, that at times opening her heart will intensify the experience. She may accept that a mental empathy with the person is another way in which she can increase the ecstatic rush. She may even be willing to engage fully, diving into the currents of a complete relationship where all these are important, so increasing the potential of the sexual encounter.

It is here that we find a skill that can significantly amplify her power, for her work is touched by another goddess. The whore may embrace her lover, offering him exquisite sanctuary in which to find the relief and pleasure of sweet deep sincerity, but the witch goes one step further. With full awareness and control, she opens her soul - not just inviting her lover in, but enchanting him to move through the scented darkness of her soul cave, as if to touch the very back wall. If he makes it, if he is able, what he finds is the essential energy of her life force. Here is the kick of the dark goddess of life's potential.

Her action isn't altruism. She knows that the touch of her energy will generate an ecstasy beyond what would normally be considered pleasure: it is too powerful and raw. She knows too that to reach that point, she needs to open herself in such a way as to assure there is complete trust, dissolving every lingering boundary of inhibition and fear, bewitching her lover into his own profound openness, his own tender and vulnerable truth, until he stands before her exposed, utterly naked. And together, as if stepping into the cold-thunder deluge of a high mountain waterfall, breathless with shock, overwhelmed with its energy and the knife-blade sensation, the slowed-vision explosion, spirit touches spirit, life touches life.

It is this moment of acutely wakeful sharing that she seeks: it is extraordinarily powerful, spiritual connection. For some it is mind-shattering, the impact of such intensity, but for the witch it is the magical draught of her craft, drawn from the deepest wellspring of ecstasy in human nature. She knows what she wants and, inspired and fuelled by such exquisite intimacy, very little can stop her from achieving it.

Now and then the witch may find a lover who knows how to work with her. When she does, the experience can be exquisite, allowing two souls to fine tune the harmony of their direction, to share in the journey of creating what they both want. Here is an anecdotal glimpse at what sex magic can feel like.

"You're like a water spirit," he murmurs, breathing the words deeply, and I'm rising and falling with his breathing like the high swell of a dusk-lit sea, "all around me - melting," sinking into him again, lost in the firelit dark, my eyes closed, my soul aching as I open a little more to him, moving my soul across his, like silk in swathes of warmth and cool, softness sliding, moving so slowly over my skin, skin on skin, with no sense of limbs distinct or fingers, just the wash of touch, touching touch, then warm breath and wet hunger upon my dry open mouth, lips moving lips, lazy curiosity deep within the hunger that I'm so awake to, the wave that's rising beneath us, like a desperate rage. And as it lifts me, my heart uncovered, I feel the winds of the night skies so vast all around me, starlight flickering sparks that burn my body, too high to breathe and I turn and taste and bite, taking him into my mouth, licking at the skin that gives so softly against my tongue. And as I hold the moment, the great wave sweeps again under me, my goddess beneath me, and I am falling into the rhythm of the swell once more, the vision flooding my mind, guiding me, leading me on.

And then he holds my head in his hands, calling out into the firelight, "oh baby, oh god - " his mind pushing against me, determinedly holding his control, and I move with him, my soul stretching out across him, reaching, encircling him with sweet soft distance, feeling him find himself again, feeling the darkness all around him, holding him, my goddess waiting, breathing, until he's back with me, grasping the vision of our purpose, and I can feel the power rise as he pours the flood of his desire into its chalice, murmuring my name, finding control, catching the swell again, higher and higher.

And now he's gliding, opening, his soul-scent surrounding me; and I rise to him, higher and higher, and in the fire's deep glow our eyes meet, gazing, then there is nothing between us. He makes the tiniest gesture, almost a nod and I almost smile, aware of our final affirmation. And we slide, with every cell open, giving, waiting, feeling the touch as it spins into blistering heat, the pain of aching, hoping, open, waiting, wet with lust and soft, silk-soft as water sliding, closer, dancing, ice melting on fire-blazing skin, closer, the wave rising. And when our eyes meet again he is shaking, not breathing, blinking, and his heart is in my belly, and time stretches as if we are on the edge of forever, the edge of nowhere, balancing so high on the tip of a wave, on water that can't hold us, and there is just one way to go -

I whisper the chosen words, filling our minds with that perfect vision. And I let go, taking him with me, falling off and over the edge, and tumbling through the storm of my goddess, until we slam crashing into the weight of life, skin and bone, vivid and screaming, hearing the sharp cry of his soul aloud, as somehow we find the glide, and make it, out onto open wings, to soar in the darkness, timeless, together.

Knowing absolutely where we are going.

If he is no accomplice, but instead a man (or woman) who is closed to his own soul, unwilling or unable to face real intimacy, the witch may not object to the use of a little alcohol or other drugs to break his inhibitions and his willingness to play. As he sobers up, he can shrug off the experience as part of the intoxication, a dream that was unnaturally intensified by the chemicals. Where he is a sensitive soul, however, the encounter can leave him reeling, his life turned upside down. With the support of a loving friend - whether that is another aspect of the same woman or a different person altogether - and a strong community, he has a chance to ride the storm that's been provoked within his soul, learning a great deal in the process.

Where he is alone, though, it is likely he will become obsessed by this witch, increasingly drained by her, weakened and confused, even if he never meets her again. If she has no moral conscience, this is the witch as succubus, the legendary demon who inspires within her lovers the most powerful sexual dreams and fantasies, and lives off their sexual energy.

Many a potential partner to the witch makes the mistake of becoming enmeshed in the kind of tomes on sex magic that have been available for the past forty years, the majority of which promote techniques that don't come from our culture. Indeed, where books on sex magic have been written in English, talking of higher sexual practice and intense psychosexual experience, they have tended to be rather dry and scientific, or embarrassingly silly. There is value in Taoism, in the Karma Sutra, in Tantra, some Eastern methods being still embedded in the ritual dance and incense plumes of their original religious practice, but all spirituality is languaged by culture; the most fundamental elements of language can only be understood within their own cultural context, and that too is only fully realised within the appropriate environmental context. When we take a spiritual teaching out of its homeland, the core of the teaching is entirely lost; the foundations, the constitutional roots, the scents and colours all fall away in the translation. Where the human mind perceives gaps, we pour in our own associations and understandings like wet grout, constructing something that is fundamentally different, something unstable or overly rigid, and potentially dangerous. A natural sense of connection and respect is lost.

When ideas are rooted within the landscape and culture within which they are taught, they are simply more effective. Not straining to gain nourishment where roots have been pulled out, they lie within a web of obvious connections and relationships, both the shared and the unspoken. Within their own context, they feel natural and real. Again and again, people struggle to grasp some technique or belief, yet laugh with relief when they realise that what they are reaching for is outside of their heritage; and furthermore, the native alternative is lying there deep within their own understanding all along.

Such roots are essential to the witch. Just as she needs to know human nature if she is to find the freedom to use her emotional energy and that provoked in others, so must she know the natural world around her and its own flows of energy. A witch, then, is entirely committed to her landscape. She doesn't just know how it functions; she aims to know every part of it. In constant relationship with it, she becomes attuned to both its short cycles of changes and its long journey of changing.

It need not be a beautiful rural environment; the witch may be happier in the big city, the suburbs, or a place needing protection or regeneration. Wherever she is, she seeks out that intensity of connection with all those who make up the ecosystem. The Pagan animist may perceive and honour the shimmering brilliance of spirit within every aspect of creation, but where a woman doesn't have that religious vision or motivation, the witch within is no less inspired to find those connections. Every action is a potential interaction, acknowledging presence, purpose and communication, and where the energy is strong, her respect rises. It may be with the mountains, the darkness, the forest or deer; it may be with the river of traffic, the wind that moves around the buildings, the sunlight on glass, the scents of anger, hunger and wit. Wherever she is, enthused by the divine hum of creativity, touched by that powerful desire to control, the witch seeks and finds her dark goddess of potential.

Indeed, in her relationship with the darkness, the witch can feel close to the young girl within us. Hag-blessed, still drenched in the confidence and naiveté of boundlessness, the world so vast with potential and adventure, the prepubescent child plays within the protective embrace of the dark goddess. Hag-blessed, she knows very little, and though she seeks experience she is not yet driven to crave certainty. Such limitations come when she starts to hide her wildness, acknowledging that not everything is possible or acceptable; such notions the witch may understand, but they do not constrain her.

She can resemble the young girl in her relationships with the nonhuman world as well. The child may be seeking a companion in play, the witch the exquisite sharing of life, but both know the need for gentleness, assertiveness, sensitivity and generosity: trust. So, where the child is naturally open, the witch opens her soul sanctuary to create ecstatic relationship with the environment around her, finding the threads of connection with the rose, robin, river, rain, snowflake, rowan, moon, always seeking that kick of life, when spirit touches spirit. She doesn't just talk to the blackbirds and the clouds; in her openness, it is as if she makes love with the power of nature itself, throwing herself open utterly to thunder and starlight, to wild wind and sea depths, a flower's scent, a sun-baked stone, the depths of grief, the tides of love.

Two feet from its edge, I pause and look around. The cars parked along the street, the sound of the city, the tatty row of shops - pizza, electrical, insurance, Asian grocer, launderette - and the bustling of so many people, all seem so momentary and insignificant. I am filled with the idea that, some four hundred years before, this oak was a sapling starting its life in this little rectangle of the grass between Queen's Street and the church.

Looking up at its glory, whispering without sound, *May I share your space, just for a moment?*, I feel myself drawn forward, and reach my hand up to touch the canopy as I take a step forward, imagining the old roots stretching out beneath me. And as I feel the tree's ease, I open my soul, and smile at the sensation of its life tingling through me.

My intention had been simply to find a place of stillness within the whir of the city, but as I sit down in the dirt and fallen leaves, breathing in the exquisite energy of the oak, I realise that there is more potential. I close my eyes and inhale deeply, letting my soul break open with my out-breath, as I lean against the tree's old trunk, and ask that we might share a little more, *Ancient blessed spirit, in honour of the gods, I ask that you find me, let me find you, let us find this moment ...*

Within an instant, I am falling back into the wood, my heart suddenly filled as if with a thousand tales of love and heartbreak, of spring and autumn, leaf buds and leaf fall. I feel my limbs rising with the sap, out to each leaf as it dances in the city breeze, laughing in the sunlight, that laughter slipping through me like cool water in the heat of the day. The sensuality of it hums through me, the earth beneath me evoking a passion, inspiring my soul too to slip down into the oak roots, into the mud beneath the grass, stretching out in the sunshine, every nerve in my consciousness alive with the sensation. On this small patch of green, I can feel football games and lovers' games, and the dancing of little feet upon me, and my soul laughs in what feels like an ancient silence. And again I feel myself intertwined with the oak, its wood exploring my history, my stories, my substance, the sap rising through me like fingertips moving across my soul-skin. It makes my soul sing - as if in response I long to share more, opening to offer to this old tree soul the lilting sounds of my own song.

I'm not sure how long I am in that state. Perhaps fifteen or twenty minutes slip away before I find myself slowly aware once more of the world passing around me. And for a long while, all I feel is the extraordinary richness of sated stillness.

When I move, it is like the disentangling of limbs after making love. I close my eyes and whisper thanks, my human language now far too limited to be the medium of communication. And unhurrying, still humming with the energy, I stride off in search of a café where I can get some writing done.

Finding pleasure in nonhuman company, through the experience of ecoeroticism or simply the rich sharing of connection, here is the hag-witch that longs to express herself in every woman. Indifferent to the pressures of social conformity, independent of any hierarchy of structure and society, she aches to experience relationships of naked intensity. Questing those that will bring her the fuel of ecstasy, she has no interest in anyone or anything that does not inspire.

She'll do just what she wants.

Then carefully, intentionally, she'll pour that energy into her soul's creativity.

CHAPTER EIGHT

The Old Bag

The last facet of the notional whole, as I have unpacked and explored it, is an aspect of our woman nature that discovers again some of the inherent integration we experienced as young children, before our responsibilities towards the world kicked in. Her task, her crisis and her wisdom is the dissolution of that conflict.

I call her the old bag.

From somewhere I find the energy to turn over and, with a heavy arm, reach out for the clock.

02:17

A weight of anger slips off some ledge where I've been keeping it, trying to ignore it as the hours have passed, and smashes into the pit of my belly, toxic fumes rising from the mess to seep through my body, erasing any last possibility of sleep. Staring at the ceiling, I listen to the giggling chattering racket below the window.

Now and then my mind wanders to summer nights of my misspent youth: dancing down city backstreets with a handful of wild companions, jeering at the 'squares' passing by, the rhythms of the songs in our heads punctuated by snatches sung out loud as if they were chants of protest, every endless moment intensified by the colourful kick of the acid that seeped through our veins and the gaudy brilliance of our brand new 'teen' revolution.

On the village green outside my window, another peel of laughter rises through the murmured chatter of their voices and I can smell the frustration in the air I'm breathing. It hasn't really been hours. They are just youngsters, sitting out in the moonlight, gossiping through a warm night, finding friendship in trivia. It isn't exactly in the same league as the idiocy of my own teenage years, uprooting plants from urban window boxes to post them through letter boxes, literally wetting ourselves with our freedom and laughter, swaying drunk as we ran clattering on metal-heeled winklepickers, yelling, meandering in the mists of alcoholic stupor.

I sigh, closing my eyes, and turn over.

Five minutes later, I'm trying the cord of my dressing gown, pulling its unnecessary warmth around me. And ignoring the sweet coolness of the grass beneath my feet, I walk straight up to them: three girls and a boy, lounging over the bench beneath the old oak. They look at me like kids unused to the word *no*, chins high but filling the air with a nervous expectation. Damn them.

"Listen, it's half past two." Immediately the words are out, I feel ancient. I breathe in, "so, can you please just keep the noise down? I'm sure I'm not the only one you're keeping awake."

The lad looks down and mumbles what sounds like an acknowledgement. The girls seem to have perfected a look of bored incomprehension. One of them smiles as her eyes stare at me, emptily.

"I don't want to - " I start, but what can I say that won't sound patronising or nervous? *Damn them.* I sigh and shake my head, turning to go. "Sleep is very precious and you are making it quite impossible. Please, will you just keep it down!"

The giggles rise as I walk away, my bare feet now cold in the lamp-lit grass.

Before I close my front door, I hear one say, "Silly old bag!"

All that we carry

The *old bag* is a wonderful term. Speaking to women for this book, funnily enough, although it is invariably used as an insult, not one of them minded if it were applied to themselves. One laughed and said, it's better than being a 'grumpy old cow', but the word she actually objected to was *cow*: grumpy, to the old bag at least, is not a derogatory term.

The old bag is that aspect of womankind that is constantly and acutely aware that she has lived. Furthermore, whenever she feels it to be appropriate, and more often when it is not, she likes to make sure that others are aware of it too. For this reason, she keeps her experiences of life with her at all times. Whether she folds them up tidily, carefully placing them in order, or just stuffs them in, she carries the memories and lessons of her living, at ease only when they are on hand should she ever need to find them.

She may use a half dozen bags, her fingers clutching them tightly, or perhaps she throws everything into a large raffia sack, or a hard-framed leather handbag with an alarmingly tight catch, or a plush velvet *poche*, silk-tassled and dog-eared, a supermarket plastic bag, a few of them, crinkly and torn, a slim designer carrier, all stiff paper and long cord handles, a Pagan pouch made from an old suede jacket found in a charity shop, adorned with feathers and wooden beads, or a massive canvas rucksack with two dozen pockets, a wicker basket with everything untidily on show. As a bag of experience, it might be a beautiful accessory, highlighting her character, her inimitable style, or it can detract, complicate and confuse; it can weigh her down until, bent double, she stumbles with the burden. Some bags seem so extensive, cavernous or complex, that experiences are lost, hidden, out of sight, forgotten from consciousness or smothered by others. Yet - adding to the weight - she carries them still, for they are a source of her creativity, and a justification for her action, a reminder of successes that would bear repeating and of moments of shame that are worth avoiding. And as they help her to remember, so the old bag brings them out in order to explain to the rest of the world just what works and what doesn't, what's true and what isn't, what should be done and just what shouldn't.

The old bag, as an individual, can be incredibly difficult.

The young woman who has been through rugged times, who has struggled with the learning curve but walked out the other side, can be a splendid old bag. She may slip the lessons learnt into the back pocket of her jeans like a mobile phone, in a way that doesn't compromise the vibrancy of her youthful movement. Or she may use some clumsy garish contrivance to carry them around in, making an awkward self-focused scene wherever she goes, needing to assert her ownership of the experience, the validity of what has happened and all that it has given her. She may believe that, now life has bitten her, she knows absolutely what is right. She has no time for the stupidity of others' misguided and naive thinking.

Just as the witch emerges more naturally in a woman's fifties or sixties, the same is true of the old bag. As an older woman, the containers of her life experience may become more numerous, but they may also drag her into a clumsiness and confusion. She may feel that she has earned the privilege to assert what she believes to be right and wrong, simply because of the years she has lived. Her bags may have rigidity because of those convictions acquired along the way, an inflexibility that causes memories and lessons to be twisted and changed as they are bundled in. Pulling out memories like pamphlets in some political protest, the old bag waves them with irritation, justifying her opinions. Sometimes it is obvious she's not read the words for quite a while, and she misquotes hopelessly without seeming to care, as if the specific issue isn't as crucial as the general expression of her indignation. There are times when her actions do poignantly remind others that their attitudes are unfounded, her experience becoming a valuable gift shared, but even then it is not necessarily presented sympathetically. She has watched others make mistakes and it's a tiring occupation.

The glamour of life is gone for her. The *miserable* old bag is a woman whose experience has been a continuing process of proving the world to be a dead end, an outdated theme park, plastic-guised and populated by con men, quacks and teasers. Resignation saturates her perception, as she sees the perpetual repetition of struggle, injustice and disappointment all around her. She's been there, done it, and she has an envelope of photographs or a sheaf of correspondence in a box somewhere to prove it. Her observation of others' hope is tight with cynicism. She is bitter and seldom hesitant when it comes to expressing it. The romantic ideologies and beliefs based on assumptions have now crumbled and dispersed as dust in the wind. The film star she so adored is just a bloke who craves attention, the mistakes politicians make are most often plans and lies, adultery is absolutely normal, altruism deceptive, love inherently and irredeemably random: nature is unjust. This sense of knowing, born of experience, offers her stability. No longer needing to grow, her ambitions either sated or dismissed, she has no need for the guy ropes of beliefs and convictions that bring certainty. Beyond what life has taught her, the world is a mystery that is unlikely to be solved by anyone.

Yet, where she has learned from those life lessons, and if she is willing and able to use her experience of life positively, the old bag can be a gloriously powerful woman. Where her experience has shown her the beauty of the world, the potential of humanity, the old bag is the facet of woman that is able to guide. She is the teacher within us. That she can at times predict responses, because she's seen the stories played out before, can allow her an easy acceptance of life, and a very real peacefulness. She knows that understanding right and wrong is not that simple and is happy to say so, even as she asserts what she believes is right *for her*. She gives not because she is seeking to make deals, or wanting something in return, but because she can give. She shares the tales of her life, explaining lessons learnt, giving out tokens and mementoes from her bag.

Standing on solid ground, her confidence also reflects an acceptance of her own life reality, for her perception of herself is now more honest than ever before. To the old bag, truth is everything; she has no willingness anymore to play with the guises used by other facets of woman. She accepts who she is, together with the extent and the limitations of her true interests and skills, her true capabilities, and without inhibition she draws her perception into free and full creative self expression. Indeed, unlike any other facet of woman, without this truth she has no creativity.

Nor does she care what others might think of her, or what she creates, because life has taught her that a sense of value is only true and useful when it comes of herself. She doesn't seek validation or affirmation from outside herself; she lives her creativity according to her own vision, not for others but for the simple satisfaction of the creating. As such, she gives the air of being a woman who may not be independent, but is nonetheless self-contained. No other aspect of woman has the same lack of fear when it comes to exploring and expressing true personal creativity.

Despite this, or because of this, she can be utterly mad. With no need or inclination to judge herself in relation to others, she can easily lose herself on the map of social references and expectations. She can wander beyond what is comprehensible, and so become distant or inaccessible, lost in her own reality. Furthermore, she may well use the contents of her bags as ammunition, like so many rotten apples hurled with surprising vigour, and sometimes for no reason anyone else can comprehend. She can be stubborn and bloody minded, asserting her own understanding while at the same time expecting the help she wants and needs, will be readily given. She may be able to function perfectly well within the world she chooses to live in, but to a wider society the old bag risks drifting into behaviour that is not quite acceptable.

The witch is indubitably crazy, talking with trees and faeries, devouring innocence with her hag-dance of intense ecstasy. The old bag isn't dangerous in quite the same way; she can, however, be quite extraordinarily rude. She can be brutal. But she isn't looking to make friends. She knows that the strongest relationships emerge and persist without artificial effort, and only where there is nothing shared but undiluted honesty. She has no tolerance for interactions based on gentle sensitivity, where issues are avoided and platitudes fill the silence.

Her skin is as soft as a peach - I almost want to bite her. And though she is round and solid, her feet barely seem to touch the ground, her soul's curiosity dancing in her eyes, glancing at everything that moves, and beside her I feel anchored by the weight of my years. She holds my hand and pulls me, as if dragging my hull along the mud. I smile and groan, "Hold on," clambering to my feet.

Just as I do manage to get up, she lets go, crying, "Liff, liff!" and she's running into the drifting path of descending autumn leaves, russet and copper, her little red coat, her arms reaching out to catch one, eyes open wide. On the grass verge, her shoes slip and she stumbles, landing on her knees; she looks up at me as if asking if it were appropriate to howl. I raise my eyebrows, she frowns, I shake my head and smile, whispering, "I wouldn't bother, little one". There's a pause as if she's considering her options, and then she turns, picking up a wide-fingered horse chestnut leaf to see what it is beneath it.

"Ah now," and I cup the shiny conker in my hand as she pads over, coming to rest in the crook of my arm, "when I was your age, my brother, that's your great uncle, he and I used to gather these on frosty mornings, until we had pockets full - " For the briefest moment she looks into my eyes.

And then she's off again, clumsily running over the grass

after the golden treasure of silent falling leaves, crying "Look, liff liff!". A wave of irritation rises in me, my body aching to sit down, and I sigh. I wonder when her mother will get back.

There's a bench beside the path a little way off.

I'd like a little silence. A moment in which to doze.

The old bag: she is the part of us that feels she has nothing to lose. Perhaps, through deep-bored cynicism, she has lost any sense of life's value and believes that anything else taken from her would make no difference. On the other hand, she may have a sense that nothing of value could be taken: surviving this far has informed her that none of the truly important elements of life are dependent on ownership. With nothing to lose, she has nothing limiting her self-expression. She can be as mad as she wishes. She can do what she wants.

As she grows older, too, the old bag comes to realise that the accumulation of knowledge is beginning to wane. While as youngsters we believe that with information we are gaining a fully functional understanding of the world, with age we see that knowledge has scant connection with wisdom. Furthermore, the more we know, the more we realise how little we know. So it is that, as years pass by, the mass of all she is keeping in her bags tangibly decreases. What was once full of substantial memories becomes filled instead with the dark emptiness of wisdom, as if the jumble stored has become fuel for its own transformation. Indeed, the wiser the old bag, the less she appears to carry at all.

All that we are

When we speak of a goddess as a dark force of nature, it is a wealth of qualities that we refer to, all of which feel to be integral to the essential darkness of the universe. She is that within nature which is not known, which is quite possibly unknowable and so provides no certainty. She may express a sense of potential, but with a complete lack of promise. She is the mystery we long for and the emptiness we fear losing ourselves within, teetering on the edge with anticipation and horror, with the dread of annihilation. She lingers in the smell of decay, whispering in the looming presence and breathlessness of death, in the gaping absence that death leaves behind. In a modern animistic language, she is the consciousness of all these qualities, holding their intention, expressing their purpose.

As the unacceptable side of woman's nature, the hag is inspired by these energies of the dark, and the hag that I have here called the old bag is no less thick with this darkness. That she presents her experiences as a banner proclaiming all she knows implies that she reaches for the light. She doesn't. In her ranting tirades and lectures, she is indicating the positions and qualities of the stars, but her awareness is very much of their insignificance within the vast darkness of the skies. Her journey is that of gradually releasing all she knows.

As with every hag, the force of nature that fuels the old bag is a specific dark goddess: in simple terms, she is honesty. In less human concepts, she is the force of openness. She is that state when the walls are down. She is the broad open moor: there is no invitation to explore, there are no barriers to stop you, yet somehow the spirit provokes reluctance. So it is with the old bag. Her sanctuary is evident, but it is not impenetrable walls that protect its integrity, allowing her to maintain it as an intimate haven; what keeps us out is merely the strength of her soul.

What makes honesty and openness a dark goddess is the nature of truth. Paganism, as an earth-oriented religious tradition, nourishing and being nourished by the environment, has never sat easily within modernist scientific thinking. Most poignantly in this regard, truth is not considered an 'objective fact', for such a notion is beyond existence. Truth is an experience. As an expression of truth, honesty is entirely transient, momentary and subjective, flowing through us in a desire to share, affirming, merging, creating, dismantling, dissolving, dissipating, in order to share again. We never know what an expression of honesty will bring.

The old bag's goddess is not, then, age or experience, for a woman can be an old bag even when all she has to give seems trivial, childish and naive to others. The autobiography of the twenty year old celebrity, ghost written by some magazine journalist barely a decade older, is a wonderfully tedious example, all too evident in our culture; even if significant events have taken place, there is seldom enough depth of life experience (in celebrity or writer) to engage with them, understand them or relate them. Yet, when this dark goddess of honesty overwhelms, we are roused to blurt out whatever it is we feel we know, allowing her to rip us open - even when the tale we have to tell is thoroughly uninspiring. Furthermore, where there isn't sufficient strength to carry the mass (or mess) of a tale under public scrutiny, the old bag can crumple; slipping away, it is often the bitch who steps in with her self-defending vitriol.

Where the woman is strong, though, the old bag radiates that strength. The power that is within her sanctuary becomes evident to those around her; the old bag is transparent. She may not wish to share the space and quiet of her soul, but she shares its content freely. And as such, she is a potent force of integration.

The loss of fertility

Through much of life as women, the various facets of our nature emerge and recede. Some of us are a mixture of two or three of those I've described; others have a tendency towards one, though others will flicker in. Although she can be of any age, the old bag is often our dominant hag face as we head into our sixties. However, from the time our menopause begins, perhaps ten or fifteen years earlier, increasingly she frequents the surface of our nature.

It is a long slow period of difficult change. A time of reassessment, for many women the menopause is a decade of challenge, of adjustment and readjustment. Just as with any aspect of our fertility and bleeding, modern medicine can describe the mechanics but at best has a vague idea of how the systems work, and often no insight whatsoever when they don't. Feeling tired, depressed, low, her body heavy, her life uninspired, a woman might head to her doctor: if she's not yet into her late forties, if her blood tides are still normal, it isn't unusual in Britain for her to be sent off with a prescription for antidepressants. If she's that bit older, tiptoeing towards fifty and her periods are irregular, a doctor will proudly declare the diagnosis as menopause, and offer her hormone therapy that will delay the effects. Either way, the old bag is not going to be happy.

The monthly drop in hormones that brings a fertile woman into premenstrual tension is, for the woman clambering through her menopausal years, increasingly the norm. Instead of a dip that then rises, over the decade of change those levels are in slow decline, but not as a sure and gentle slide, fraction by fraction; the dips are sometimes cataclysmic plummets, and apparently randomly, at other times, they are barely evident at all.

There is little order to the journey. Most start with the low energy and mood swings, feeling premenstrually grumpy or miserable but all the time. This may continue for a few years before the next symptoms appear. The feelings are not helped by the fact that what natural muscle which had existed to keep our breasts looking vaguely attentive appears to disappear overnight. The bathrooms scales may swear that we've not put on weight, but our thighs have gained a few inches overnight. Our bellies crinkle and sag, and the notion of 'pulling your tummy in' becomes just a memory. The clothes we've been wearing for years suddenly no longer fit.

At what point the menstrual cycle itself changes differs from woman to woman. It may take five years of irregularity, with periods when we bleed by the bucketful and others that can barely be bothered to start; slowly they peter out completely, ending with one final burst four months later, no doubt when it is least expected or convenient.

Then there are the hot flushes. Some women find them easier to hide than others; that they tend to be a response to the slightest stress or excitement means that often they happen at the most inappropriate times. They can keep us warm if we need it (a photograph of Brad Pitt will provoke a flush in me), but they can also leave us sweating, aching and faint, revealing our raw nature and our age for all to see. Society may smile or chuckle, but in a world powered by men and youngsters, to be suddenly sweltering with an inner heat can be judged as distracting, unprofessional, unattractive: unacceptable.

As hard to admit is our changing scent. As women we're allowed a hint of sunshine and perfume, but as we get older, hormones dropping with the release of our fertility, the rich juices of our vulva drying, the scent of our sex is not so sweet: we smell muskier, somehow dustier. The years of sleepless nights can be equally challenging. Dream-filled snatches of sleep are broken, again and again, by the need to pee, by the soaring heat, our muscles twitching and cramping. Many women suffer with crippling headaches through these tangled years.

For the majority who are hit hard by the process, this is a large chunk of life through which to pretend nothing is happening. Like a snake sloughing off an old skin, wriggling and stretching, our soul is desperate to break through it. We lie awake at night, feeling a desperation for change but unsure how to create it. Opening the window, gazing out into the night, sweat dripping down our bodies, we can feel a new world calling, another world we can almost stride into, an otherworld of spirits, of ancestors' voices, a world that most often feels formless and free, and just beyond our perception. If we are lucky, this is when the old bag gets to her feet within us, prodding us to wander out into the garden, to cool our fevered bodies in the night air, and to listen to the whispers of nature - inside and around us.

When the heat crashes in, it is the old bag who stays with it, laughing with its surge, riding it like a roller coaster, at times aware of its wealth of emotion, at others just breathing its extraordinary high of life energy. And if we haven't been fighting it, hiding from it, hating it, when the peak passes, inspiration comes like cool rain on our hot skin: we ache to express these new glimpses of truth. In the interviews for this book, women told me of the childish urges that come - to yell, to paint, to write, *this is really me*, calling out to be heard. It is as if they are facing the last opportunity to do so, but in some ways it is the first: the current of this wild goddess of openness is with us, baking us with a soul heat that breaks apart the structures we have crafted through our lives.

Through that decade, with its beginning and its end often too pale to be perceived, most of us journey through two distinct periods of menopausal crises, each one marked by a flood of utter desolation: during the first we lose the *joie de vivre*, the second erasing any remaining sense of purpose. The point of being alive slips from our tired and sweaty fingers. If we move through those years, lying in bed, crouched on the bathroom floor, sitting at the kitchen table in the dark, with the hum of the fridge giving a relentless rhythm to our irrational and unjustifiable grief, the desolation can be unbearable. If we let her, it is the old bag inside us who takes us in hand, giving us the necessary bloody-minded determination, guiding us through.

Of course, not all women struggle, some managing to glide through just as some bleed lightly and hardly ever feel the presence of the hag's blood hound (or any other dark goddess). Not all women are broken apart, but for each one of us the horizon of our lives does change. Oestrogen, that softening and feminizing hormone whose tides flowed through our bodies enabling us to mother, to care, and to multitask, is not being released in the same way that it has been throughout our fertile years. The result is an increase in aggression, which the old bag uses to her advantage. She can be hard, sharp, cutting, like a chill autumn storm that drives the leaves from the trees, leaving a clearer, cleaner, brighter land. The menopausal woman can find it hard to contain her emotion, exploding in rage and dissolving into tears, feeling herself out of control, her self-esteem battered; the old bag doesn't care, expressing what rises in her when it rises, considering there to be no reason why she should hold herself back. The black sniffer dog, that hag-hound of PMT, can help us by following the scents of each and every aspect of our lives that we don't want anymore. Finding every action we can no longer do truthfully, the dog snarls, pulls and barks, until we make the changes we must make, dragging us towards a place of integration.

As *old bag*, we don't care what we look like: our bodies have dropped leaving us more pear-shaped than ever, with cellulite and wrinkles, with fruzzy thinning grey hair, but the old bag laughs, a rich deep laugh that comes from the belly and makes our soft-muscles shake. Coming to terms with the changes brought by the end of our fertility, we come to terms with ourselves: without self-consciousness, without shame, and with the strength of the old bag, we can provoke society to question its inability to acknowledge and accept weakness, age, mortality and decay.

For a while we've held the position of pivotal generation, in our family, in our community and in the workplace, but our inspiration is no longer the driving force. The world around us appears to have altered its speed and our ideas seem out of synch. Society is asking us to take the back seat, to let the younger ones get behind the wheel. It's a difficult thing to do, as if it were an admittance of defeat and worthlessness, but the fight can be exhausting and humiliating. We may have friends and colleagues - even the law - on our side, but society isn't, and slowly we come to understand that neither is nature.

With the old bag's honesty, with the wisdom of her experience, giving up the wheel can be deeply empowering. It can feel like taking to the air after the weight of being grounded: exhilarating, it offers an expanse of freedom. What used to be gold toys are - to the wise old bag - merely a clutter of irritating distractions. She is not interested in the struggle. She can't be bought. She won't compromise.

The other sides of our hag-nature bow and step aside, allowing the old bag to stride out into the limelight.

A time of celebration

Though we may struggle to consider what we are and what we can be, the old bag laughs: with the burden of fertility gone, menstruation behind her, ambition and pretension abandoned, life lies ahead as a wealth of opportunities. She has let go, and for her this is a time of ease and celebration.

Indeed, to mark the release is a powerful act. Just as the young girl moving into her years of fertility can be profoundly changed by a rite of passage that acknowledges her first bleeding, so the woman leaving behind her blood tides can feel the benefit as powerfully. We honour the young girl, accepting her new status, sharing gifts and guidance in order that she might feel recognised as an individual growing up; valued as a distinct member of her family, community, society, she is better able to take the responsibilities, needing less to assert herself aggressively, rebelliously, destructively, able better to express herself creatively.

For a woman stepping out of her fertility, the act of acknowledging her changed world can be poignant.

Like any rite of passage, this is one that can be done formally, with an invited gathering and with a qualified priest to guide and bless the event, and it can be done with all the informality and spontaneity that is desired. Some feel the value of human friendship, support and sharing, needing those who share her life to recognise the shift in her soul and in her relationships within the tribe. For others the desire is to walk the steps themselves, recognising, understanding, reflecting upon the change, witnessed only by the spirits of the land and the ancestors.

The old bag is nature as the power of autumn. The last of the sloes are to be gathered in, the plums, apples and maize, the late roots and brassicas. She emerges as part of the process of that harvest, the cycle of growth completing, experience cutting through like the scythe in the barley. Yet once the harvest is done, what the land needs is rest. The stubble is turned that the frost of winter can break up the soil, the storms taking the last of the leaves from the trees. Expressing the need to accept and embrace this potent time of falling leaves and gathering in, the old bag seeks whatever it requires for her to walk in balance on her journey between summer and winter.

Acknowledging in her rite all she has gained through her life's experience, while also acknowledging all that she has lost or is soon going to lose, she opens her soul to the freedom of the wild, and the deep inner strength which that gives her. She steps into a commitment to walk the path, beautifully integrating her inner self with the world around her.

I'm not here as her celebrant, to guide her or create sacred space: my presence as a witness is merely to accentuate the poignancy of what she is about to do. As yet, I've no idea what that might be. Neither does she.

The wind whistles around us, chill and sharp, blurring the sound of the distant road as it blurs my vision and makes me sniff. From where we sit on the old stone wall, fields stretch out to the horizon, broken only by patches and swathes of copse. Not a word has passed between us for a long time now. I watch the fallen leaves floating, swirling, on the water, wondering at the silence of this ancient spring, the endless surge of pure and soundless water.

Then suddenly she's on her feet. "Bugger it," her words have more determination than felicity. "I'm going in." I nod, *fine, absolutely*, not wanting to speak in case my anxiety dissuades her: the water will be freezing. The wind is bad enough. Yet she pulls off her fleece and jumper, kicking off her boots, and before she can think sensibly she's completely naked and shuddering, and mumbling, making her way down through the grass, the horsetails and reeds, to the pool. I breathe in and make a quiet prayer, following her path, watching her toes sink into the deep muddy clay.

Then she's in, up to her neck and she's howling, yelping with pain and delight. She takes a deep breath and disappears underwater. The autumn leaves, in a thousand colours of ochre and rust, settle on the surface, lilting with the swell. The wind rises through the trees, pulling leaves into its wake, and I watch the water, whispering my prayers, aware of the thumping of my heart. And then she's there, with eyes closed, for a brief moment intensely still.

And five minutes later, shaking, shivering wildly and laughing, dressed in all her clothes and some of mine, muddy and damp and positively glowing, we are embracing. "Well?" I ask. "Did you do what you wanted to do?"

"Yes," she smiles, with chattering teeth, pushing her wet grey hair from her forehead. "And from now on, I'm doing nothing but what I want to do. Do you know, I feel cleansed." I can't help but laugh: she has mud on her face and leaves in her hair. She squeezes my hand, still shivering, as we turn to make our way back over the fields. "All that's left is me. Yes, I feel thoroughly bloody *me*."

In the medieval Welsh myth of Cerridwen, the goddess uses her cauldron like the container of her life's experience, and indeed the old bag within each of us can tote her memories about in such a pot. The rough black iron has a use beyond the leather handbag: it's heavy and clumsy, but you can cook in it.

Cerridwen in the story, the *bent white* hag goddess of the crescent moon, is preparing a brew for her son, Morfran (*cormorant*), a child so ugly that he is called Afagddu (*utter darkness*) by the people of the neighbourhood. Cerridwen believes that with this brew she can impart to him the gift of pure *awen*, the sacred flow of inspiration, and taking a year and a day she wanders the hills of her homeland gathering every sacred ingredient she might need.

In the tale, however, instead of Afagddu, it is a young child of the village that gains the magical power of the brew. Set to stir the cauldron while she is out collecting, his name is Gwion Bach (*little innocent*) and, wide eyed in his open childish receptivity, when the brew bubbles, splashing his hand, he jams the scalded thumb into his mouth in an age-old manner of suckling innocence. The three drops he imbibes contain all the magic imparted by the goddess, and little Gwion is transformed into Taliesin, the foremost Bard of the Welsh tradition.

The story isn't as simple as that, for in the telling Gwion is chased by Cerridwen, both of them shapeshifting in an attempt to outmanoeuvre the other, over land, through water and up into the skies, until exhausted, with her magic he changes into a grain of wheat, hurling himself into the mess of a threshing floor. She herself transmutes into a fat black hen, whereupon she pecks him up and swallows him whole. In her goddess form, so does she become pregnant with him, giving birth to the beautiful child that would quickly become the great Bard.

Creating what she desires, Cerridwen is goddess as witch in the tale; she is mother too, for those questing the wisdom of that aspect, but in this one respect the goddess is the old bag: into the cauldron she places all the ingredients of her life. In the tale, she collects them from the landscape of her home, expressing the circular horizon-based perspective of the Pagan tradition, the inherent integration of a people and their environment. Each ingredient she drops into the pot is of her experience and treasured relationship with the land, and this she stirs over a blazing fire, boiling it down to its pungent essence.

It is a potent brew and, used badly, it can be toxic. It is the powerful smell of her own soul and like a skunk it can be give off a stench that overwhelms the senses of anyone else. It can be frightening. Yet used well, it can be the enchanting wine that others long to taste; indeed, it can be intoxicating with its powerful inspiration. It can, like any good magical brew, be exquisitely transformative.

Letting another drink from her cauldron is an act of intimacy for the old bag. As concentrated liquor, it imparts the true sense of her own being, her truth. In practice, she might do it through any media of creativity, in a poem written and shared, a meal made with special care. A distillation of her experience, the brew is poured into a specific form that is intended as a gift, as communication. It may not be easily palatable, the taste may take some getting used to, but the intention is poignant.

Although the old bag's sanctuary is not defended by high walls and distrust, instead being naturally protected by the strength of her soul, her nature is not to invite people in. Her inclination, her desire, is to share her experience through the process of integrating her inner self with her outer world, but that doesn't mean she has no haven for intimacy, nor a need for one. In her sanctuary, the old bag sets down all those bags she carries. For her, this is a place of absolute privacy, stacked with boxes, perhaps even the odd padlocked chest. Here there are love letters, tied up with old ribbons, newspaper cuttings, hand written recipe books, that box filled with photographs, flower seeds in old envelopes. There are shelves stacked with books, records warping seldom played, a silver cup, dusty, everything veiled in spiders' webs.

Yet the chances are that her life experience has taught her the value of true intimacy. She may be bloody stubborn and alarmingly rude with her uncompromising honesty, but she knows there is nothing in the world like the magic of sharing moments, soul to soul, soul-naked. It may be that not many come her way, not many are invited, but when they do there's a kettle, a couple of mugs for tea or maybe something stronger, and a dog-eared old sofa in the midst of it all.

But how does she share? And with whom?

Intimacy with the old bag is a wild adventure.

When she's in her prime (usually the other side of fifty), using the strengths she has gained as a sweet source of inspiration, she is the most exceptional guide. She may take you on a tour of dusty trunks and old letters, paper brittle with age. She may draw you into stories, reliving them again on heady currents of aged emotion, swells of fear and anticipation, empathy steering the course like a stiffly-moving rudder. She may take you into the depths of her knowing, where you are blindfolded by your own lack of understanding, and down into caverns where she knows her way in the darkness but which to you feel endless, dangerous and new. Holding onto her hand, you are dependent on her experience, yet she may well guide gently, sympathetic to your not-knowing, holding your naiveté.

But with a sharpened wit, at times she has a merciless sense of humour.

Her sexuality is distinct from any other facet of woman. She may or may not have significant experience in sex itself, but her experience of life as a whole will affect her attitude. The empowered old bag will have a deeper confidence and awareness of her body, a better sense of what will work for her and what she wants. She'll know her limits, yet not be afraid to step beyond the boundaries of where she's been before. She is open.

Most importantly, though, for the old bag, sex is about celebration. She's not interested in the whore's pleasure deals, the witch's magical change, nor the political control crafted by the bitch. She is past thinking of reproduction, probably beyond the need for contraception, and the mother's focus on holding another's creativity is to her abhorrent. The only point of sex is the art of celebration.

The miserable old bag doesn't get much sex, of course. Potential partners are few and far between, her negative view of the world and her open honesty ensuring she is left alone. When prospects are pessimistic, there is no reason to make the necessary effort. For many women, of any age but particularly those in the second half of the lives, sex exists only as an old package tucked away somewhere in one of their bags of experience.

Yet, for the old bag who is awake and willing to share of herself, her sexuality is the very best it has ever been. She is humming with physical sensitivity. She doesn't care what she looks like, nor is she tangled up in fears of rejection. If she decides to share her sanctuary in physical intimacy, she's not going to hold back. She's shameless, and she'll do just what she wants.

Although the soul is battered by changes through the ten years of the menopause, for most women remaining sexually active throughout this period is one of the most powerful ways of facilitating the transition. Just as sexual pleasure is often a very effective way to alleviate pre-menstrual cramps - mental, emotional and physical - so does sex ease the symptoms of the menopause. Furthermore, retaining a habit or willingness to share intimacy helps us move into that post-fertile part of our lives. The affirmation that comes with sharing intimacy - on our own terms, where there is trust, respect, empathy, caring - is a beautiful and effective way of reminding ourselves that we are still alive. We may be transmuting into some redundant wrinkly sagging monster, no longer needed by the species as a baby-making machine, no longer essential to our now adult children, no longer quick enough to beat the competition, no longer able to remember why we've gone all the way upstairs (*and it is always for something really important*) but we can still feel the exquisite hum of life in our souls, we can still find its kick in the connection with another. Indeed, even if love isn't involved, the old bag has the wit and experience to know the value of what is: the caring, sharing wonder of attraction and sweet intimacy that allows an opportunity to *celebrate*.

Indeed, being sexual through the changing years and beyond can make a big difference to our physical wellbeing, as well as the way that we engage with life. It's great exercise if done with appropriate care, keeping the muscles toned, prolonging hip flexibility, ensuring the pelvic floor is strong (avoiding that pee dribble problem that comes after childbirth and with age). It can help to keep the vaginal juices flowing, evading the associated itchy friction problems of dryness, on a day to day level as well as during sexual play.

For the wild old bag, sex can be exceptional. It may take longer to reach the highs, but she knows that it's worth it, because those highs can be the highest of her life, shuddering through her for long depthless moments. While men may begin to struggle with gaining or maintaining an erection, there are no such issues for the older woman. For many I spoke to for this book, the focus of sex was also not as orgasm-led as it had been in their younger days; the celebratory play of sexuality was about the experience of physical intimacy shared, the easy comfort and pleasure rather than the big explosion. They had learned to make time and take their time, and learned that in doing so the beauty of the whole experience was significantly enhanced. Sex is better than ever.

When sex has no purpose but celebration, it allows a much greater freedom of partners, too. The old bag may find a delicious sweet certainty with a long term partner, but she may also break the expectations society has laid upon her. She has no need to choose a partner for his genetic potential; nor does she need a man who will stick around to care for her while she bears and rears the children. She has been there and done that (the photographs are in a box somewhere). Indeed, the old bag who is truly able to use her life experience as a source of inspiration finds partners in the most unlikely individuals. She follows the scents that intrigue her, that provoke her curiosity; the unattractive can be interesting, the twisted and broken can be exciting, the weird and unfamiliar can be fascinating. She seeks out those who can add to her experience, who can teach her, whom she can teach, sharing in the wonders of new discovery.

I'm laughing, "You're too old for my daughter!"

And he shrugs, "Yeah, man, I'm not sayin' ... " Then he grins, that little-boy grin, putting the photograph back on the table. "Oh, you a bad woman, you windin' me up. How old's she, anyhow?"

"26." I smile, asserting the point. Lifting the kettle from the hob, I fill the mugs with steamy water, smiling, the aroma of dark chocolate filling my lungs, feeling his eyes on me in the kitchen lamp-light of evening. Then he's behind me - he has the ability to sneak right up to me - and his broad dark arms are sliding around my waist.

"But not too young for you, baby," he whispers.

"Oh, I think you probably are," and I turn, our mouths meeting, the soft give of his lips, like warm silk as we kiss. He's in his late thirties, closer to her age than to my own. And as I taste him, his tongue, I taste all that he is, the gentle curiosity in his big brown eyes when I moved to the bar stool beside him that night, the wide open laughter of that first meeting, the anticipation. *Why not?* I'd thought, *Why bloody not?!* I'd been celibate for over eight years, since Jack's death. And the way he looked at me across the bar, him drinking American beer out of the bottle, and me sitting there reading a novel - barely able to read a sentence once I'd noticed his gaze. He kept on looking at me. Well, maybe I'd got it all wrong and he wouldn't dream of it in a thousand years of blue-balled solitude. But, hell, *I may as well find out,* I'd thought.

Something inside me sighed deeply, disapproving whole-heartedly.

"I believe the question one asks is: do you come here

often?"

He'd watched me take the stool and place my whisky on the bar, his eyes all sparkling with the smile inside, a smile that broke across his face as he listened to my words. And he nodded, emphatically with a frown, "Oh yes, uh-huh, now that is the exact perfect thing that one has to ask".

His smile made me smile. "Well, do you?"

He gestured at the barman wiping glasses, "He's a mate".

"Ah," I nodded.

"So, um," that beautiful smile, "do you ... come 'ere offen?"

"No. I'm not really a ... " I looked around at our surroundings, "neon lights and rodeo sort of girl. But it seemed a reasonably quiet place in which to linger for an hour".

He laughed, his eyes still fixed on my face, "So this is you lingerin', yeah?"

"Er ... yes. What do you think?"

"Oh baby," he said, lifting his beer in a salute, "You tha best at lingerin'."

Then there was this delicious long silence between us, as he just looked into my face and I felt myself appreciated in a way that I hadn't felt for very many years.

It was me who broke it. "So," I said, horrified at myself, *what on earth are you doing, girl?!* "I'm going to the cinema at eight. Would you like to join me?"

And now, three months later, he's here in my kitchen, and we've made love all afternoon, as we have done so many times now, and bathed and eaten pasta that he cooked as if he were dancing, singing to music in his head, while I sat and watched, the rhythm of his hips, the swirl and dexterity of his body, still alive with youth.

So much moves through my mind in this one kiss.

In the half light, I look into his eyes. I want to say, *I love you*, but I know it isn't true. He exhausts me, and invigorates me. I don't understand him very well, but I don't believe I need to. *I'm loving this* is what I mean.

I slide gently down onto my knees, untying his robe (one of Jack's, actually). Jack always used to say this was one of my best skills.

"Oh baby," he murmurs.

And I wonder what my daughter would think: her mother here, in a silk robe, fellating a black man on the kitchen floor.

When intimacy is integrated

The sheela-na-gig is an aspect of our heritage that is wonderfully debated: carved in stone, this is a woman often shown squatting, her hands between her legs, holding apart her labia to reveal the glory of her vulva. She is found in churches, castles and other medieval buildings. Like the green man, many believe these figures to be remnants of old Paganism, a folkloric image with roots that stretch back to ancient goddesses of sexuality, fertility, sovereignty and tribe. Yet, like gargoyles, many are grotesque, which some say backs the more academic belief that they are warnings against female lust, or perhaps symbols to frighten away the succubus, the devil and other evil spirits. She is seldom luscious, more often thin, even skeleton, with no evidence of breasts.

For me, the sheela-na-gig is a powerful image. She is the perfect hag. She is flagrant, outrageous, shameless. Without a trace of subtlety, sometimes even with a smile, she sits there with no effort to hide her ugliness, revealing to all the dark, mysterious and altogether female source of human pleasure and creativity. It is sweet provocation.

For an older woman to be overtly sexual can be as provocative. She's lost the tight, smooth curves of her youth. Just as many can't bear the idea of their parents wrapped up in the uninhibited sticky throes of animal passion, our society too often recoils at the idea of older people being sexual. By and large, to the younger generations old folk are not seen as attractive, so the images brought to mind aren't especially *nice*. It is altogether preferable to believe that old folk are not involved in sex.

In reality, in most relationships sex doesn't last. After the first swell of passion, a couple will often settle into a rhythm of what works, and after a while the predictability of it can become boring. The chemical rush of anticipation fades. The come-on signs peter out, and the reasons not to make the effort begin to fill the space that was once created by lust. Life becomes busy with children always somewhere at hand, with work pressures building. The midlife crises clatter in raising their awkward questions about values, priorities, opportunities missed and taken, provoking us to drink more, sleep more, crave more space in order to wonder who we really are. In menfolk, stress, uncertainty, a few too many flickers of rejection, can lead to confidence breakdowns and erectile dysfunction, while women become grateful that they no longer have to reveal their sagging crumpled bodies for pawing inspection. The same tales and explanations have been told me by people of all ages, social situations, sexual inclinations, from twenty seven to seventy.

Sometimes what remains is a supportive companionship. For a while there may be sex now and then, affirming the love or friendship, until that affirmation is rightly or mistakenly assumed and sex simply slips away, no longer a part of what makes up the relationship. When such partnerships do work, they can be invaluable and last many years, or even throughout the couple's life. Indeed, where sex continues, as a habit, without love or friendship, the effect can be far more damaging.

Where it works, though, sex in later life can be truly wonderful, but what makes it work is the sharing of intimacy. Looking ahead, beyond her menopause, the old bag sees a life that is rich with potential: it's a world in which she can be herself and that, to her, is fundamental. Perhaps more so than any other part of life, she knows that sex without the naked honesty of intimacy is no longer worth it. She knows too much for it to be otherwise. She recognises doubt, insecurity, pretence; she can see longing and fear and all the ways that human nature endeavours to hide. Making love when those lies are hanging like veils between her and the soul of her lover is simply a waste of time and effort. It's more than frustrating: it is dull.

When the old bag is younger, age is not on her side. Age, after all, naturally aids us in the inevitable and dreaded process (or the deliciously conscious art) of becoming naked. Each dent, ridge and scar of some old wound, each crinkle in what used to be smooth skin, each new freckle and blemish that create new patterns of colour, each wrinkle that emphasises an expression, each ache that twinges as we find the slowness of our limbs, all reveal a little of who we are. And if we are hoping to make a relationship, to discover the soul of the person before us, all these marks of our living can be genuinely beautiful.

Intimacy may be what sustains a good sexual relationship, but it is the intimacy that is important, not the sex. As human beings, most of us crave it: intimacy provides the most profound nourishment of affirmation, allowing us to feel ourselves fully alive and not alone. It is not just experience of hurt that dissuades us from it, though; society is not supportive, letting us know that its intensity is messy and indecent, complicated, dangerous, and liable to entangle us to the point of harm. Easy superficiality, relationships without deep investment, are safer, more dignified and tidy. As we grow older, it can seem sensible to set aside the desire for intimacy. To get into an emotional muddle in our later years is far worse that to do so in our youth: after all, we should know better. Closing down, hunkering down, settling into a self-contained distance is the more acceptable state. Yet loneliness and lack of self-worth come all too easily when our place is society is slipping away. With the old bag's desire for honesty, her impatience with guile and deceit, the openness of intimate relationships can be more important than ever.

Furthermore, as age reveals our nakedness, and increasingly we fail to hide behind assertions, pretence and illusion, it is the wisdom of the old bag that brings us so much strength. Here there is no drama, no emotional opening of the doors to her sanctuary. She doesn't open her soul for others to walk in: she just isn't hiding anything. There is a simplicity in her sharing: she is simply honest.

Her honesty shines out. And like an older body, that honesty can be exquisitely beautiful, scarred with the old wounds of a life that's been lived, crumpled and wrinkled with use, worn soft and worn rugged. She shrugs, not worried that what she reveals is not sweet naive eagerness. She is content in her confidence that what she is is all she is, albeit thoroughly marked by years of experience. And as she lets go her own need to hold on, releasing the convictions that her living has given her, her ability to make relationships, soul to soul, naked and free, evolves into a beautiful acceptance. Finding the wisdom that lies as a foundation of nature, beyond the need to trust, she breathes peace.

Her dark goddess quietly present in every cell of her body, in every shadow cast by knowing, softly and increasingly saturating all that is inside, underneath, behind what is there to be seen, the old bag is at ease. She is quite aware that the nakedness of intimacy, of profoundly sharing all that we are, can happen fully clothed, with a look and a gentle touch.

Sunshine touches the tip of his foot. I wonder if it feels warm on his toes.

I must darn those socks.

He breathes in and sighs, turning the page of the newspaper, shaking it out a little to smooth the page, in the way that he does.

It's Tuesday, a little after ten. His breakfast plate is still at his side, toast crumbs, a little marmalade. My book lies half open in my hands, and I gaze out over the garden, last night's frost still crisp, a haze on the grass, spiders' webs revealed, outlined in frozen dew. It feels like Sundays used to feel.

And I think of Sundays when we were young, staying in bed until hunger drew us out, drinking milk from the bottle, the smell of the gas under the kettle. I can feel the thickness of his hair again in my fingers, see the light in his eyes, the hope and the energy, the firmness of his muscles, the strength of all that could be. And we'd make love with such passion, the sheets in disarray, pushing the big wide world so far away.

He picks up his Earl Grey and sips, still deep in the article.

We don't need to push it now; the world seems a long way from our door these days anyway. It's no longer our world, no longer our concern. If I lost him, when I lose him, I know, I shall be thrown back upon its harsh and cacophonic rhythms, at least for a while. But until then we drift in this bubble beyond. I smile, to myself, within myself, gazing at his gentle face, this man whom I adore.

Some whisper of my thoughts touches him and he looks up, our eyes meeting, and slowly he joins me there in the moment, letting go the words of the page, feeling my presence. And I know in the stillness he truly sees me, this blend of mother and wild young thing, washer and carer, my success writ in flashing lights and such tearful failure, my glory, my wisdom and my stupidity. He smiles. And in his eyes he says everything, and nothing at all. There is no judgement, just acceptance, with such tender warmth, such gratitude shared for all that we've shared. There, upon the rugs in the privacy of our own world, I can almost sense those suitcases in which we have carried our lives, our memories, lying open, easy and so well-worn, comfortably dishevelled, like the sheets of our bed in the days when our lovemaking was exuberant and wild.

When you're younger, you don't realise a heart can be this open. He would smile and tell me I'm as unpredictable a mystery as ever I have been, but I feel completely known in the gentle gaze of this most beautiful old man. I let my eyes close, and slowly, so slowly, the sanctity of the moment streams through me, cool liquid fire, and it lifts me with such an exquisite surge of life, taking my breath, and filling me so deeply.

Oh my love ...

And when I open my eyes, I feel awash with serenity. He smiles at me, as if he were a cat with a bowl of cream, as if reaching out a hand, fingertips touching, as if showering me with petals of a deep red dew-wet rose, stolen from some other time. I breathe in and catch the glistening scent of certainty, though of what I don't know. Nor do I care.

That smile shared is everything.

There is nothing to do.

CHAPTER NINE

The Hag

The old Arthurian tale that is *The Marriage of Gawain*, related as prologue to this book, speaks of the deep mystery of womankind. What does she most desire? The subtext: given her incomprehensibly complex, pugnacious and perpetually changing nature, just how is it possible to make a woman happy? When asked around Arthur's court and across his lands, the question evokes numerous responses, each woman giving her answer of the moment, an expression of her immediate dream's desire. The answer required by the Black Knight, however, is specific: *what a woman most desires is to have her own way.*

It is not the only answer that holds truth or validity, but it is the hag's answer. And as such, it delivers all the Black Knight is seeking. For, if the king were able to acknowledge this most difficult aspect of woman's nature, he would doubtless be able to live with all the rest. The uncompromising, inaccessible, wild, disruptive, bleeding, needing, independent woman will, after all, always ask for more than is easy to give.

Yet if we are to read meaning into the tale, replacing it within the context of medieval storytelling, we might see how the knight's question is challenging far more than the king's worth as a husband, lover or father. He is questioning the king's ability to understand the goddess of the land, and thus his right to sovereignty. Is Arthur truly able to acknowledge and accept the landscape as both tender and wild, as fertile in swathes and in other places always unwilling to give anything at all? Can he care for this goddess with a sensitivity that is genuinely ready to yield when her will rises against his own - when she says no? Can he craft and nurture a relationship with her that is truly honourable, and thus sustainable?

It is easy to see a poetic environmentalism in such an interpretation of the myth. In many ways it expresses the foundational vision of Paganism, where the law (lore) of nature supersedes the laws of humanity. The latter is all too often born out of the insecurities and greed, the politics of power and ownership that are based upon our fearful belief in scarcity; the lore of nature is instead a coherence that is rooted in the tides and balances of relationship which gently proffer the potential for sustainability.

Needless to say, such a vision, as a spiritual challenge, is more poetry than religious, scientific or rational decree. Yet if we are considering the environment of nonhuman nature, like the myth of Gawain's bride such a perspective inspires us to reflect carefully on how we interact with the earth. It dares us to contemplate how we might allow the land to exist in peace, beyond the effects of our human needs and wants. However, just as his bride shows herself as both hag and maiden, as Arthur's land is no doubt as much winter-barren as flushed green with summer, the forces of nature are not all gentle. And if we were to give way to the 'desires' of each natural deity, our species would not survive. In Paganism, submission to the gods is seen as dishonourable, both to nature itself and those ancestors who have lived before us, leaving us their legacy of human wit and experience. At the same time, where we push too hard and with insufficient respect, demanding too much of nature, we destroy or are destroyed: the diseases that are spreading through livestock in the meat and dairy industry are an example of such dishonour, the inevitable crises of populations living in floodplains, the depletion of topsoil that has been over sprayed and overused. The gods can't be tamed. They are not elusive giant humans susceptible to influence; they are forces of nature and no more. So does Paganism teach us to find the courage we need to express our respect, learning how to engage with responsibility, riding the currents of the gods, and so living viably as an integral part of nature.

In this book, however, my focus has not been an exploration of how we could better engage with the earth in what we might call a sacred environmentalism. I have looked instead at a handful of the forces that move through us as human beings, and particularly as women: the gods of our own human nature. Just as we do with the forces of flood and fertility, if we are to live with the peace and satisfaction of real personal creativity, we must learn to ride these currents of our nature, finding the balance between letting them career through our lives unchecked and learning how to evade them, exploring how we can manage and utilise their elemental energy, and understanding how their natural creativity inspires and reflects our own.

So when we consider that *a woman must have her own way*, as the hag's answer it is not a directive. With a gnarled and bent finger, she is simply pointing out a part of our nature - one that is both potentially dangerous and yet humming with a wealth of opportunity.

The young girl, wild and uninhibited, pushing against the forces eager to tame her, has no regard for whether or not she is justified in her desires. As she grows, bleeds, discovering the world, taking on the weight of her fertility, life requires that she find ways to juggle her own desires with the needs of others. She starts to realise how often she must put her own wishes to one side. Though most of us do learn how to balance self-expression with self-control, accepting the need for compromise and trade, the wild spirit within us continues to snarl for her own way, ever itching for space to play. That inner conflict - empathy and responsibility tussling with natural selfishness - is a powerful part of the journey of our lives as women.

It's an important part. When a woman loses that wild self, she has lost access to the layer of woman nature that is her well of imagination, inspiration, innovation - all so crucial to the human wit that crafts a path for our species' future. Where she still feels it, it shows: there is a sparkle in her eyes.

It's a sparkle that some see as life's essence shining through, the dance of a soul's vitality. I've heard it attributed to the closeness of some benevolent yet transcendent god, revealing the individual as especially blessed. In a young girl it is often seen as the vibrant mischief of a bright seeking mind. In a woman it can be beautiful, compelling, even bewitching, or startling, threatening, an overt yet impenetrable lucidity. With the hag glinting in her eyes, she challenges simply by shining so brazenly amidst the crowd.

The choice
Like moonlight upon the black surface of a pool of deep water, that sparkle is most potent when it is in contrast. When a woman can feel the ancient wellspring of creativity, that legacy of her ancestry, her heritage, her woman-nature, the depth of her soul shows in her eyes. Conscious of her soul's cauldron, letting that energy fuel all she is, it is obvious when her power is sourced in both light and darkness, in knowing and mystery, in the acceptance of growth and of decay. She is open to nature.

Of course, as I've made clear in preceding chapters, every aspect of nature can be destructive, overwhelming our lives without respect or responsibility. However, unless she is irrecoverably disabled with mentally illness, every woman can learn to ride the currents. It is seldom easy: life isn't easy. Indeed, often it is when we are under the most pressure that we learn how to survive in the barrage of untamed nature, when the wearying winds have become driving hurricanes, the dismal rain has turned into torrential flooding storms, metaphorically or literally. Yet it is perhaps more important to know how to ride these forces when they are no more than persistent and barely conscious irritants; so do we change the course of each insignificant day, waking ourselves fully to nature, and finding our creativity within it.

Sometimes we can ride a current for years, sometimes just

moments: each force, each surge, each flood of nature has a limited span. The energy peters out, naturally. Summer's harvest leads us into autumn's fall. Such tides are an integral part of our hag-nature, some dark goddess rising through us and moving on. For the old bag within, this process is pertinent, particularly as we head towards the last years of our lives. As the old bag finds true integration, she naturally lets go. Embracing the autumn, she has nothing more to lose, her steps steadily taking her towards winter, there to be released into the elemental form of the hag. The journey isn't dissimilar to each day's dusk: as the darkness creeps in, edges disappear, allowing a gentle dissipation of identity, of meaning. The art of dying well is one taught us by nature.

Though Pagan traditions emphasise the importance of such teaching our secular society shies away from it. So many have so little experience of living well, that the necessary release into death is beyond comprehension. Certainly, if we have no sense of autonomy within (as opposed to authority over) nature, we will feel as if we have no choices, not only at the end of our lives but throughout their course: instead of learning to live with the gods, we blindly fight their brutality, railing against their injustice, ever searching for someone we might blame for our misfortunes. Nature is *not* fair, and the Pagan gods are not bothered by human suffering. It is by learning how to ride the forces of nature - human nature as well as that around us - that we can retain (or regain) the reins to our own lives.

Like so many, I live with the limitations of physical pain. The condition has been with me all through my life, and has proved an extraordinary teacher albeit at times thrashing me to the brink of utter despair. In my adolescence, carried by the confusion of desolation, I made a number of clumsy attempts at ending my life. The final occasion bears relating.

Any minute now I know it will come, that feeling, the falling, when the life-weight disappears. I know it will. Because it does. Sometimes it comes when I'm sitting in the dark and the endorphins are so thick in my brain, the scream in my spine so excruciating I'm too tired to feel anything, and suddenly I'm on the outside, drifting free, like a bubble in sunshine, so tender, temporal, just waiting to burst and, *blink*, be gone.

But I'm still here, filled with lead, watching the gap between the bottom of the door and the grey fluff-dust of the carpet. My eyes won't move. Blurred with water, with lack of effort. Any minute now, it will happen.

My hand is swollen thick, a little way from my face. Now and then my heart stumbles, jilting me, jerking me, my belly rolling in on itself like molten life, lava heat, disappearing down some crack into nowhere. I would so like to close my eyes.

Then it comes, that blessed moment, the darkness filling the light with the softest, warm, breathless water, and matter becomes the dream, deliriously intangible as I'm spinning, reaching for the certainty of it, filled with the wonder of such intense relief. But instead of falling, I'm kicked again, silently *slammed* again, cheek down, right here by the gap, my eyes fixed on the gap between the door and the carpet, and I don't understand what the fuck is going on. I just want to close my eyes, *just let me close my eyes.*

My hand is like a creature lying on the road. If it got up, if it found the strength, it could crawl out of the inevitable squealing onslaught of traffic, the wide black wheels, if only it could get up. It would just need to take one breath, one breath.

I was 21. I breathed, and I threw up. Albeit within that dissociated state, I had made the choice to live and its effect stayed with me, sinking into me as I found my feet once more. There was no rational comprehension, no flash of realisation, and I felt myself beyond the grip of an instinct to survive. The need in that moment was simply to make a decision: live or don't live, but stop pissing about in the middle. Don't waste it. That night it felt as if I were making that choice for the first time.

My life turned around. Yet, crucially, it is a decision I continue to make, consciously, every day - not because I live with despair, but because that moment of choice taught me the power of being awake. At times it is useful (even pivotal) simply in that choosing affirms the motivation, setting or clarifying the day's intentions and walking them through; sometimes restating the decision is enough to inspire.

Some people live easier lives, and may dismiss the need for such purposeful awareness: we may accept the value of learning how to ride the forces of nature when they are battering us to our knees, but those lessons are of extraordinary value in our day to day lives as well. It is all too easy to shrug off responsibility, to sink into apathy, blaming others and breathing resentment; that's no way to live. *Choosing* to live, we can choose a life that is vibrant with energy, with the joy of creativity, a life that is genuinely worth living.

So many shuffle through their lives with such half-hearted resignation. Their choice is to dull their boredom with a constant drip-feed of soul sedative, the pacifying drugs that are acceptable in our culture - another bottle of wine, a pint of beer, another spliff, another night in front of the television, prescription antidepressants, the drama of celebrities and gossip. When we dull the pain, using the toxins of drugs and alcohol, passive entertainment, we lose our ability to make true relationship. Our minds blurred, our energy slurring, what we believe to be connections with others are in fact no more than tangles of reflections and projections.

When we dull our perceptions, evading any risk of danger, of rejection or pain, avoiding the darkness of the unfamiliar, we barricade ourselves, separated from what were (or could be) our sources of inspiration. Without a muse, what creativity we have feeds upon itself; it loses any intention of communication, becoming self-indulgence, increasingly rank, bitter, acrid, or simply bland. Soon enough, it dries up and disappears altogether, intensifying our sense of life's futility, our lack of value, our stupefied depression. And society shrugs, accepting it as normal. *Have another drink, switch on the telly.*

And the hag within us snarls and spits, crouched in the stench of her suppression. She may find cracks through which to kick and scream; she may even sneak through and cause the kind of devastation that only comes when such energy is kept contained, under pressure.

Or we can choose to live.

The edge

In these pages, I have explored the most potent source of our creativity: our own wild nature. Crafting eight distinct elements from the storms of its energy and consciousness, I have presented each as formed and fuelled by a force of human nature, a face of the dark goddess: the young child untamed, the girl bleeding with fertility, the virgin claiming her independence, the whore making deals for her own pleasure, the mother holding others for her own nourishment, the bitch deconstructing, the witch in control, the old bag claiming her right to be. Each marks a broad progression through the years of our living, but is also potentially accessible in each moment of our lives. Thick with the complications inherent to all nature, each can provoke the kind of truth of self-expression that is wholly unacceptable. So have I used one word to encompass that power in woman: the hag.

It is a word with long and tangled roots stretching back through our European heritage. The principal root is to the Old English *haegtesse*, a particularly female word meaning a seer, the Old High German being *hagazussa*. The *haeg* or *haga* is the hedge, that which delineates the edge of a community from the wilderness beyond, the second part of the word implying the *riding* of this edge. In many ways synonymous with the folkloric witch or she-demon, it is possible the *haegtesse* was the wild woman, she who lived at the edge of the village, on the edge of society, on the edge of madness or comprehension.

When first considering the word, it seemed to me this edge was wholly appropriate: the hedge-snaggled wind-blown soul whose vision of the world, thick with the fey colours and shapes of energies and intention, was hard to reconcile with conventional life. This hag isn't the witch of black velvet and gothic fashion, of spellcasting and magical invocation; she is simply the woman who can't quite manage to be or do what it takes to be accepted.

Though the sources are more poetic, folklore speaks of the temple groves in Northern Europe called *hagi*, and some say that from the old practice of divination by the entrails of sacrificed animals came the Scottish *haggis*, a pig's bladder of tripe boiled and eaten in fear and honour of the Cailleach, the hag goddess who stalks the living on the longest nights of winter. Even more doubtful in terms of etymology, the word is poignantly close to the *heq* of ancient Egyptian mythology, a holy woman, one who held the invocations and incantation to the gods, a magician of words and deeply feared. From Egypt she became the Greek goddess Hecate, holding power over life and death, incarnate through her priestesses. Always at that point we most desperately fear, she sits at the crossroads and watches as we tear ourselves apart not knowing which way to walk.

It's a delicious word. Hag: it holds all that is not conventionally *nice*, like armfuls of rotting autumn leaves, smelling of the sweet earth and decay, wet with mud and wriggling with spiders and slugs. She is alarming, the hag, the fascinating outsider, ostracised and yet somehow also integral to the whole. She whispers in our souls what we long to scream aloud, yet we are scared of what she'll say, what she'll do: the horror of being outcast is a terrible fear.

At times we may let her energy move through us, within us, but letting her out into the world to touch our relationships is quite another thing. Between women the cutting ice-words and screaming winds that are hag-storms are not uncommon; contained, they are shrugged off as normal, cat fights, all hiss and claws. Nor are they necessarily apocalyptic; many women's friendships survive, growing deeper after the blizzard of hag encountering hag, truth hurled as blades across the raging balefire. Some women revel in friendships based on haggish wit, each relishing the other's seethingly unacceptable opinions, slanders and desires, each knowing that their hag conversations are only that: hag energy exhaled.

When the hag emerges in one woman and not in the other, however, the game is often too cruel to bear. When that 'other' is a man, the story is one which has been played out in bars and bedrooms, theatres and myths, of every culture around the world. It need not be gender specific, but few men have access to pure *hag* energy within themselves, those who do usually populating the centre ground of the gender spectrum.

The hero

For a man with no understanding of the hag, her behaviour can be utterly baffling.

Deep in his soul an ancient fear wakes, a warning that has been passed from father to son through countless generations. His survival instinct kicks in; his trust dissolves and he pushes her away. Where there is neither love nor strength sufficient, he may simply turn from her, feeling himself wronged, declaring her behaviour unfair, unreasonable, unacceptable, ugly. If his own mother expressed her hag with brutal ferocity, it may be that he is just too scared or scarred to deal with the hag again. If, on the other hand, he was brought up with a woman who suppressed her hag nature, teaching him through her own determination that such behaviour was unnecessary and *wrong*, faced by the hag his fear may be heightened by what he sees as her madness. Emotionally at sea, feeling harshly rejected, he is likely to withdraw, closing down, cutting communication completely. If he has the strength to try, he may repeatedly ask her to explain, not understanding why he can't understand, blaming her for what appears to be a cruel and irrational unwillingness to untangle what is going on.

When the hag arrives in a man's life, human nature plays out the conflict, as ever it has done. He falls in love with a woman's beauty, her strength, her vulnerability, her caring - he may fall for any number of qualities, but seldom is it her untamed force of disruption. Most men, if subconsciously, do perceive the hag beneath, and for some that wild, dark mystery is a very powerful part of the inherent attraction, but however much he is expecting it, when the hag emerges he is shaken.

Of course, some men respond with violence, emotionally impotent in the face of her dark storm, asserting themselves with their physical strength. Some simply walk away, perpetually frustrated when time and again they find the hag resides in the women they get close to. Some learn to choose carefully, finding women whose hag is weak, hidden or broken.

If there is love, though, or some other drive that holds him to her (and most often love is the only drive that is strong enough), even though he is hurting, he desperately seeks out the courage to stand his ground. She has the power to humiliate him completely, and he knows that. Tearing him apart, she will question his courage, and throw him naked out into the street. She can reveal to society the full extent of his impotence, the weakness that is hidden in the depths of his soul. She perceives the little boy trembling, the uncertainty that cowers beneath his manly guise. In the darkness of her eyes, with the coldness of her touch, she can make him face his own truth and failure with a simple look. In the devastation she leaves behind, he is left in the dark silence of his own soul, with nothing making sense. He may feel a part of himself trembling, wounded, dying. As the Black Knight of the Arthurian tale well knew, it takes more courage for a man to face the hag than anything else he may ever do.

Yet the hag longs to be met. Indeed, in every woman there is a crying need for surety that all her hag energy will be accepted, embraced. So does she seek out the male principle, in whatever form he comes, as partners, lovers, father-figures, even other women, anyone who will engage with her. If a man can't cope, if he runs or she destroys him in the process of expressing her hag-self, then he is no use at all. She will find another.

When he holds his ground, he has every right to feel proud: he is strong enough to be what she needs him to be. Like every hero, certainly along the way he has been broken. A part of him has died in the vicious moments of battle. With the last of his strength, though, and without comprehension, the hero does what he needs to do. He must not give way, must not give in. But he kisses her, accepting her in all her disruptive rage. And in return, the hag recedes, the woman before him transforming. She has expressed her wild blizzard of winter, and now, before his eyes, she becomes the most beautiful woman he has ever seen. In the old myths, she is the maiden. She is spring.

And he, in all his most dreadful weakness, is fully accepted by her.

So is he reborn.

" - with your stupid bloody half-witted so-called friends sitting around the fucking table like a shagged-out posse of ageing bloody pigeons drinking that tasteless goats' piss by the bucket like we don't need any money to buy food and pay the fucking mortgage, and why? Every bloody week, why? To watch a crowd of bloody half-wits chanting playground songs at a huddle of more bloody half-wits brawling on a field over a bloody plastic ball, so that you can get so bloody drunk you end up brawling on the pavement like fish in the bottom of a bloody rowing boat. You don't even play the game! - "

It's those last six words that make the impact. He's heard the rest so many times before, and I've cringed knowing that he can hear his mother's screaming words in mine, words then hurled at his father, the club scarf wrapped around his neck, feet on the table. And still I have yelled, watching him standing there, protected by some veil of his own making, half hearing but only enough to know when he might get away, bored by my ranting, knowing it will go away. But those last words hit home. I've never said them before. And for a moment I feel victorious. I have reached him. Somewhere inside me I feel a smile I know I must not show.

A moment later, I feel devastated. In a voice battered with sorrow, I add the totally inappropriate and counter productive, " - anymore". He stares at me.

I can feel his mind tumbling over itself, without words or thoughts, searching for something he can't identify, and his beautiful mouth moving to shape words that are really not within his reach. He breathes in, sighs, shrugs and shakes his head. If he walks away now, if he turns and walks out, heading for the pub or the computer, the TV, the pain inside me will be like red hot gravel falling. I lift a hand to my forehead and close my eyes.

When I look up, he is holding his head in his hands.

"How do you manage to be such a total cunt?" he whispers.

I gaze at the floor, seeing nothing in the space between us, the storms with their vast black clouds still tumbling through my soul. If I move, or say a word, I'm not sure if I'll shriek or weep.

"Yeah, well, that's just me," I murmur.

And he looks up, desperately tender but smiling. He almost laughs. "Fuck it, babe," he says quietly, "fuck you, you crazy fucking beautiful harpy." And he sighs, "Come on, let's go and sit down".

It is the perennial myth: the woman goddess, life-giver, nurturer, destroyer, and the man as supreme hero, lover, fighter. Brutal she can be, but without her disruptive challenge he stagnates, failing to grow either emotionally or spiritually. Yet this is no feminist tirade: she needs him.

When her disruptive energy is too much and overwhelms those around her, when there is no place for her to place that wildly charged dynamic self, the hag suffers, taking the rest of the woman with her. Lost in the winter, she keeps calling to the sun to touch her frozen body, to melt her that she may return to fertility. Her soul starves in the endless darkness.

The nature of love

However they operate, the power of our relationships flows as an undercurrent in our lives. Where there is bright water, sparkling with vitality, we find confidence, energy and courage, which in turn feeds back to us, strengthening our souls and our connections with others. The more able we are to be open with another, respectfully, appropriately, consensually, the more deeply we allow that relationship to work, the more we expose ourselves in our naked truth, revealing, discovering, all that we are. Where we are sharing intimacy and ecstasy in trust, allowing our sexuality to infuse the connection, that powerful inspiration slides deep into our core.

Sex is one of the basic drives within humanity. She is a divine force of nature, a dark and disruptive goddess, providing an extremely potent adjunct to emotional, intellectual and spiritual intimacy. If we recognise her presence, knowing when she is close and when we need to invoke or turn away from her, forging a relationship with her in the Pagan way, it is possible for us to explore our understanding of how her currents play through nature, both our own and that of the world around us.

As a part of our basic human nature, she fuels the way we behave, both directly and indirectly, individually and socially. The sexual act moves energy within us, fuelling and altering not only our limbs and drives, but the energy of our beliefs: it stirs the cauldron that lies at the heart of our soul's sanctuary. The more deeply we are touched, the more holistically we are entered, the more we are able to share, the more effectively our cauldron is stirred, which in turn affects our sense of what is real, what is possible. How we accept her gifts and use the energy of our sexual need, and of our sexual play, can shape us as individuals, provoking different facets of our nature, forming the world within which we live. It doesn't matter if we are *virgin* or *whore*, expressing it in open physicality or feeling it move within the privacy of our soul, as long as we let it flow. If we inhibit her energy, we inhibit our creative process.

But what of love? It is a word I've barely mentioned. In a book about woman, about the power of nature, relationship, darkness and creativity, that may seem strange, but I have avoided it consciously. Love is an energy that can arrive in our lives at any time, emerging through any facet of our being. As such, it would have been all too easy to sprinkle it over every chapter like sieved sugar. Yet love is more complex. To begin with, it isn't always *nice*.

Love: it's a compulsion. It is not something we can control. Another dark goddess of nature, those seeking certainties may analyse observations and declare evolutionarily justifiable rationales for its motivations, but love is a force beyond our capacity to understand. *Why do you love me* is a question that has no answers.

Love changes us. It turns our priorities upside down. It makes a tired person run, a lazy person get off the couch, a late one early and someone usually punctual always horribly late. It makes a drunk sober up and a sober person drunk. It tears away our inhibitions, pulling us out of our apathy to start to blunder forward, allowing us to dance where before we could only stumble, leaving us feeling incomprehensibly carefree. Drenched in love, everything is possible! Love demands spontaneity - of expression, of action - regardless of the risk of rejection. Love strips us naked. It hurls us tumbling into raw vulnerability, leaving us wading in confusion, broken but breathing, witnessing our weakness, our failings and our strengths. It paints bright our insecurity and our self-negation, laughing with the rain of forgiveness. Yet we can't invoke love. We can create space for the goddess, but she doesn't come just because she is asked. Furthermore, she is even harder to evict than the gods of lust.

She is brutal. Love hurts like hell. Even when it is beautiful, untouched by doubt and fear, it can ache more deeply than a physical wound, tearing open our heart, our nemeton, our soul, breaking down the doors and walls that have held us. The simple inability to express all that we feel can fill our minds with storms of confusion. It's wild. Definitively beyond the reach of being tamed, it can make us intensely selfish, blind to all but ourselves and perhaps the one we love. It is utterly and self-indulgently disruptive.

Clearly, love is another goddess of the hag.

Being loved is an exquisite gift, for it presents to us the offer of acceptance. However idiotic and unattractive we are, if someone loves us there is a glimmer of hope that we may be OK. But love means nothing if we can't take that gift. If we can't believe we are truly loved, we can spend years alert with the anxiety that the person will wake and realise just how awful we are, how worthless and ugly. We know the flip side of love is hate. And when we don't wish for the love, when we can't love in return, that love can become obsessive, intrusive, horrifying.

When it is us who loves, when we are fully in love the hag dances within us. It can feel as if she is dancing in stomping heavy steel-capped boots, or as lightly as a butterfly, ever fluttering, leaving us breathless. When we love, it disrobes us. It leaves us desperately naked, vulnerable to ridicule and rejection. When our love is not received, we ourselves feel the pain of its flow dammed, rising, flooding and overwhelming, suffocating, destroying. Yet in that process of loving are we given the opportunity to face ourselves, to learn to accept ourselves, hag and all. Only then are we able to accept that we can be loved, and so feel fully loved, and, understanding love, love more deeply in return.

Indeed, what changes us more effectively than the power of love? Even when love's expression is mutually received, its hag power disrupts our lives. Waking us to who we are, we see better our potential, possibilities and paths ahead. It breaks up who we were. Yet loving and loved, we find courage to express the wild self, getting out of the box of expectations and convention, doing what we wish to do when before there seemed no hope.

The effect can be intensified when physical intimacy is a part of this love's compulsion. The hag energy of love is spiked with sexual dynamite. Anything could happen. Letting go into the lust of physical love, we submerge in the dark thrilling water of touch. We lose control. The fear of drowning may keep us stalling, but the hag calls us on, always letting us know that there is more we could feel, more ecstasy to taste, more intoxicating pleasure to drink so deeply.

Hag-blessed, we fall *madly* in love. We become crazy with it, tumbling head over heels, losing our minds, breaking the rules, helpless, enchanted -

I touch his face with my fingertips, knowing so completely every curve, every line, every mark, every idiosyncrasy, yet feeling my heart soar with wonder as if for the first time, such serene wonder, my mind so wide open, horizon to horizon, yet utterly filled with this vision of him, with every detail that I touch, his whole beautiful face. Nothing exists but this moment, his skin, the rich colours of his eyes as he searches mine, the dark line of his eyebrow, the hard curve of his jaw, the first scratch of stubble, the dents and ridges of scars, each one telling stories, stories I know so well. Oh, how I love this love. I feel my soul relax as if every last chore of living were done, the journey complete, my body instinctively moving closer to his, the final task simply to dissolve into his, two rivers merging into one perfect flow.

I close my eyes, and feel his fingers, the cup of his hands about my face, holding me before him. Our foreheads are almost touching as he sighs, whispering, "I love you so much". And, so close, every breath overwhelms me all over again, as I breathe all he is, breathing his breath as he breathes mine, lost in this timelessness. Forever.

- until we find our feet again. And scrambling for certainty, doubting, realising that love's motivations are not altogether rational or *sane*, we step away. Our wild expression of love may have lasted a few hours, a few months, a few years, but slowly all too often we begin to push the hag away. Securing our soul sanctuary, putting love in the box of all that is dangerous, disruptive, unacceptable, we damage love by containing its wild free spirit. Love may continue, nourished and warmed by the comfort of familiarity, but no longer does it shine with inspiration and creativity. Without the hag, there is no dynamic connection. It is her dark goddess of love, shimmering with that primal and essential energy of conflict that shows us how edge meets edge, inspiring us to find a way to touch, soul to soul. Our true awareness of life is woken with that touch, energy flowing through us, bringing new vision, strength and creativity.

In a world of change, relationships not fraught with the energy of this love-hag are safe, nurturing, holding, offering us security, stability, companionship, reliability. Indeed, these are the relationships that glue our communities together. When such bonds support our dynamic self, their value is obvious; it is often only with their gentle support that we find the strength to face the hag in other parts of our life, to dance with her and step beyond the edge of our known world. When these relationships are all we have, though, our lives become dull, purposeless, mundane.

As the glue of our society, these relationships express too what is acceptable in our society, so affecting the dynamism of our culture as a whole. Where the hag's gifts - intimacy, passion, death, disintegration, the wild and unpredictable - are not acceptable, neither is nature. Where the hag is rejected, society lacks innovation, regeneration, inspiration; the cycle is jammed and cannot complete. Pulling away from the dark, unashamed and seething tides of muddy nature, Western society does its utmost still to tame and control its environment, its cravings, its passion, love, anger and ecstasy, its storms and currents, clouds and torrents. Rules are laid down, some written into law, others taught us in early childhood, some almost unspoken.

With walls towering above our heads, these boxes are the parameters we are supposed to live within, boxes constructed of the rules of acceptability. If we aren't afraid to get out of the box, very quickly we discover those walls are made of paper.

Kissing the hag

Another powerfully disruptive aspect of nature is illness and disability. The discomfort caused by the presence of illness is acute, particularly in the kind of antiseptic environments that increasingly exist in some parts of our Western world, promoted by those massive pharmaceutical companies selling drugs and disinfectants. The contagiousness of 'flu makes us shy away only in part because of fear about catching the virus. We do the same with a person disabled by blindness, mongolism, Parkinson's, anything else, stepping back from the danger. If I am limping with pain, people may ask with a sympathetic smile whether I've hurt my leg, most often genuinely wishing me a full and speedy recovery, but when they discover it is not a clean and curable mishap but a lifelong condition most often the expression changes, the smile becoming tense, concern turning to uncertainty, quickly diluted by the distance they cast between us.

We teach our children to do the same. A child's natural curiosity is quashed when he or she comes into contact with illness and disability, their instinctively seeking minds keen to check out what and why. Yet children are taught not to draw attention to the difference, instructed that to do so is wrong; such an intrusion may be impolite, but more commonly it is the adults' discomfort that is revealed, their fear and unwillingness to confront it themselves. Such difference drags them out of the comfort zone, disrupting a world they are trying to control.

When I worked as a spiritual healer in my late twenties, I recall watching a young boy lying beside his mother, his hand exquisitely gently moving over the huge bulbous swelling on her naked belly, the focus of a cancer now grown out of control. The woman, haggard but calm, just days from dying, stroked the boy's hair, and he looked up and smiled tenderly. He was six; it was an exquisite acceptance and intimacy I knew he would remember all his life. At another such house, I witnessed a child of the same age shaking with grief and confusion, desperate to see his mother but not allowed to enter the room for fear that he would see her pain: his beautiful mother as hag. She lay weeping in desolation, having lost access to her son's love and warmth just when she most needed it, the household brittle with the fear of the hag.

We are afraid but so much of that fear is of our very own making, fear exacerbated by fear of nature's power within and all around us. Bodies twisted and scarred from birth, or from accident, elicit more fear if they are kept covered, distanced, unexplored, untouchable, and consequently nurture far more ignorance and prejudice. How would it be if we were free to show curiosity, to run - with consent - a finger down the deep wrinkled path or hard ridge of a scar, to feel the hair on the dark splash of a disfiguring birthmark or the tight silk of burned skin, to understand how a limb could bend the wrong way, to share the shaking of neuralgic pain? Even where the disability is in the mind, how much less would our society shun those scarred or born in such a way if we were to listen to their visions, to hear their stories and imagine life through their eyes, without judging their experience as deluded, erroneous, devoid of value and learning? And for those who live within the enclosures of pain, disease and disability that cannot be aided by our mechanist medical profession, so much fear provoked by anticipating social rejection could be dissolved if the hag energy of their *difference* could be accepted. Lives and creativities, often so drastically restricted, could be opened out with such profound value as individuals find freedom to reveal and express their own hag-touched experience.

Nature's power of disruption will always cause us to feel out of control. It takes the lid off the box of all that is conventional, acceptable, complacent in its bounded knowledge, and thoroughly shakes up what it finds inside. Disruption as disease, as cyclones, as madness and plague, is nature feared. Within women it comes in the form of hysteria, rage, birthing, bleeding, seething, passionate loving, grieving, needing, manipulating, the shuddering of her drawn out pleasure and pain. This is woman, as unacceptable: woman as hag. It is woman's nature.

There are now more women than men at university in the Western world. Their school grades are higher. Female infant mortality rates are lower than male rates, with little girls generally healthier than boys. The fraction of women in gaols is tiny, the number who commit suicide equally small, and so the statistics go on. It has been said that, now women in Western culture are letting go the shackles of male ownership, their natural physical and emotional superiority is starting to shine through. Emerging out of the era that began with our wandering ancestors first settling, when land was first possessed, sown and defended, and community hierarchies became clearly estab-lished, we are beginning the return to a level playing field between the sexes. Where women are not suppressed by ownership and childbirth, their innate strengths give them the edge. Yet where does this take us?

Women are still trapped, still crippled by fear. But so much of that fear is generated within themselves. I do not deny that many millions of women around the world, and a small proportion within our own culture, are still suppressed by men's dread of their wild nature. However, my words here focus upon women's own fear, projected upon anything that will hold it, that keeps them still bound into lives that are insidious, valueless, and wholly uncreative. Where that fear creates aggression that pounds men into submission, we suffer even more for the lack of heroes. Women retain and nurture only their isolation, the hag angry within, disallowing creativity, too intent on (self)destruction.

It is time to shake off the fear. Having broken through the suppressive chains of ownership, we must fully recognise that life heavy with negativity is unendurably tedious and wholly unnecessary. We must stop complaining and stop blaming others. Life is hard. Escaping from it in any of the ways society encourages us to use does not help it get easier, most often exacerbating the problems. Instead we must engage with it. Facing the power of our own woman nature, we must learn how to let that flow through our bodies, shimmering in our souls, brilliant in our spirit, not fearing that it will tear us apart, not fearing the muddy, the bloody, the dark.

Only by acknowledging the fullness of our nature, with its disruptive, untamed and unashamed potential, can we find the wholeness that allows us health and wellbeing. Only when we stop reaching off-balance for the light, and equally welcome the darkness of our souls, will we find the exquisite inspiration that comes from being rooted, nourished and blessed by nature. Open to the sanctity of nature's currents, can we then experience the vibrant flood of energy that is offered us as *life*, finding the deep resources of wisdom and fuel within our nature, and exploring the freedom of perfect self-expression. Only then do we have a chance of touching the joy of exquisite relationships and true creativity.

Making life worthwhile.

So have I told my tale.

In a breath, a sighing outbreath, I have told you the twists of my tale. And I find myself again here upon this hard wooden bench, the sunlight now higher in the winter sky, sunlight no longer able to warm what it touches; it reaches us in silence as if now still sleeping. And, while not making me sleepy, it reminds me how much I long to sleep, to sleep like the leafless forest, blurred with icy mist, to sink into a sleep undefined by time, a sleep that could only be ended by the kiss of some sweet young tender courageous prince. Yes, that would be perfect: people would find me where I lay in these dirty ragged clothes, a homeless old hag on a cold park bench, and each take no more than a moment to recoil from my stench. If one came close enough to lift the hood from my face, he would retreat soon enough, stepping away from the wrinkled grime, the flabby pale skin, knowing all too well that I am no maiden, no princess, no damsel in distress.

I shift my fat arse and sigh with my dreams of sleep.

Something hits my foot.

A ball, plastic white and strangely clean: I stare at it for a moment, hearing a child's voice calling, footsteps running on the cold muddy ground, heading my way. Looking up I see the little boy, all colour-splashed with life, blue socks and red face, so vibrant he shimmers. I lean forward, staggering to my feet, and give the ball a bloody good kick. It glides right past him, away down the hill, the child yelling with indignation as he charges off in pursuit. I watch them, boy and ball, *That got rid of that,* and I sigh, sliding back onto the bench.

"That wasn't very nice."

His voice is softened with a smile.

"Yeah well, I don't feel very *nice*."

He sits down beside me, his long coat open. His neck is bare.

"Ah."

"Piss off."

"Ah."

A couple of mallards squabbling on the pond rise up into the air in a flurry of splashing wings which the winter trees ignore.

"Is this a good time to say, 'hello, I love you'?"

"Piss off."

"Maybe not."

"I've got womb ache."

"Right."

I turn to him, where he has sat down at the other end of the bench, his warm open face, hands in his coat pockets, waiting, patiently. He's very beautiful. And I can see in his mind a dozen ideas rising, falling - chocolate cake, a deep bath, the hot water bottle, perhaps wild dirty sex, or maybe the teddy bear - as he tries to work out what he should-could do. I know he's wondering if it is worthwhile or if he will just piss off; he has every right to. He sighs, his breath lazy and misty in the cold air, and turns to me.

"OK, so what do you want to do?"

I smile somewhere deep inside.

"Kiss me?"

Do you dare?

BOOKS

SOME RECENT O BOOKS

Living With Honour
A Pagan Ethics
Emma Restall Orr

This is an excellent pioneering work, erudite, courageous and imaginative, that provides a new kind of ethics, linked to a newly appeared complex of religions, which are founded on some very old human truths.
Professor Ronald Hutton, world expert on paganism and author of *The Triumph of the Moon*

9781846940941 368pp **£11.99 $24.95**

Switching to Goddess
Humanity's Ticket to the Future
J. Lyn Studebaker

A hard-hitting get-up-and-go book that challenges the reader with its racy style and punchy arguments. Backed up by scholarship, it is a clarion call for our times. **Claire Hamilton,** author of *Maiden, Mother, Crone*

9781846941344 432pp **£11.99 $24.95**